BIG LEARNING

for

LITTLE LEARNERS

Easy Guide for Teaching Early Childhood Activities

by Sally Stavros and
Lois Peters

Illustrated by
Sara Mittlestaedt

©1987 by Sally Stavros and Lois Peters
ISBN 0-933212-30-5

Published by Partner Press, P.O. Box 124, Livonia,
MI 48152
Distributed by Gryphon House, Inc., 3706 Otis Street,
Mt. Rainier, Maryland 20712.

Cover Design: Graves, Fowler & Associates

A DEDICATION TO YOU AND TO LITTLE JUSTIN

A special dedication to the big helpers. It is not possible to keep young children from learning. What they learn depends on the adults with whom they spend their time. Your young learners are supremely fortunate that you are the adult with whom they will be spending their time and experiencing these learning activities.

A special dedication to Little Justin. To Little Justin who is the hero in the June chapter. Justin now lives in California, eats all of his vegetables and is getting bigger every day.

ACKNOWLEDGEMENTS

Special thanks and acknowledgement to Cindy Fowler who designed the cover.

Recognition also goes to Robert J. McKnight, RBP, who did the photograph of Sally Stavros.

TABLE OF CONTENTS

DECEMBER

MARCH

INTRODUCTION

The activities in this book are teacher developed and carefully selected. They are learning fun for both the little learners and the big helpers. Everything has been done we could think of to make this an easy-to-use resource book.

The components in each chapter are:

Parent Page (may be duplicated) - an overview of monthly activities

Art - art and crafts (material chart included)

Literature - stories, fingerplays, poems and nursery rhymes

Music - new words to favorite tunes

Science - activities and background information

Social Studies - information for discussion

Math Cooking - opportunities to illustrate Math concepts with concrete ingredients

Books - selected to relate to chapter activities and be available in your local or school library

Physical Education - exercises and games to develop young minds and bodies

Patterns (may be duplicated) - very helpful especially if you are not an artist

Coordinate - You may:
Use all of the activities in each chapter
Add and subtract some
Select those you prefer

If you wish to coordinate activities, a monthly learning calendar is provided as the second page in each chapter except for the chapter for summer (July and August). A materials chart is provided at the end of each Art section.

BOOKS

The "Books From The Library" section can be used as a guide. A few weeks before you need the books, contact your librarian and make arrangements to pick up those you have selected from the list. If your librarian has the time, a box of books may be ready when you need it.

A special word about books, stories, nursery rhymes and finger plays.
Research shows the best way to develop comprehension and critical thinking skills is to ask a few simple questions before, during and after reading. The following are recommended questions to ask:

1. Before:
   a. This is a story about . . . (name main character or show some pictures in the book).
   b. What do we already know about . . .
   c. What do think may happen in this book?

2. During:
   a. What has happened so far?
   b. What do you think may happen now?

3. After (immediate):
   a. What happened?
   b. Were some of us correct when we guessed what would happen?

4. After (recall at a later time):
   a. What was the story about?
   b. How did it end? (if not already answered)

Repetition of the questions is very important so the child begins to ask the questions of himself/herself. Take the time to ask the same questions over and over with each new book, story, nursery rhyme, and finger play until the children can ask the same questions of you.

FIVE STEPS TO SUCCESSFUL USE OF SCISSORS

The use of scissors helps prepare the young hand muscles for future printing and writing activities.

Before beginning organized cutting activities children will:

1. Practice holding scissors appropriately several days in a row without cutting.

2. Practice holding scissors appropriately and cut a random "fringe" around the outside edges of ½ sheet of construction paper or large index card.

3. Cut a four inch paper circle or square in half.

4. Master cutting on short lines and very gently curved lines before moving to more complex material.

5. The key is to move slowly and let the child's success dictate moving her/him to more complex material.

The use of pencils and crayons:

This sequence is also excellent for children who are inexperienced with crayons and pencils. Just remember to let the child be your guide on how fast to progress from merely holding the crayon or pencil correctly to following more complex designs.

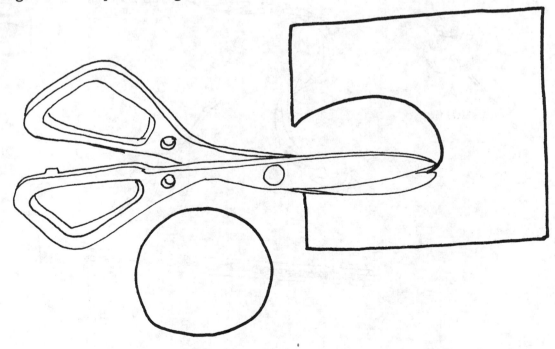

TRICKS WITH PAINT

Take your favorite paint recipe and add soap or detergent. You may also use a recipe below. The soap or detergent helps make paint shiny and it also will help it wash out of clothes.

Finger Paint   Mix: 1 quart water
                                ½ cup corn starch
                                    Cook until clear.
                                    Take from heat.
                                Whip in ¼ cup soap flakes
                                Add coloring as desired.

Regular Paint   Mix: 1 cup powdered paint
                                    2 cups detergent
                                    2 cups water

You can use brushes and a variety of other objects to paint. They include:

Eye droppers	Straws (blow gently!)
Yarn	Filled roll-on deodorant bottles
Leaves	Sponges

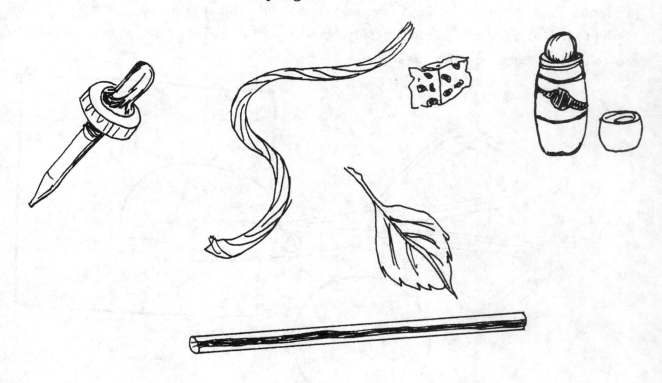

SEPTEMBER

Dear Parents:

Each month you may receive a Parent Page. This is the first one. Parent Pages will give you a very brief overview of some of the contents of each month's learning activities.

This month we will be focusing on "Fall."

SOCIAL STUDIES
Safety rules to remember

SCIENCE
Watch the weather change
Make a leaf scrapbook
Find a cocoon

MATH COOKING
Caramel Apples
Applesauce

BOOKS FROM THE LIBRARY

LITERATURE
Johnny Appleseed
Autumn Leaves and
Red Apples finger plays

ART
Leaves make pictures
An apple person or an apple puppet!
Traffic light

HAPPY SEPTEMBER!

Parent Page ART - Finger Paint Leaf Picture LITERATURE - POEM "Fall or Autumn" PHYS. ED. - Exercise 1 & 2 MATH COOKING - Caramel apples	ART - Seed and Yarn Pictures LITERATURE - POEM "Little Acorn" SCIENCE - Discuss Fall Activities A & B 1-3 MUSIC - Falling Leaves BOOK - Sometimes Things Change by Patricia Eastman	ART - (Complete) Seed and Yarn Pictures LITERATURE - FINGER PLAY- "Summer Birds" SCIENCE - Discuss Fall Activity 4 PHYS. ED. - Exercise 1-3 (five times) BOOK - Fall Is Here! by Jean Belk Moncure	ART- Leaf Prints LITERATURE - NURSERY RYHME - "Early To Bed" PHYS. ED. - Exercise 1-3 (five times) BOOK - Sun Grumble by Claudia Fregosi	ART - Spray Paint A Leaf Picture LITERATURE - FINGER PLAY "When the Leaves Are On The Ground" PHYS. ED. - Exercises 1-4 (four times) BOOK - Johnny Maple-Leaf by Alvin Tresselt
ART - Leaf Wall Hanging LITERATURE - POEM - "Autumn Leaves" MUSIC - Leaves of Gold and Red and Brown PHYS. ED. - Exercises 1-4 (four times) BOOK - Henrietta Goes To The Fair by Sydney Hoff	ART - (Complete) Leaf Wall Hanging LITERATURE - FINGER PLAY - "Summer Birds" PHYS. ED. - Exercises 1-5 (four times) MATH COOKING - Applesauce	ART - Leaf Placemat LITERATURE - FINGER PLAY "Five Autumn Leaves" SCIENCE - Activity 5 PHYS. ED. - Exercises 1-5 (Two times slow; two times fast.) BOOK - Hard Scrabble Harvest by Dahlov Zorach Ipcar	ART - Beans and Seeds Wall Hanging SCIENCE - (Complete) Activity 5 SOCIAL STUDIES - Discuss Safety A PHYS. ED. - Exercises 1-6 BOOK - Let's Find Out About Fall by Martha and Charles Shapp	ART - Mr. Squirrel With A Bushy Tail LITERATURE - POEM "Mr. Bushy Tail" SOCIAL STUDIES - Discuss B PHYS. ED. - Exercises 1-6 BOOK - Squirrels by Brian Wildsmith
ART - Vine Wreath LITERATURE - FINGER PLAY - "Leaves Are Floating Down" PHYS. ED. - Exercises 1-6 BOOK - The Great Green Turkey Creek Monster by James Flora	ART - Cattails In A Can SCIENCE - Activity 6 SOCIAL STUDIES - Discuss Safety C PHYS. ED. - Exercises 1-7	ART - Beautiful Weeds SCIENCE - Activity 6 PHYS. ED. - Exercises 1-8 MATH COOKING - Nutritious Snack BOOK - Mouse Days: A Book of Seasons by Leo Lionni	ART - (Complete) Beautiful Weeds SCIENCE - Activity 6 SOCIAL STUDIES - Discuss D PHYS. ED. - Exercises 1-8 BOOK - The Sandwich by Dorothy Z. Seymour	ART - Blow Paint Apple Tree LITERATURE - "Grandfather's Story Johnny Appleseed" MUSIC - "Oh, Apple Tree" PHYS. ED. - Exercises 1-8 (Fast then slow)
ART - Print A Pattern LITERATURE - Complete (recall & discuss) "Grandfather's Story "Johnny Appleseed" NURSERY RHYME - "Wee Willie Winkle" SCIENCE - Activity 6 PHYS. ED. - Exercises 1-8 and B BOOK - Weather by Jan Pienkowski	ART - An Apple Person MUSIC - "Apples For You and Me" PHYS. ED. - Exercises 1-8 (Do them as big as possible; do them as small as possible.) BOOK - Dick Bruna's Animal Book by Dick Bruna	ART - Paper Mache Apple LITERATURE - POEM/FINGER PLAY - "Red Apples" SCIENCE - Activity 6 SOCIAL STUDIES - Discuss E PHYS. ED. - Exercises 1-8 (Fast, slow, big, small) BOOK - The Growing Story by Ruth Krauss	ART - A Miniature Apple Tree LITERATURE - FINGER PLAY "Sharing" SOCIAL STUDIES - Discuss F PHYS. ED. - Exercises 1-8 and B MATH COOKING - Apple Face	ART - Apple Puppet LITERATURE - FINGER PLAY "Ten Red Apples" PHYS. ED. - Exercises 1-8 and B BOOK - I Can Dress Myself by Dick Bruna

SEPTEMBER

I. ART

Children will develop skills in:

Organization

Sequence

Use of small muscles (small motor)

A. FINGER PAINT A LEAF PICTURE

Use fingerpaints on glossy paper, swirl the background with either gray or black. Allow it to dry. Then, dab orange, brown, yellow and red with your fingertips to make it look like leaves being blown by the wind.

B. SEED AND YARN PICTURE

Use white glue and yarn to make the outline of a leaf on stiff cardboard. Fill the inside of the leaf with either seeds or colored aquarium rocks. Glue to hold seeds or rocks in place.

Another idea: Instead of making the shape of a leaf, use the shape of an apple. Use red aquarium rocks and put on a stem and two green leaves.

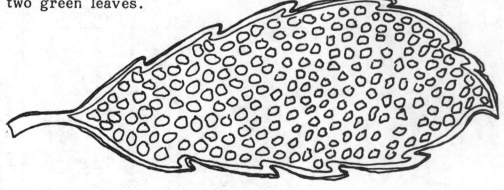

C. LEAF PRINTS

Select a leaf or leaves. Place newsprint or tissue paper on top of the leaves. Rub crayon, using the flat side, over the paper to make an impression of the leaf or leaves.

Use one color for the impression or use a different color for each leaf. For a special effect, trim around the edges of the paper with the leaf impression and glue it on black construction paper.

D. SPRAY PAINT A LEAF PRINT

Select a leaf or leaves. Select a spray paint. Use a dark paint on white paper or white paint on colored paper. Tape the leaf or leaves to the paper. This will hold them in place.

Spray paint over the leaves, especially around the leaf edges to make a good outline. When the paint is dry, remove the leaves to see the pattern outline.

E. ## LEAF WALL HANGING

Gather leaves of different colors and shapes. Discuss types of trees and leaves such as maple, oak, etc. Place several layers of newspaper on the table. Measure rectangles of waxed paper, 9" x 12". Place leaves between two pieces of waxed paper. Put a piece of newspaper on top. Press with a warm iron until wax melts and seals it together.

Punch holes at the top and use yarn or string to hang.

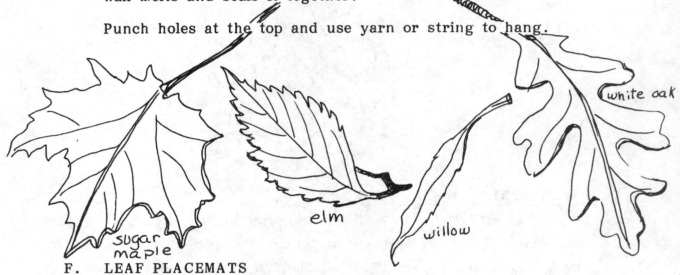

sugar maple

elm

willow

white oak

F. ## LEAF PLACEMATS

Gather leaves that are colorful. Cut two pieces of clear contact paper. Place a few leaves on the sticky side of one piece of paper. Carefully place sticky sides of contact paper together. Push any air bubbles from the center toward the sides until all are removed. Now trim or cut placemat into any shape you desire.

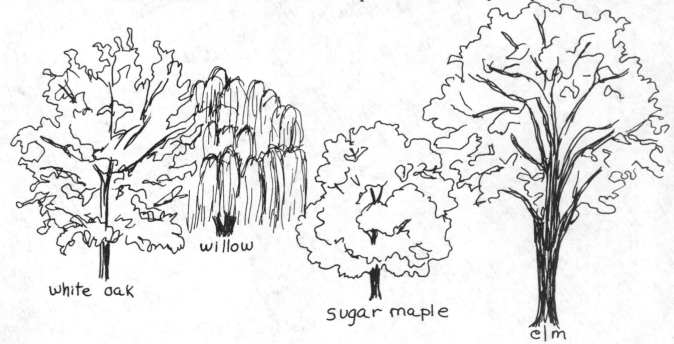

white oak

willow

sugar maple

elm

G. BEANS AND SEEDS WALL HANGING

Take a piece of cardboard or the foam platter from under meat or vegetables. An oval paper plate will also work.

Make several sections on the cardboard or the foam platter with colorful yarn. Glue to the base. Put a different kind of seed or beans in each section and glue in place. Peas, rice, lima beans, kidney beans, coffee beans are just a few kinds that would make an excellent project. When this is completely dry, attach string or yarn or ribbon to hang. Punch two holes in the top to tie on the yarn or ribbon or use a stapler to secure it.

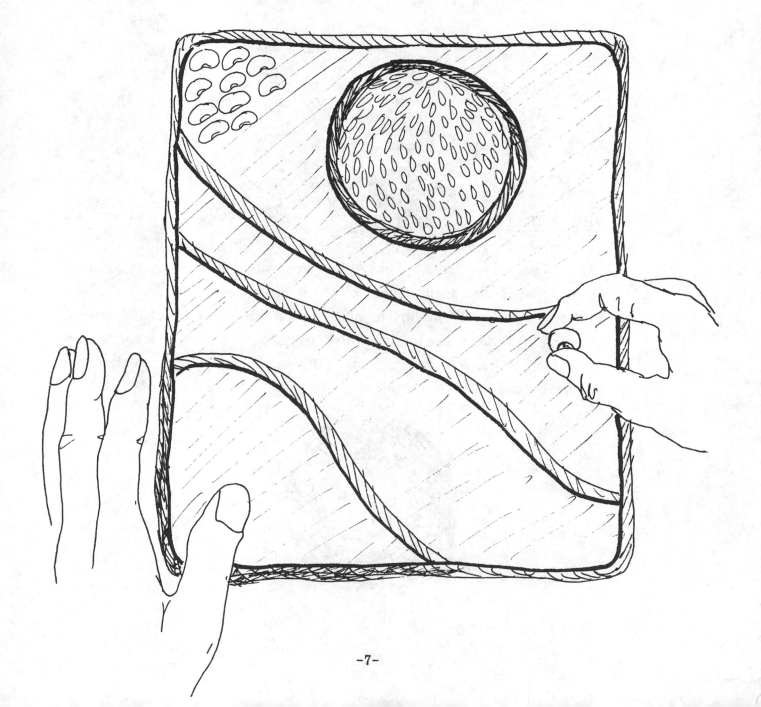

H. MR. SQUIRREL WITH A BUSHY TAIL

Trace squirrel pattern on 9" x 12" sheet of construction paper. Color in body of squirrel but not the tail. Cut small squares of brown crepe or tissue paper. Dip paper into paste or glue and then place inside outline of the squirrel's tail. Completely fill the tail with the pieces of paper. This will give the squirrel's tail a very bushy look. Color in a background, adding grass, sky or leaves.

Another idea: For a better effect, glue on real leaves, twigs or berries gathered from a nature walk.

I. VINE WREATH

Gather dried grape or other vines from the fields or woods. Arrange the vines in a circle - any size you wish. A wreath with an eight inch or ten inch diameter would be a good size for children. Use small pieces of string to hold the vines in place. Wind ribbon or yarn around the vine and tie the bow. The pieces of string can then be cut and removed. Place a bow either at the top or the bottom of the wreath.

J. ## CATTAILS IN A CAN

Collect cattails from a marshy place. Spray the cattails with a hair spray or with spray lacquer to keep "bloom" intact. Unsprayed cattails go to seed.

Decorate a coffee can or large fruit can with colored construction paper, tissue or colorful contact paper.

Place clay in the bottom of the can and stick the cattails into the clay.

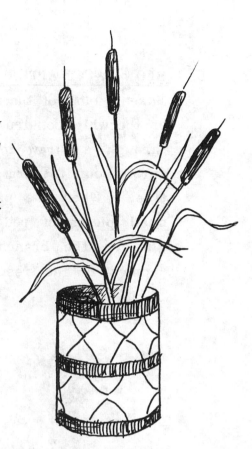

K. ## BEAUTIFUL WEEDS

Gather interesting dried weeds. Spray paint the weeds white, gold or any other color you would prefer. Wrap and paste burlap around a can. Anchor weeds in the can with a piece of foam stuck to the bottom of the can or a piece of clay. To make this fancy, glue sparkle or sequins to the tops of the weeds. Tie a bow around the can to finish.

L. **BLOW PAINT APPLE TREE**
Make a blop of black or brown paint
on the white construction paper. Blow
through a straw to make the paint
spread out to form "branches" of a
tree. When the paint is dry, use
small pieces of red tissue paper to
glue on the branches to make the
"apples" on the tree.

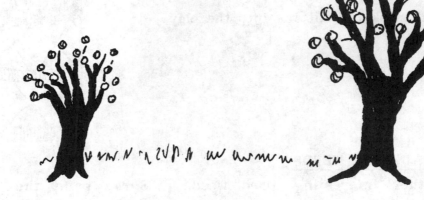

M. **PRINT A PATTERN**
Cut a raw potato or apple in half. Cut a shape in the half apple
or potato. For example: fish, hen, flower, leaf, butterfly,
etc. Use this shape to dip into paint and stamp onto paper or
cloth. Make a design and then allow time to dry.

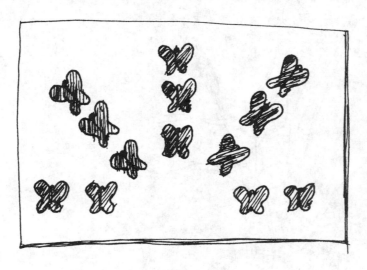

N. **AN APPLE PERSON**

Cut red 9" x 12" construction paper in the shape of an apple. Paste four black paper strips (1" x 6") on as arms and legs. The face can be drawn in with crayons.

O. **PAPER-MÂCHÉ APPLE**

Cover inflated balloon with layers of torn newspaper and glue or wheat paste. Layer glue and paper until entire balloon is covered with about three layers. Allow time to dry. This should take about two or three days. When thoroughly dry, puncture balloon and remove through a small hole in the top. Make green leaves from construction paper or green felt. Glue over small opening in top of apple.

Optional: Make a stem with a pipe cleaner. Glue or puncture stem through the leaves.

P. A MINIATURE APPLE TREE

Find a twig with several extensions that look like branches. Anchor the twig in clay on a piece of stiff cardboard or in a small margarine container. Paint or cover cardboard or container with contact paper, or glue on material (felt works well).

Glue pieces of red felt or red tissue paper to the branches to look like an apple tree.

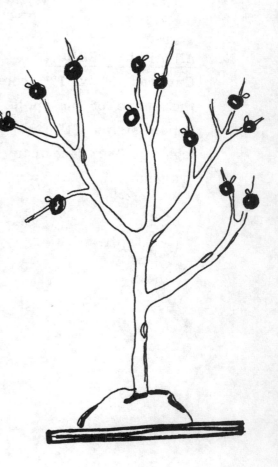

Q. APPLE PUPPET

Let an apple get dried and shriveled. Use seeds or peas for eyes, nose, and yarn or cotton for the hair. A wooden tongue depressor inserted into the bottom of the apple will hold the puppet. Scraps of material or felt will make a hat, cape or other clothes for the puppet.

NOTE: It takes approximately three to four weeks for an apple to dry.

-12-

MATERIALS CHART

SEPTEMBER

A. FINGERPAINT A LEAF PICTURE
- Glossy paper
- Finger paint - gray, black, orange, brown, yellow and red

B. SEED AND YARN PICTURE
- White glue
- Yarn
- Seeds
- Colored aquarium rocks

C. LEAF PRINTS
- Leaf/leaves
- Newsprint/tissue paper
- Crayons
- Black construction paper

D. SPRAY PAINT A LEAF PICTURE
- Leaf/leaves
- Spray paint
- Tape

E. LEAF WALL HANGING
- Leaves
- Newspaper
- Waxed paper 9"x12"
- Iron
- Yarn

F. LEAF PLACEMATS
- Leaves
- Clear contact paper

G. BEANS AND SEEDS WALL HANGING
- Cardboard/foam platter or oval paper plate
- Yarn
- Glue
- Seeds
- Ribbon
- Beans

H. MR. SQUIRREL WITH A BUSHY TAIL
- 9"x12" construction
- Crayons
- Crepe/tissue paper
- Paste/glue
- Leaves/twigs/berries (optional)

I. VINE WREATH
- Grape vines/vines
- String
- Ribbon/yarn

J. CATTAILS IN A CAN
- Cattails
- Hair spray/spray lacquer
- Coffee can/large fruit can
- Colored construction paper/tissue/contact paper
- Clay

K. BEAUTIFUL WEEDS
- Dried weeds
- Spray paint
- Burlap
- Foam/clay
- Sparkle/sequins
- Ribbon

L. BLOW PAINT APPLE TREE
- Black/brown paint
- White construction paper
- Straw
- Red tissue paper
- Glue

M. PRINT A PATTERN
- Raw potato/apple
- Paint
- Paper/cloth

N. AN APPLE PERSON
- Red 9"x12" construction paper
- Black paper
- Crayons

O. PAPER MACHE APPLE
- Balloon
- Newspaper
- Glue/wheat paste
- Green construction paper/felt
- Pipe cleaners

P. A MINIATURE APPLE TREE
- Twig with extensions
- Clay
- Stiff cardboard
- Contact paper/glued felt
- Red felt/red tissue

Q. APPLE PUPPET
- Apple
- Seeds/peas
- Yarn/cotton
- Wooden tongue depressor
- Material scraps/felt scraps

II. LITERATURE

Children will develop the ability to identify and enjoy:

Characters

Main characters

Details

Sequence of events

A. GRANDFATHER'S STORY ABOUT JOHNNY APPLESEED - AN AMERICAN LEGEND

Amy and Tommy finished their lunch, drank the last few drops of milk and, looking at Grandmother, they spoke together, "We're all done. May we be excused?"

"Are you children sure you've had enough to eat?" asked Grandmother.

"I'm really full," said Amy, rubbing her tummy. At six years of age, she was a curly-headed bundle of energy who was more interested in action than in eating.

Eight year old Tommy was just as anxious to leave the table, but patiently waited until Grandmother said, "Well, if you children have had enough to eat, you may be excused."

"Come on, Grandpa," said Amy. "You said you were going to take us for a walk around the farm after lunch."

"All right, all right," chuckled Grandfather. "Let's see what we can see."

Outside the sun was shining and a warm wind was blowing. It was a perfect day to explore the farm. Amy and Tommy had waited all summer for the chance to visit Grandmother and Grandfather on the farm. Now, at last, they were here.

At first, the children were content to hold Grandfather's hands as they walked down the path. But, soon the excitement of being outside and seeing so many new and interesting things, the chance of making a new discovery, caused them to let go of Grandfather's hands and skip on ahead.

The path led them past the barn, up and over a small hill and soon they reached the orchard. Grandfather was proud of his apple trees for he had taken good care of them and, as a result, every tree was filled with large, shiny red apples.

Grandfather asked, "Would you like to have an apple? You know, there's an old saying, 'An apple a day keeps the doctor away.'"

"What does that mean?" asked Tommy.

"Well," said Grandfather, "that means the apple is considered to be a very nutritious fruit and is good for boys and girls to eat. If you eat one a day, you'll stay healthy."

"How did all these apple trees grow?" asked Amy, who had been listening.

"Would you like to hear a story about the first apple trees in America?" asked Grandfather.

"Yes, yes," Amy and Tommy shouted together.

GRANDFATHER TELLS A STORY

Many years ago, before we had automobiles or television or airplanes, there lived a man named John Chapman. John was a pioneer in the early 1800's. He knew a lot about plants and herbs and how they could be helpful to people. He was also a very religious man and he traveled all over the states of Ohio and Indiana preaching and teaching religious sayings. He carried his herbs and apple seeds with him as he went from town to town. His pockets bulged with all the apple seeds as he started out on his journey. He was so enthusiastic about giving his seeds to other pioneers that he often gave them away for nothing. As the pioneers planted his seeds, apple trees grew and flourished in the rich farming areas of Ohio and Indiana. People stopped calling him by his name. Instead, he soon became well-known as "Johnny Appleseed." He was responsible for making apples such a valuable crop for farmers. To this day, as we pass an apple orchard or see the apples in a store, we have to remember "Johnny Appleseed" and the great part he played in spreading apple trees throughout the country. He made the apple a favorite crop of farmers and a favorite fruit of boys and girls.

When Grandfather finished telling the story, both Amy and Tommy decided they wanted to share the story of Johnny Appleseed with their class when they returned to school in a few days.

"I'm going to think of Johnny Appleseed every time I eat an apple from now on," said Tommy with determination.

"Me, too," echoed Amy.

And they did.

POEMS/FINGERPLAYS/NURSERY RHYMES

Children will develop the ability to participate in and enjoy:

Rhythm

Poetry

Sequence

Characters

B. POEMS

1. FALL OR AUTUMN

Sometimes we call it Autumn,
Sometimes we call it Fall,
It really doesn't matter,
Which name we use at all.

We know it is the season
When flowers fade and die,
The leaves on the trees
Turn from green to brown,
And we bid summertime goodby.

For the days are getting shorter,
The balmy wind has a chill.
We welcome Fall or Autumn,
Its season to fulfill.

2. AUTUMN LEAVES

(Cut leaves out of construction paper. Use red, yellow and
brown.)
The leaves are turning colors,
Yellow, red and brown.
And when Mr. Autumn wind comes by,
He'll blow them all down.
(Teacher makes sound of wind, "Woo-o-o" then tosses leaves
in the air. Children try to catch leaves.)

3. LITTLE ACORN

Little acorn can it be
That you're the beginning
Of a great Oak tree?

How can an acorn
That is so small
Grow into an Oak tree
So big and tall?

4. MR. BUSHY TAIL

Hi, Mr. Bushy Tail,
How are you today?
You should be gathering nuts,
You don't have time to play.
For winter time is coming,
And snow will be all around,
Then you'll have your dinner,
Safely hidden in the ground.

C. FINGERPLAYS

1. SUMMER BIRDS

Fly south, fly south, little summer birds.
   (Wave arms like wings.)
For winter is coming and the cold wind will blow.
   (Hold arms, make wind sound.)
Fly south, fly south, where the warm sun is shining.
It's time to leave before we have snow.

2. FIVE AUTUMN LEAVES

(Cut from construction paper: one yellow leaf, two red leaves, two brown leaves.)

Five pretty Autum leaves,

One yellow, two red, two brown. (Teacher points to each color.)

A little breeze came by

And blew the yellow one down. (Take yellow leaf away.)

Four colored leaves

Are left up in the tree,

A red leaf floated down,

Now there are three. (Take a red leaf away.)

Three Fall leaves

And the wind whistles through,

The red leaf twisted loose, (Take other red leaf away.)

And now there are two.

Two little leaves,

Both of them are brown.

One broke off

And fluttered to the ground. (Take a brown leaf away.)

Now we see there's only one,

The last one fell, (Take last leaf away.)

And now our story's done.

3. RED APPLES

Oh, pretty red apples in the tree,

Send one down just for me, (Hold up one finger.)

It would be a delicious treat,

If only I had an apple to eat.   (Rub tummy.)

4. SHARING

If I had two apples, (Hold up two fingers.)

Do you know what I would do?

I'd shine them up and keep one for me,

   (Shine apples on chest.)

And give the other one to you.   (Extend hand to friend.)

5. TEN RED APPLES

Ten red apples grow on a tree (Both hands high.)

Five for you and five for me (Dangle one hand and then the other.)

Let us shake the tree just so (Shake body.)

And then red apples will fall below (Hands fall.)

1, 2, 3, 4, 5, 6, 7, 8, 9, 10, (Count each finger.)

6. **WHEN THE LEAVES ARE ON THE GROUND**

When the leaves are on the ground, (Point to floor.)

Instead of on the trees, (Hands clasped over head.)

I like to make a great big pile of them,

Way up to my knees. (Hands on knees.)

I like to run and jump in them, (Jump once.)

And kick them all around. (Kicking motion with foot.)

I like the prickly feel of them,

And the crickly, crackly sound. (Click fingernails.)

7. **LEAVES ARE FLOATING DOWN**

Leaves are floating softly down, (Flutter fingers)

They make a carpet on the ground.

Then, swish! The wind comes whirling by,

   (Bring hand around rapidly.)

And sends them dancing to the sky. (Flutter fingers upward.)

D. **NURSERY RHYMES**

1. **WEE WILLIE WINKIE**
    Wee Willie Winkie runs through the town,
    Upstairs and downstairs in his nightgown.
    Rapping at the windows, crying through the lock,
    Are the children all in bed, for now it's eight o'clock?

2. **EARLY TO BED**
    Early to bed, early to rise,
    Makes a man healthy,
    Wealthy and wise.

III. MUSIC

Children will develop the ability to participate in and enjoy music.

A. <u>FALLING LEAVES</u>

(Tune: Here We Go Round The Mulberry Bush)

Watch all the leaves come sailing down, sailing down,

Sailing down.

See them fall upon the ground,

When Autumn time is here.

B. <u>LEAVES OF GOLD AND RED AND BROWN</u>

(Tune: Farmer In The Dell)

Oh, Autumn time is here,

Autumn time is here,

The leaves turn gold and red and brown,

The wind will bring them floating down,

When Autumn time is here.

C. <u>APPLES FOR YOU AND ME</u>

(Tune: London Bridge Is Falling Down)

See the apples on the tree, on the tree,

On the Tree.

There's one for you and one for me,

They're so yummy!

D. OH, APPLE TREE

(Tune: Oh, Christmas Tree - Oh, Christmas Tree)

Oh, Apple Tree. Oh, Apple Tree. How lovely are your branches.

Oh, Apple Tree. Oh, Apple Tree. How lovely are your branches.

They're filled with apples that are sweet,

They make a snack for us to eat.

Oh, Apple Tree. Oh, Apple Tree.

Your fruit is so delicious.

IV. SCIENCE

Children will develop skills in:

Distinguishing differences and similarities of attributes

A. FALL

Days start to grow shorter and the air becomes cooler in the fall. People wear warmer clothes. Sometimes the air becomes so cold we can see our breath. The temperature drops at night when the sun goes down and in the early morning we may see a light frost on the ground.

The leaves start to turn from green to yellow, orange, red and brown. Some leaves fall off the trees. Nuts, pine cones and other types of seeds may start falling to the ground. Some trees may remain green throughout the winter. We call these trees "evergreens." In the warmer climates, palm trees remain green all year round. However, old leaves turn brown and fall off while new leaves continue to sprout.

In some places the grass and plants turn brown and wither. Soil gets hard and plants are brought indoors to keep them from freezing. Bulbs are dug up and stored. Tulip and crocus bulbs are planted so they can bloom in the springtime.

Farmers start to "harvest" their crops. Apples, squash, potatoes and pumpkins are picked. Various kinds of nuts are harvested, too.

B. IN THE FALL WE CAN:

1. Take a walk and collect leaves of different colors and shapes. These colorful leaves can be used for several different kinds of art and science activities.

2. Walk through the woods and listen to the crunch of the dry leaves.

3. Make a pile of dried leaves in which to jump and roll.

4. Take a walk through fields or woods. Look for a cocoon. Look in a milkweed patch for a chrysalis. If you are lucky, you may find the Monarch larva. Take the caterpillar and a good supply of milkweed leaves. Place these in a box with a twig leaning or suspended so the caterpillar can attach its chrysalis. Wait and watch. In about two weeks, you'll see the beautiful Monarch butterfly hatch.

5. Make a leaf scrapbook. Find a beautiful tree while the leaves are green. Make certain that it is the type of tree which changes color in the fall. Take a leaf from the tree every few weeks as the leaves change color. Paste each leaf in the scrapbook (or pages of construction paper stapled together). Watch the changes in the leaves.

6. Use Fall items such as acorns, leaves, apples, pumpkin seeds. The teacher and children should have identical sets of fall items. The teacher will lay out a simple pattern, explaining while she does this. For example: "I'll put down an acorn and then an apple." The children will then lay out the same pattern. Continue this activity by changing the items or by adding more. Encourage the children to describe what they are doing.

V. SOCIAL STUDIES - SAFETY RULES TO REMEMBER

Children will develop an awareness of holidays, traditions, seasonal changes and personal safety.

A. STREET SAFETY

Don't run in the street to chase a ball.
Stop! Or you may never play at all.

B. MATCH SAFETY

Don't play with matches, you have learned.
For matches are dangerous,
You might get burned.

C. POISON SAFETY

Don't eat berries from bushes and trees,
They could be poison. So, don't eat these.

D. STRANGER SAFETY

Don't go with strangers. Don't get in their car.
They might take you away some place very far.

These rules are important for you to know.
They'll help keep you safe.
They'll help you grow.

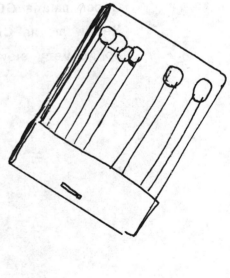

E. TRAFFIC LIGHT

Cut circles out of the red, yellow and green construction paper. Paste colors on a 6" x 12" piece of black construction paper in the same order as on a traffic light.

Punch a hole in the top and string the yarn through so it can be hung up in a room.

F. SAFETY POEM

Point to green, red and yellow on the traffic light and say the Safety Poem:

Red means STOP,
Green means GO,
Yellow means CAUTION,
So go very slow.

VI. SEPTEMBER PHYSICAL EDUCATION FUN

Children will develop skills in:

Rhythm

Imaging

Use of large and small muscles

Good sports conduct

A. MOVE AS IF YOU ARE

1. Putting on a very tight sweater.
2. Putting on warm pants and shoes.
3. Sewing buttons on your jacket.
4. Picking a bushel of apples.
5. Carrying a heavy basket of apples.
6. Johnny Appleseed spreading apple seeds along the highway.
7. Eating a big apple pie with no spoon or fork.
8. A squirrel running up a tree.

B. WHAT AM I DOING?

(To be done after all children have done above.)

Person who is "It" pantomimes (moves) as one of the above eight exercises.

Person who guesses correct exercise becomes "It." If no one guesses after four tries, the child who is "It" chooses the next "It."

VII. MATH COOKING

Children will develop skills in:

Number awareness

Counting

Measuring

A. CARMEL APPLES

Apples	Brown sugar
Sticks to hold	Water

Melt 1½ T. butter

Add 1½ cups brown sugar

Add 6 T. water

Stir ingredients until sugar is dissolved. Bring to a boil. Cover and cook about three minutes until steam has cleaned the inside of the pan. Uncover and cook, without stirring, to soft ball stage – 238°. Cover apples with caramel.

Math: set timer for three minutes – discuss three.

B. APPLESAUCE

Apples	Water
Sugar	Cinnamon

Wash apples, peel and slice into small pieces. Add small amount of water, cover and cook slowly until tender. Add sugar to taste and sprinkle with cinnamon, lightly. Eat warm or chilled.

Math: Count apples – discuss ½ and ¼ as you cut – guess, then time, how long apples will take to become tender.

C. <u>NUTRITIOUS SNACK</u>

      Apples

      Raisins

      Nuts

Mix apple slices, raisins and nuts for a healthy treat.

Math: count apples and nuts - which is the greatest number?

D. <u>APPLE FACE</u>

      Apples   Raisins

      Carrots   Peanuts

      Red candies

Make a face on an apple. Use raisins for eyes, carrot curls for hair, peanut for a nose and ears, heart candies for the mouth. When finished, eat it up.

Math: count apples and raisins. How many raisins will each child need to make two eyes for each apple?

READ ALOUD BOOKS FROM THE LIBRARY
SEPTEMBER

BOOKS

Children will develop the ability to enjoy and gain knowledge from books.

1. I Can Dress Myself
    Bruna, Dick
    Methuen, New York, 1978
    Unpaged, color illustrations

    Uses few words to tell about each article of clothing a young girl and her brother put on to go to a party. It also shows the outer clothes they wear during cold weather like boots, gloves and hats that "Granny made." This is a small book with few words, very large print and bright illustrations.

2. Dick Bruna's Animal Book
    Bruna, Dick
    Methuen, New York, 1976
    Unpaged, color illustrations

    Very simple strong drawings of animals. The only words are the animal's names on every other page opposite the pictures. This book contains domestic and zoo animals and ranges from dogs to hedgehogs. Excellent for pre-readers who will be able to supply the one word that goes with each picture after the book has been read to them several times.

3. **Sometimes Things Change**

Eastman, Patricia

Illustrated by Seymour Fleishman

Prepared under the direction of Robert Hillerich, Ph.D.

Children's Press, Chicago, 1983

30 pages, Colored illustrations

(A Rookie Reader)

This book illustrates how things change. It shows the changes many things go through to get to their final state. It includes: flowers (seeds), raisins (grapes), children (babies), and many, many more. There is a word list on the final page which has forty-seven words on it.

4. **The Great Green Turkey Creek Monster**

Flora, James

Artheneum, 1979

32 pages

The Great Green Houligan Vine creates laughter and disorganization as it grows out of control. Trombone music is finally discovered as the answer to controlling the vine, but not until the whole town has been affected.

5. **Sun Grumble**

Fregosi, Claudia

McMillan, New York, 1974

Unpaged, color illustrations

Can the sun get crabby? In this book it certainly did and as a result it quit it's job and started doing mean things to stars and meteors. The people and plants on earth began to freeze. The sun visited the earth in disguise and felt sorry its absence caused such hardship and it began to shine again. Simple words and bright pictures will help young children realize how important the sun is to the earth and human beings.

6. Henrietta Goes To The Fair
   Hoff, Sydney
   Gerrard Publishing Company, Champaign, IL, 1979
   48 pages, color illustrations
   (Imagination Books)

   > Mr. Gray, the farmer, decided that a big pig should be his entry
   > into the state fair. Henrietta, the chicken, hitched a ride to
   > the fair. After a series of adventures ending in another pig
   > winning the ribbon, Henrietta went to sit with the other chickens
   > and was awarded the first prize. She rode home triumphantly
   > in the front of the truck. Simple vocabulary.

7. Hard Scrabble Harvest
   Ipcar, Dahlov Zorach (1917)
   Doubleway, Garden City, New York, 1976
   Unpaged, color illustrations

   > Rhyming story of a farmer's problems as he plants and protects
   > his crops from animals and birds. At last, he can harvest before
   > his crops freeze. He makes cider, brings in the pumpkins and
   > squash and gets ready for winter just before Thanksgiving and
   > Thanksgiving dinner.

8. The Growing Story
   Krauss, Ruth
   Illustrated by Phillis Rowand
   Harper, 1947
   Unpaged, illustrated

   > Green, red, black and white pictures illustrate this book about
   > growing. A little boy puts his warm clothes away for the summer.
   > He watches plants and animals grow throughout the summer. Only
   > when he gets his warm clothes out in the fall and they are too
   > small, does he realize that **he** is growing too.

9. **Mouse Days: A Book Of Seasons**
    Lionni, Leo
    With text by Hannah Solomon
    Pantheon Brooks, New York, 1981
    Unpaged, illustrated

    January through December each month has two or three sentences
    and a picture of mouse activities which relate very closely to
    the type of human activities which may take place during that
    month. The mice appreciate nature, celebrate holidays, take vacations
    and eat ice cream cones.

10. **Fall Is Here!**
    Moncure, Jane Belk
    Illustrations by Frances Hook
    Child's World, Elgin, IL, 1975
    Unpaged, color illustrations

    A picture word page introduces this book which tells about a
    young boy's activities during the fall. He plays football with
    his friends, rolls in leaves, watches the birds go south, cooks
    hot dogs over a fire, eats an apple and buys a pumpkin. He
    sees seeds, squirrels and chipmunks. On the last page is a
    song with music - "Autumn Leaves."

11. **Weather**
    Pienkowski, Jan
    Illustrated by the author
    Judian Messner, New York, 1975
    Unpaged, color illustrations

    One word per every other page and two pages of pictures illustrating
    weather makes this a perfect book for very young children to
    put correct words to different types of weather. The pictures
    are colorful and fun and include one all gray page to indicate
    fog.

12. The Sandwich

Seymour, Dorothy Z.

Illustrated by Richard C. Lewis

Grosset, New York, 1965

Unpaged, illustrated

(An early start pre-school reader)

> Pictures and an eleven word vocabulary tell the story of a young boy and girl making a huge sandwich. Two of the pictures also show the children taking things off of the sandwich and the words on the page indicates "Less of this!" Less of that!" This could be helpful in explaining the concept of "less than."

13. Let's Find Out About Fall

Shapp, Martha

Illustrated by Laszlo Roth

Watts, New York, 1963

Four pages, color illustrations

> People, animals and plants change in the fall as they get ready for winter. Birds fly away and frogs find the bottom of the pond where they spend the winter sleeping. The caterpillar sleeps in his cocoon and becomes a moth in the spring. Halloween and Thanksgiving are in the fall.

14. Johnny Maple-Leaf

Tresselt, Alvin

Illustrated by Roger Duvoisin

Lothrop, New York, 1948

28 pages, illustrated

> This story is called "gently rhythmic" in the Library Journal. The words tell, and the pictures show, the details of spring and summer and fall as seen by a maple leaf named Johnny who lives deep in the woods. When winter arrives, Johnny falls from the tree and happily snuggles his way between the other leaves and goes to sleep.

15. Squirrels

   Wildsmith, Brian

   Watts, New York, 1975

   32 pages, color illustrations

   Large beautifully color watercolor illustrations help show young
   children the activities and abilities of squirrels. The uses of
   squirrel's tails and surprising facts about squirrel's diets will inform
   the adult reader as well as the young listener.

MR BUSHY TAIL

LEAVES

OCTOBER

Dear Parents:

It's October and, of course, October is the month for all of the funny, scary Halloween activities!

ART
Witches, hats and black cats

MUSIC
Halloween Is Here!

LITERATURE
Ghost stories and poems
Finger plays and nursery rhymes

SOCIAL STUDIES
Interesting facts about Halloween

SCIENCE
Migration and Hibernation

MATH COOKING
Caramel Corn
Toasted Pumpkin Seeds

BOOKS FROM THE LIBRARY

PHYSICAL EDUCATION
Pretend you are a witch combing her long stringy hair!

HAPPY OCTOBER!

SUGGESTED DAILY LEARNING PLANS

OCTOBER

Parent Page ART – Paint A Pumpkin LITERATURE – POEM – "Mr. Pumpkin" SOCIAL STUDIES – Discuss Halloween – A PHYS. ED. – Exercises 1-1 & B BOOK – Clifford's Halloween by Norman Bridwell	ART – (Continue) Paint A Pumpkin MUSIC – "Halloween Can Be Scary" PHYS. ED. – Exercises 1-2 & B MATH COOKING – Caramel Corn	ART – Jolly Jack-O-Lantern LITERATURE – POEM – "Jolly Jack-O-Lantern" PHYS. ED. – Exercises 1-3 (five times) BOOK – That Terrible Halloween Night by James Stevenson	ART – Let's Make A Black Cat LITERATURE – POEM – "Halloween Night" PHYS. ED. – Exercises 1-3 & C MATH COOKING – Popsicles BOOK – The Witch Kitten by Ruth Robinson Carroll	ART – Paper Mache Pumpkin LITERATURE – ACTION POEM – "Mr. Pumpkin Face" PHYS. ED. – Exercises 1-5 & L BOOK It's The Great Pumpkin Charlie Brown by Charles Schulz
ART – (Continue) Paper Mache Pumpkin LITERATURE – FINGER PLAY – "Five Little Jack-O-Lanterns" PHYS. ED. – Exercises 1-5 (do fast, do slow) BOOK – The Jack-O-Lantern Trick by Lillie Patterson	ART – Paper Bag Pumpkin SCIENCE – Discusss PHYS. ED. – Exercises 1-5 & D (do very slowly, do very, very, very slowly) BOOK – The Cat In The Hat Comes Back by Dr. Suess	ART – Stretchy Black Cat LITERATURE – FINGER PLAY – "Wide Eyed Owl" PHYS. ED. – Exercises 1-6 & B MATH COOKING – Finger Jello	ART – (Complete) Stretchy Black Cat MUSIC – "Halloween Is Here" PHYS. ED. – Exercises 1-6 & C BOOK – The Old Witch and The Ghost Parade by Ida DeLage	ART – Kleenex Ghost LITERATURE – STORY "A Ghost Story" SOCIAL STUDIES – PHYS. ED. – Exercises 1-6 & D
ART – Surprise Pumpkin Painting LITERATURE – Recall "A Ghost Story" PHYS. ED. – Exercises 1-7 (three times) BOOK – ABC Halloween by Ida DeLage	ART – Halloween Noise Maker LITERATURE – FINGER PLAY – "Five Little Ghosts" PHYS. ED. – Exercises 1-8 BOOK – Haunted Houses on Halloween by Lillie Patterson	ART – (Complete) Halloween Noise Maker SCIENCE – Discuss "Hibernate" SOCIAL STUDIES – Recall A & B PHYS. ED. – Exercises 1-8 & E	ART – Chinese Jack-O-Lantern LITERATURE – NURSERY RHYME "Peter Pumpkin Eater" PHYS. ED. – Exercises 1-8 & E MATH COOKING – Cupcakes BOOK – Pumpkin Moonshine by Tasha Tudor	ART – Another Chinese Jack-O-Lantern LITERATURE – NURSERY RHYME – "Little Miss Muffet" PHYS. ED. – Exercises1-8 & D BOOK – Detective Mole and the Halloween Mystery by Robert Quackenbush
ART – (Complete) Chinese Jack-O-Lanter LITERATURE – POEM – "Carving Mr. Pumpkin" SCIENCE – Discuss "Woodchuck" PHYS. ED. – Exercises 1-8 & F BOOK – Scat, The Witches Cat by Geraldine Ross	ART – Halloween Placemat MUSIC – "Sing A Song of Halloween" PHYS. ED. – Exercises 1-8 & G BOOK – Halloween Surprises by Ann Schweninger	ART – Triangle Witch LITERATURE – POEM – "Scary Halloween" PHYS. ED. – Exercise 1-8 & C BOOK – The Witch Who Went For A Walk by Margaret Hillert	ART – (Complete) Triangle Witch SCIENCE – Discuss "Butterfly" PHYS. ED. – Exercises 1-8 (do very small and very fast) BOOK – Humbug Witch Lorna Balian	ART – Black Skeleton LITERATURE – FINGER PLAY – "Halloween", NURSERY RHYME – "Wise Old Owl" PHYS. ED. – Exercises1-8 and F, G. H MATH COOKING – Toast Pumpkin Seeds

OCTOBER

I. ART
Children will develop skills in:
Organization
Sequence
Use of small muscles

A. PAINT A PUMPKIN
Cut large newsprint paper in the shape of a pumpkin. Paint it orange. When the orange paint is dry, children will paint facial features of pumpkin in black.

B. JOLLY JACK-O-LANTERNS

Pre-cut squares, triangles, circles, diamonds, stars and ovals from black paper. Also, cut assorted mouth shapes. Pre-cut pumpkins out of orange paper. See pumpkin patterns.

Children will paste black shapes on pumpkins to make eyes, nose and mouth from shapes they select. This will give the children a chance to be creative as they decide how they want their Jack-O-Lantern to look.

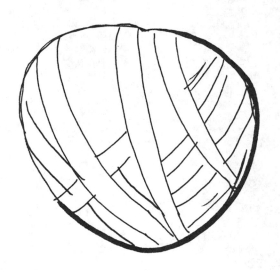

C. **PAPER-MÂCHÉ PUMPKIN**

Dip newspaper strips in wheat paste, wallpaper paste or white glue and apply to balloon. Continue overlapping strips until covered with two or three layers of paper.

Place on wax paper or paper toweling to dry. It will take several days to dry. Puncture balloon. Paint and decorate when dry.

D. **PAPERBAG PUMPKIN**
1. Stuff a large bag with crumpled newspapers.
2. Tie the top closed with string.
3. Paint the pumpkin part of the bag orange.
4. Paint the top that is tied green to look like a stem.
5. Use the black paint to put on the facial features.

E. LET'S MAKE A BLACK CAT

1. Cut one large circle for the cat's body from one 9" x 12" sheet of construction paper.

2. Cut smaller circle for cat's head from half of a 9" x 12" sheet of construction paper.

3. Cut two triangles for ears, two strips 1" x 4½" for feet.

4. Cut six white strips for whiskers.

5. Cut one curved black strip for tail.

6. Cut two green circles for eyes and cut two smaller black circles for pupils of eyes.

7. Assemble and paste.

F.   STRETCHY BLACK CAT

Cut a piece of black paper into 5" x 6" pieces. Fold in half, shape ears at one end and round off other end - making a small tab at the botton:

Make oval green eyes, orange circle for nose and large circle for mouth:

For the body, cut one strip orange and one strip black (2" x 8").

For arms and legs, cut two strips black 2" x 18".

To make the body, place orange strip and black strip at right angle, then fold alternating black then orange until strip makes accordian appearance. Attach the head and arms to the body. Then, attach legs to the body. Finish off the cat by curling ends of arms and legs around pencil.

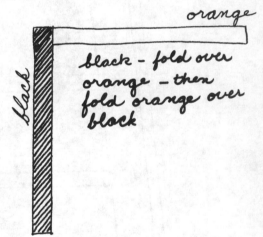

black - fold over orange - then fold orange over black

Give the cat whiskers if you like.

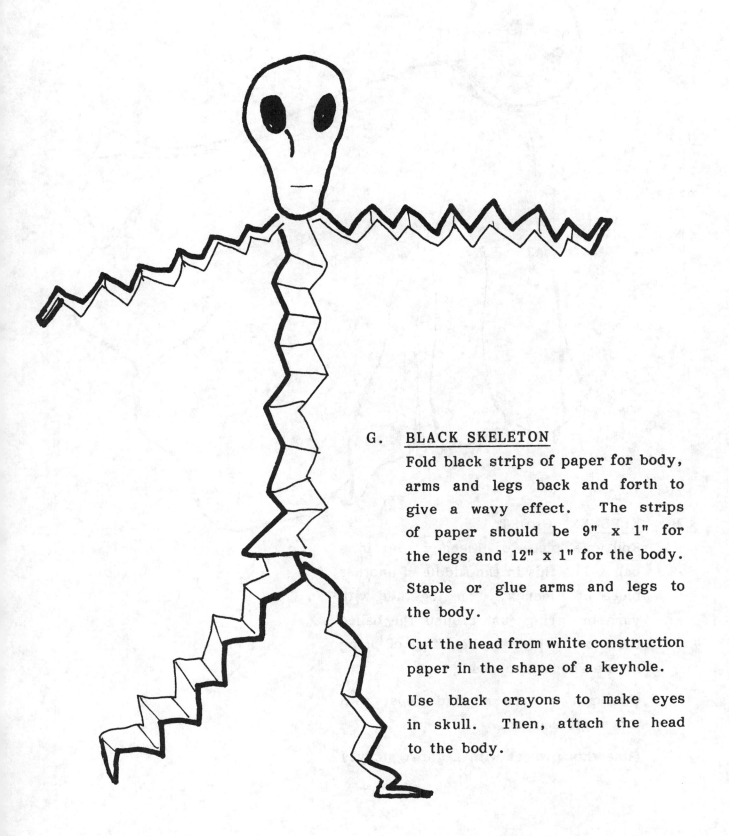

G. **BLACK SKELETON**

Fold black strips of paper for body, arms and legs back and forth to give a wavy effect. The strips of paper should be 9" x 1" for the legs and 12" x 1" for the body.

Staple or glue arms and legs to the body.

Cut the head from white construction paper in the shape of a keyhole.

Use black crayons to make eyes in skull. Then, attach the head to the body.

H. KLEENEX® GHOST

Roll one piece of Kleenex® up in a ball. Put this in the middle of another piece of Kleenex®. Tie together with yarn or string just around the balled Kleenex® to give it the effect of being in the shape of a head.

Now put a face on the ghost with the magic marker.

(Use this project with a ghost story.)

I. SURPRISE PUMPKIN PAINTING

Draw a pumpkin or other Halloween type picture on newsprint. Instruct the children to press down hard on the crayon.

When the picture is finished, paint over it with black paint.

The orange picture will show through.

J. HALLOWEEN NOISE MAKER

Staple two paper plates together with a few beans inside. Decorate by painting or coloring on a Halloween design.

K. CHINESE JACK-O-LANTERNS

Fold orange construction paper in half lengthwise. Cut from folded side approximately ½" apart to within 1" of the edge of the paper. Open and attach short ends of paper with stapler.

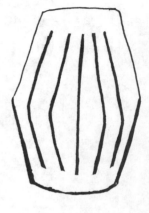

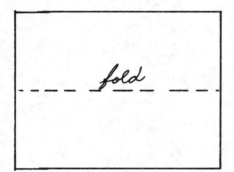

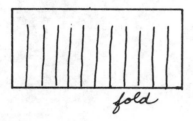

L. ANOTHER CHINESE JACK-O-LANTERN

Fold orange construction paper in half the long way. Fold it in half again. Open up the last fold.

Cut into paper from folded side making cuts 1" apart and stopping at the center fold.

Open the paper all the way. Now, fold the uncut sections in the center and overlap them. Staple ends to form a three dimensional pumpkin.

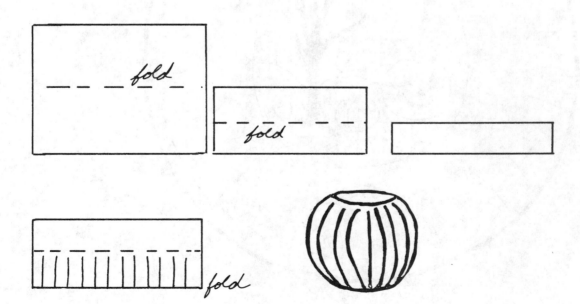

M. HALLOWEEN PLACEMENT

Children draw a Halloween picture on a piece of 9" x 12" construction paper.

Fringe the edges of the paper.

This can be used as a placemat for party time.

N. TRIANGLE WITCH

Cut one white circle for the head.
Cut one large black triangle for the body.
Cut three small black triangles (one for the hat and two for the arms).

Paste the head, body and arms on a piece of newsprint.

Draw in the hands, feet, facial features and witches hair.

MATERIALS CHART

OCTOBER

A. PAINT A PUMPKIN Large newsprint Orange paint Black paint	**B. JOLLY JACK-O-LANTERN** Black paper Paste Orange paper	**C. PAPER MACHE PUMPKINS** Newspaper Wheat paste/wallpaper paste/ white glue Wax paper/paper toweling Paint	**D. PAPERBAG PUMPKIN** Large paper bag Newspaper String Orange paint Green paint Black paint
E. LET'S MAKE A BLACK CAT 9"x12" black construction paper White construction paper Green construction paper	**F. STRETCHY BLACK CAT** Black construction paper Green construction paper Orange construction paper	**G. BLACK SKELETON** Black construction paper Staple/glue White construction paper Black crayons	**H. KLEENEX GHOST** Kleenex Yarn/string Magic marker
I. SURPRISE PUMPKIN PAINTING Newsprint Orange crayons Black paint	**J. HALLOWEEN NOISE MAKER** Two paper plates Beans Paint/crayons	**K. CHINESE JACK-O-LANTERN** Orange construction paper Staple	**L. ANOTHER CHINESE JACK-O-LANTERN** Orange construction paper Staple
M. HALLOWEEN PLACEMAT 9"x12" construction paper Crayons	**N. TRIANGLE WITCH** White construction paper Black construction paper Newsprint Crayons		

II. LITERATURE

Children will develop the ability to identify and enjoy:

Characters

Main characters

Details

Sequence of events

A. A GHOST STORY

Once upon a time there lived a family of ghosts. There was Mother ghost and Father ghost and their three little ghost children. Mother and Father ghost were very proud of their ghost heritage. Ghosts are very special and they have special duties to perform on Halloween. Their job as ghosts is to scare people by moaning and groaning.

Most ghosts can moan and groan so well, they send shivers up and down your spine. They can make your hair tingle. Some can make you so scared, your heart will start to pound like a drum. Mother and father ghost had taught their children to be very scary.

Two children learned their lessons well. They could moan and groan so well it would make your heart quiver. Mother and Father were very proud of their two children. But, the little baby ghost was such a happy little ghost he spent his time smiling and laughing and enjoying himself. When he was supposed to moan and groan, all he could do was chuckle. Now, whoever heard of a chuckling ghost?

Mother and Father hoped as the baby grew he'd learn that he had to moan and groan to be a good ghost. Sorry to say, as time went by, he, instead of moaning and groaning, became happier. His laughter now came in great "Ho, Ho's" and "Ha, Ha's." Sometimes he laughed so hard he rolled around on the floor laughing and laughing.

His mother and father were greatly concerned about his unghostly behavior. They were embarrassed about having a child so different from all the other ghost children.

Their concern became even greater as Halloween time approached. It is the duty and responsibility of each and every ghost to make this a scary night. This is the night when witches ride their brooms, black cats howl and cry and skeletons rattle their bones. On Halloween night, the ghosts of all sizes must moan and groan and make Halloween a night for all to remember!

Mother and Father discussed this with the baby ghost but, somehow, he couldn't seem to understand how serious they were. Baby ghost only thought of how much fun the children were going to have on Halloween night. He wanted to see all the children in their costumes and hear their excited cries of "Trick or Treat."

Halloween night finally arrived and the baby ghost was watching a group of children as they walked, hurrying from house to house.

"Tommy," shouted someone. "Where have you been? Come on with us."

The children thought the baby ghost was their friend Tommy dressed in a ghost costume. Before he knew what was happening, he was walking along with a witch, a robot, a cowboy and a fuzzy black cat. Tumbling up porch steps, the children all shouted, "Trick or Treat." The lady of the house smiled when she saw the little group.

"My, oh my. Just look who's here!"

As she was talking, she was putting a candy bar in the witch's basket. The cat carried a bag and each one had something to put their treat in except the baby ghost.

"Where's your bag?" asked the lady. But before the baby ghost could answer, she ran back into the house and quickly brought a brown bag for him to carry.

"There you are," she said. "That's because you have such a good ghost costume.

"Thank you," the children shouted, and they ran down the steps and hurried along to the next house.

The baby ghost thought this was great fun. The children kept calling him "Tommy" as they walked from house to house, collecting treats. The baby ghost thought this was great fun! He enjoyed the children so much, he went to every house in the neighborhood with the children. At last his bag was so full of goodies it was getting heavy to carry. They finally reached the last house on the block. Then, in a flurry of "Goodnights" and "Goodbyes" the children scattered to their various homes and the baby ghost found himself standing with a bag full of treats. He skipped home, barely touching the ground.

When he arrived home, no one was there. Since Halloween only comes once a year, the witches and ghosts wanted to enjoy every minute of it and they were still out moaning and groaning. The baby ghost sat down with his bag of treats. One by one he ate each delicious piece of candy, each apple, each popcorn ball and each caramel until the bag was empty. Not one piece was left! He smiled with contentment.

Soon, however, the smile faded. He didn't feel well. What could be the matter? Poor baby ghost. His little tummy hurt so much that he started to moan and groan.

Just about this time, Mother and Father ghost came home. What did they hear? The whole house rang from top to bottom with the saddest, the most sincere, the most heart rendering moans and groans they had ever heard.

"Could it be!" said Mother in wonderment.

"Could it possibly be?" said Father in amazement.

And sure enough, poor little baby ghost was uttering the best moans and groans they had ever heard.

Mother and Father ghost were so happy with baby ghost's moans and groans he began feeling better and better.

Every Halloween after that, the baby ghost remembered how terrible his tummy felt after he had eaten all of the Halloween candy and his moans and groans were the loudest, most scary of all!

POEMS/FINGER PLAYS/NURSERY RHYMES

Children will develop the ability to participate in and enjoy:

Rhythm

Poetry

Sequence

Characters

B. POEMS

1. MR. PUMPKIN

Mr. Pumpkin so orange and round,
You look so lifeless on the ground.
But children will smile and clap with delight,
When you're a Jack-O-Lantern on Halloween night.

2. HALLOWEEN NIGHT

On Halloween, On Halloween,
Goblins and witches can be seen.
Jet black bats fly through the air,
Moaning ghosts give us a scare.
Children in costumes can be seen,
Parading around on Halloween.

3. SCARY HALLOWEEN

Witches and ghosts are scary things,
And so are bats with large black wings.
They make us tremble and shake with fright,
When they come begging on Halloween Night!

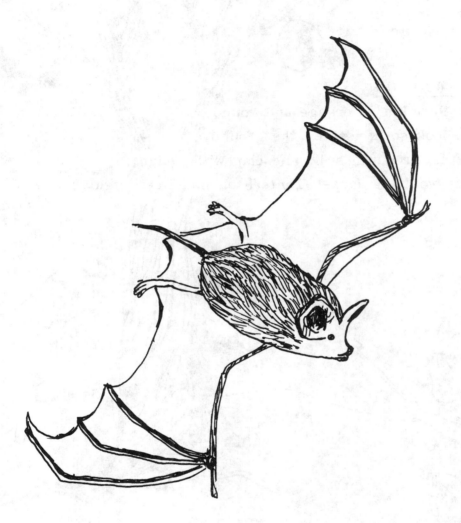

4. JOLLY JACK-O-LANTERN

Jolly, jolly Jack-O-Lantern,
I'll light a candle to make you shine.
With your slanted eyes and toothsome grin,
I'm happy that you're mine.

5. MR. PUMPKIN'S FACE

(Use a real pumpkin and black construction paper features
to tape onto the pumpkin, or use a felt shaped pumpkin
with black felt features.)

Look at Mr. Pumpkin,
Sitting in his place.

Let's get a knife,
And carve a funny face.

Two triangle eyes,
And an oval nose.

Look how funny
Mr. Pumpkin grows.

Now for a mouth,
We'll make a toothy grin.

And then we'll light a candle,
And place it in.

Mr. Pumpkin's smile,
Will surely bring delight,

To all of the children
On Halloween Night.

6. **CARVING MR. PUMPKIN**

Here sits Mr. Pumpkin,
He is quite plain as you can see.

When you start to carve him,
Think how he should be.

You can make his face like this,
And he'll look glad.

Or make his face like this,
And he'll look sad.

If you want him scary,
To fill our hearts with fright,

You'll make him look like this,
On Halloween Night.

Or, maybe you'll cut him in pieces,
Can you guess the reason why?

To turn our Mr. Pumpkin,
Into Pumpkin Pie!

C. FINGER PLAYS

   1.   HALLOWEEN

Witches in their pointed hats,	(Place a hand on each side of the head and then meet over the head to form a point.)
Rattling skeletons,	(Shake arms and legs and head.)
Scary cats.	(Make fingers form whiskers.)
Ghosts dressed in their Sheets of white,	(Wave arms up and down.)
Parade around on Halloween Night.	(Children move around in a circle waving their arms like ghosts.)
"Trick or Treat. Trick or Treat."	(Place hands around mouth like a megaphone.)
What goodies do you have for us on Halloween Night?"	(Hold out hands as though holding a bag to receive a treat.)

2. <u>WIDE-EYED OWL</u>

Here's a wide-eyed owl,   (Bring pointer finger and thumb of both hands together and place before eyes.)

With a pointed nose,   (Make a peak with two forefingers and place before nose.)

And claws for toes.   (Hands arched before chest, fingers curled.)

He lives high in a tree.   (Hands clasped high above head.)

When he looks at you,   (Index finger and thumb of both hands together before eyes.)

He flaps his wings,   (Bend elbows, flap hands.)

And says, "Whoo, whoo-o-o."   (Make "whoo" sound.)

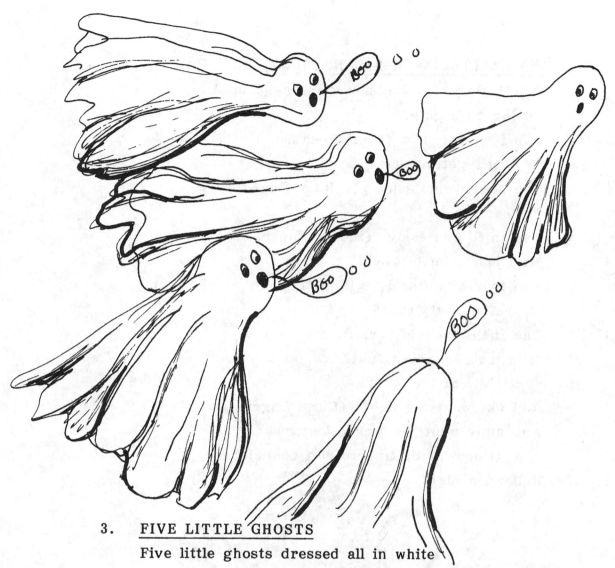

3. <u>FIVE LITTLE GHOSTS</u>

Five little ghosts dressed all in white
Were scaring each other on Halloween night.
"Boo!" said the first one. "I'll catch you!"
    (Hold pointer finger.)
"Whoo," said the second, "I don't care if you do!"
    (Hold up middle finger.)
The third ghost said. "You can't run away from me!"
    (Hold up ring finger.)
And the fourth one said, "I'll scare everyone I see!"
    (Hold up little finger.)
Then the last one said, "It's time to disappear!"
    (Hold up thumb.)
See you at Halloween time next year.

4. ## FIVE LITTLE JACK-O-LANTERNS

Five little jack-o-lanterns (One hand up.)

Sitting on a gate.

The first one said (Point to thumb.)

"My, it's getting late!"

The second one said, (Pointer finger)

"I hear a noise!"

The third one said, (Middle finger.)

"It's just a lot of boys!"

The fourth one said, (Ring finger.)

"Come on, let's run!"

The fifth one said, (Litte finger.)

"It's just Halloween fun!"

"Puff!" went the wind.

And out went the light (Close fingers into fist.)

And away went the jack-o-lanterns

    (Open hand, fingers run behind back.)

Halloween night.

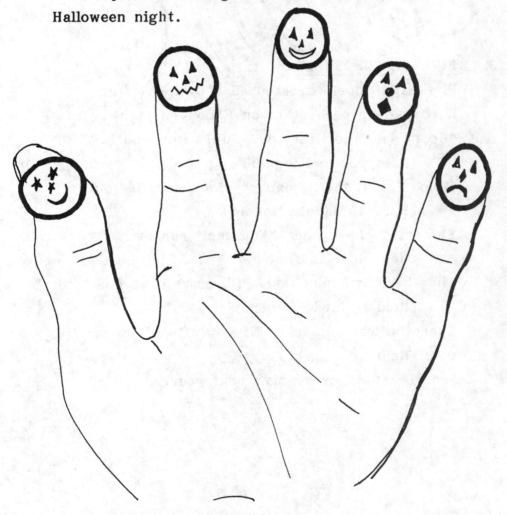

D. NURSERY RHYMES

1. PETER PUMPKIN EATER

Peter, Peter, pumpkin eater
Had a wife and couldn't keep her;
He put her in a pumpkin shell,
And there he kept her very well.

2. LITTLE MISS MUFFET

Little Miss Muffet,
Sat on a tuffet,
Eating her curds and whey.
Along came a spider,
Who sat down beside her,
And frightened Miss Muffet away!

3. WISE OLD OWL

A wise old owl sat in an oak,
The more he heard the less he spoke;
The less he spoke the more he heard,
Why aren't we all like that wise old bird?

III. MUSIC

Children will develop the ability to participate in and enjoy music.

A. <u>HALLOWEEN CAN BE SCARY</u>
(Tune - make up your own tune.)
Strange things happen on Halloween,
All around us can be seen,
Little people dressed so cute,
Someone wears a cowboy suit.
There's a witch, a ghost, a bunny, a cat,
A robot, a hobo in a stove pipe hat.
Who's little face hides behind that scary mask?
No one is telling, but if you should ask,
Get ready! Get set! Count, one, two, three,
'Cause behind the mask is little me!

B. <u>HALLOWEEN IS HERE</u>
(Tune - The Farmer In The Dell.)
Oh, Halloween is here,
Oh, Halloween is here,
With costumes on we'll walk around,
We'll knock on doors all over town,
When Halloween is here.

C. SING A SONG OF HALLOWEEN

(Tune - Sing A Song Of Sixpence.)

Sing a song of Halloween,

What a scary night,

Ghosts and bats and big black cats,

Give us all a fright.

Shining jolly Jack-O-Lanterns

Fill our hearts with fun,

But if the black witch comes along,

We'll all run!

IV. SCIENCE

Children will develop skills in:

Distinguishing differences and similarities of attributes.

A. <u>Birds start flocking together</u> as they prepare to fly south. <u>This is called "Migration"</u>. Birds that migrate to a warmer climate for the winter are: robins, bluebirds, red winged black birds, wrens, hummingbirds, bobolinks, Baltimore Orioles and most wild ducks and geese. Birds migrate because the ice and snow make it hard for them to find their food in the winter. No one really knows how birds manage to find their way south. However, birds have sharp eyes and even though some of them fly at night, they are sensitive to wind currents, temperatures, moisture and light. These conditions help them find their way. Not all birds have to migrate when it turns cold. Cardinals, nuthatches, English sparrows and chickadees have a warm down that keeps them warm during the cold winter.

B.   Some animals "Hibernate" when the cold winter arrives. Hiber
     means "winter sleep." Some animals go into a deep sleep
     some are in a half-sleep state. The body functions of the an
     slow down and the animal is able to live through the winter months
     when it would be difficult to find food. Animals that hibernate
     to escape the cold weather are: skunks, squirrels, prairie dogs,
     badgers, bats and dormice. Bears hibernate but, on a warm
     winter day, may wake up and they will move around. Snakes,
     toads, frogs, turtles and lizards know when summer is over and
     they will burrow down into the mud where they stay until spring
     arrives and it is warm again.

C.   The woodchuck, or ground hog, as it is more commonly called, becomes fat, lazy and sleepy in the fall.   Late in the fall, the woodchuck will go into his den, curl up into a ball with his head between his hind legs and go into a deep sleep.   There is a legend that has come down through the years that on the second day of February, the woodchuck will come out of his den.   If the sun is shining and he can see his shadow, he will return to his den to sleep for six more weeks.   However, if the day is cloudy and the woodchuck or ground hog could not see his shadow, the ground hog wouldn't go back to sleep and this would signal that spring had arrived.   We call that special day "Ground Hog's Day."

D. <u>The Monarch or Milkweed Butterfly</u> is distinguished by its beautiful orange and black coloring with white dots along the edge of its wings. This butterfly hatches from a caterpillar that has black, yellow and white stripes around its body. The larva, or caterpillar, feed on the milkweed and, for this reason, the Monarch is often called the Milkweed Butterfly. The caterpillar has a big appetite as it feeds on milkweed leaves, which incidentally, give the caterpillar a bad taste which the birds don't like. Then, the caterpillar spins a chrysalis that is apple green in color and edged in gold. In less than two weeks, the butterfly will emerge and soon the Monarch Butterfiles will swarm together and start on their long journey south. Some Monarchs may even cross the ocean. The butterflies travel together and they make quite a sight when they stop to rest as they will all swarm on one tree turning it a beautiful orange color.

V. SOCIAL STUDIES

Children will develop an awareness of holidays, traditions and seasonal changes.

A. <u>Halloween</u> is a time of excitement and fun as boys and girls plan the costumes they will wear October 31st. Children, dressed in costumes and often wearing masks, go around their neighborhood to "trick or treat" as they collect goodies to take home and enjoy.

Halloween is always celebrated October 31st. The name came about because Halloween comes before "All Saints Day" and means "hallowed" or "holy evening." This holiday goes back over 1,200 years to the 700's when the Roman Catholic Church named November 1st as "All Saints Day."

B. There are many superstitions connected with Halloween. These superstitions came down through the years from an order of priests from France and Britain called the Druids.

The Druids believed that on Halloween, ghosts, fairies, cats, witches, and elves came out to harm people. The Druids also had an Autumn festival called "Samhain" or "summer's end." In the 700's, the two celebrations were combined and became known as "Halloween."

VI. OCTOBER PHYSICAL EDUCATION FUN

Children will develop skills in:

Rhythm

Imaging

Use of large and small muscles

Good sports conduct

A. **MOVE AS IF YOU ARE:**

1. Carrying a great big pumpkin.
2. A witch combing her long, stringy hair.
3. A little baby ghost.
4. Putting on your Halloween costume.
5. Carving a little, tiny pumpkin.
6. Going up and down a porch's steps trick or treating.
7. Jumping up to say Boo-oo-oo.
8. A big black cat.

B. **HIDE THE WITCH'S HAT**

Make a witch's hat or a picture of a witch's hat. One child leaves the room while others hide the hat. Child that is "It" returns. The children clap (or slap the floor) very slowly as "It" comes into the room and speed up as "It" gets closer to the hat. They slow down to very slow clapping as "It" gets away from the hat. A new "It" is chosen if, after a few minutes, the child does not find the hat. If "It" finds the hat, he/she may choose a new "It" and the process is repeated.

C. PIN THE NOSE ON THE PUMPKIN

Preparation: Draw a large picture of a Jack-O-Lantern with all his facial features except his nose. Cut a large triangle or circle to be the nose and place a piece of tape on one side. Blindfold a child, turn him around a few times, then aim him toward the pumpkin. He will try to stick the nose on the pumpkin. One by one the children will each get a turn.

D. LET'S PLAY A PUMPKIN GAME

Preparation: Adult cuts a pumpkin out of orange felt and makes several black felt shapes for a pumpkin's mouth, nose and eyes.

A child uses black mouth, nose and eyes to make a pumpkin face while the others watch. Recite pumpkin poems found earlier in this chapter to go along with this activity.

E. LET'S PLAY "I SPY"

This game can be played any time and with any theme. For Halloween we will use the colors orange, black and white. Show the children a piece of orange paper. Then say, "I spy something orange in this room." See if they can guess what you see. Give clues if you need to. Anything that has orange in it will be the right answer. Use the other colors and when children catch on, give them the chance to say, "I spy something orange."

F. **PAPER PUMPKIN HUNT**

Preparation: Cut paper pumpkins from orange construction paper. Hide the pumpkins around the room. Then have the children try to see how many they can find.

G. **WHAT'S MISSING**

Preparation: Find or draw pictures concerned with Halloween. For example: pumpkins, witches, bats, ghosts, etc. Discuss each picture with the children. Then choose someone to close their eyes. Take one of the pictures away and see if the child can guess which one is missing. This is a good memory game.

H. **MATCHING HALLOWEEN COLORS**

Preparation: Cut four circles each of orange, black and white construction paper.

Place the circles on the table. Pick up an orange circle and ask the children what color it is. Then, have children give all circles of the same color to you. Let them point them out to you and you pick them up. Do this with all the colors. Purposely make a mistake so the children can correct you.

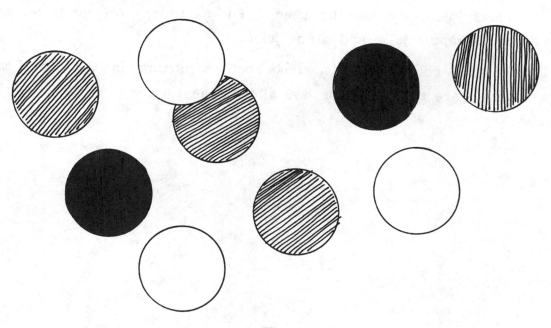

-77-

VII. MATH COOKING

Children will develop skills in:

Number awareness

Counting

Measuring

A. CARAMEL CORN

Pop the popcorn.

Mix together:

 1 cup molasses

 1 cup corn syrup

 ½ cup sugar

 ½ t. salt

 1 T. butter

 1 T vanilla

Pour the mixture over a bowl of popcorn and fold over and over until all the popcorn is coated.

Math: measurement awareness, larger and smaller -- kernels before and after popping.

B. POPSICLES

Mix orange kool-aid according to directions. Pour into a muffin tin. Place a popsicle stick in each tin for holding after the kool-aid is frozen. (They will freeze and lean at an angle.)

Fruit juice may also be used. For example: orange juice, apple or pineapple juice and grape juice.

Math: count popsicle sticks before putting in the tins, count tins - are there more or less sticks than tins?

C. <u>FINGER JELLO</u>

       3 small envelopes orange gelatin

       4 envelopes of unflavored gelatin

       4 cups boiling water

Stir gelatin powder before adding water. Add boiling water and stir until gelatin is dissolved. Pour into pan and allow to cool. Allow to set in regrigerator. When set, cut into cubes and serve.

Math: count ingredients and measurements, count cubes.

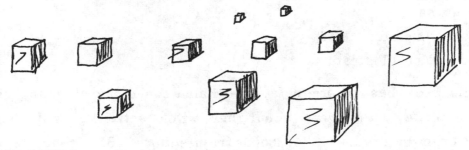

D. <u>CUPCAKES</u>

Make cupcakes from small box of prepared mix. Frost with orange frosting. Using M&M's, make a face on the cupcake. You can make these look like Jack-O-Lanterns.

Math: count cupcakes, count M&M's on each cupcake.

E. <u>TOAST PUMPKIN SEEDS</u>

Carve a pumpkin as children observe. Clean insides. Pull seeds from pulp. Rinse the seeds well and dry on a cookie sheet. Place the seeds in an oven at 350° for 10 minutes after coating seeds lightly with oil and salting them.

Math: count pumpkin seeds before baking and children can count them again as they eat them.

READ ALOUD BOOKS FROM THE LIBRARY
OCTOBER

BOOKS

Children will develop the ability to enjoy and gain knowledge from books.

1. Humbug Witch

    Balian, Lorna

    Abingdon, Nashville, 1965

    Unpaged, color illustrations

    > This book has become a favorite Halloween story of young children. The little witch goes about her witch activities with her black cat named Fred. She looks frightening. She concocts a Magic Potion. She makes attempts to change Fred into a hippopotamus or a candy bar. Piece by piece she takes off her costume to reveal an ordinary little girl. Then she goes to bed.

2. Clifford's Halloween

    Bridwell, Norman

    Illustrated by author

    Four Winds Press, New York, 1966, 1969

    Unpaged, color illustrations

    > Clifford dresses up as a ghost for Halloween. It's pretty hard for the big red dog who is bigger than a house to disguise himself. It's even harder for him to play Halloween games. Trick or treating with Clifford scares everyone out of the houses. But, he had a good time and asks the reader to make suggestions about his costume for next year.

3. The Witch Kitten
    Carroll, Ruth Robinson (1899)
    Walck, New York, 1973
    Unpaged, illustrations

    A wordless book and the pictures do not need words to tell this
    wild tale of a kitten's adventures after he unties a witches broom
    and is taken for a ride to nearby houses in the woods. After
    he is attacked by a predatory bird, the witch and her friends
    save him. He happily returns home.

4. A B C Halloween Witch
    DeLage, Ida
    Illustrated by Lou Cunette
    Gerrard Publishing Company, Chicago, IL 1977
    32 pages, color illustrations

    An alphabetic book showing witch activities. The drawings are
    amusing and populated with witches, black cats, children, unicorns
    and a particularly appealing yellow and red striped caterpillar who
    is destined to end up in the witches brew. Many good little
    Halloween sayings to help young children remember the alphabet.

5. The Old Witch and The Ghost Parade
    DeLage, Ida
    Illustrated by Judy Taylor
    Gerrard Publishing Company, Champaign, IL 1978
    47 pages, color illustrations

    After a series of adventures, an old witch wins only second prize
    in the jack-o-lantern contest. Not a gracious loser, the witch
    snatches her prize and zips off on her broom.

6. __The Witch Who Went For A Walk__

Hillert, Margaret

Illustrated by Krystyna Stasiak

Modern Curriculum Press, Cleveland, 1981

31 pages, illustrations

> A pre-primer vocabulary of sixty-seven words (vocabulary list included) and full color drawings tell the story of a witch's adventures on Halloween night.

7. __Haunted Houses On Halloween__

Patterson, Lillie

Drawings by Doug Cushman

Gerrard Publishing Company, Champaign, IL 1978

> The first of the two folk tales in this book tells of poor Ivan who seeks shelter in a small house that the owner has told him is haunted. Because he wasn't afraid, a skeleton gave Ivan some money. Ivan split the money with the owner of the haunted house and lived happily ever after. In the second story, Blackcat-witch, a witch who has been disguised as a cat, attacks a hunter but his dogs protect him and the witch disappears. Good Halloween stories for young children because they are not really too scary.

8. __The Jack-O-Lantern Trick__

Patterson, Lillie

Drawings by William M. Hutchinson

Gerrard Publishing Company, Champaign, IL 1979

38 pages, color illustrations

> Two pioneer girls use their jack-o-lantern to scare away some unfriendly Indians who visit them when the girls' parents have gone to the village.

9. **Detective Mole and the Halloween Mystery**

Quackenbush, Robert M.

Illustrated by author

1st edition, Lothrop, Lee and Shepard Books, New York, 1981

32 pages, color illustrations

> Detective Mole was called to solve the mystery when every jack-o-lantern from every front porch in town was stolen. The whole town become involved in solving the mystery. They discovered the jack-o-lanterns had been stolen to be lighted and used as a landing signal for a witch when she returned from the witches council. A happy ending was had by all.

10. **Scat, The Witch's Cat**

Ross, Geraldine

Illustrated by Kurt Werth

McGraw, New York, 1958

30 pages, illustrations

> Scat the cat wanted to escape from the witch he lived with because he hated her. He wanted to live with nice children. But, when he finally managed to escape, it was an accident. He fell from the witch's broom into a Halloween beggar's bag! The story is written in rhyme and after being read aloud several times, children will be able to start filling in the rhyming line if the reader stops to let them.

11. **It's The Great Pumpkin Charlie Brown**

Schulz, Chas. M.

Random House, New York, 1980

Unpaged, illustrations

> Charlie Brown and Sally wait in the Pumpkin Patch for the Great Pumpkin, as all of the others go trick or treating. The Great Pumpkin never shows up but Charlie never loses faith.

12. **Halloween Surprises**
    Schweninger, Ann
    1st edition, Viking Kestrel, New York, 1984
    32 pages, color illustrations

    This story is written in cartoon style with dialogue balloons over the speaking characters. The rabbit children make costumes, go trick or treating and end an eventful Halloween party with all of their friends. Charming soft pastel drawings illustrate this gentle story.

13. **That Terrible Halloween Night**
    Stevenson, James (1929)
    Greenwillow Books, New York, 1980
    Unpaged, color illustrations

    Louie and Mary Ann fail to scare Grandpa. Grandpa tells them that he cannot be easily scared since a night years ago when he became an "old man." He tells them about terrible monsters that he saw in a haunted house and one final terror which he refuses to describe. He tells them it made him the old man he is today. This amusing book provides happy Halloween ghost story.

14. **The Cat In The Hat Comes Back**
    Suess, Dr. (pseud.)
    Random House, 1958
    61 pages, illustrations
    (Beginner Books)

    The Cat in the Hat returns to get into all kinds of trouble in the children's house. He gets the house dirty, introduces little cats in the hat with alphabet names and finally cleans up his mess and departs with the whole alphabet back in his hat.

15. Pumpkin Moonshine

Tudor, Tasha (1915)

Walck, New York, 1962 (1938)

Unpaged, illustrations

> This is a small book which is dedicated to "a very sweet wee person." It is the story of a small girl who finds a very large pumpkin on her grandparents farm. She wants to make Pumpkin Moonshine from it, so she takes it back to the farm house. it is so big that she soon finds she has a run-away pumpkin on her hands and it terrorizes most of the animal and human residents of the farm. Grandfather cuts the pumpkin into a Pumpkin Moonshine. (After the little girl finally gets it to the farmhouse.) We can see by the picture that a Pumpkin Moonshine is the same as a Jack-O-Lantern.

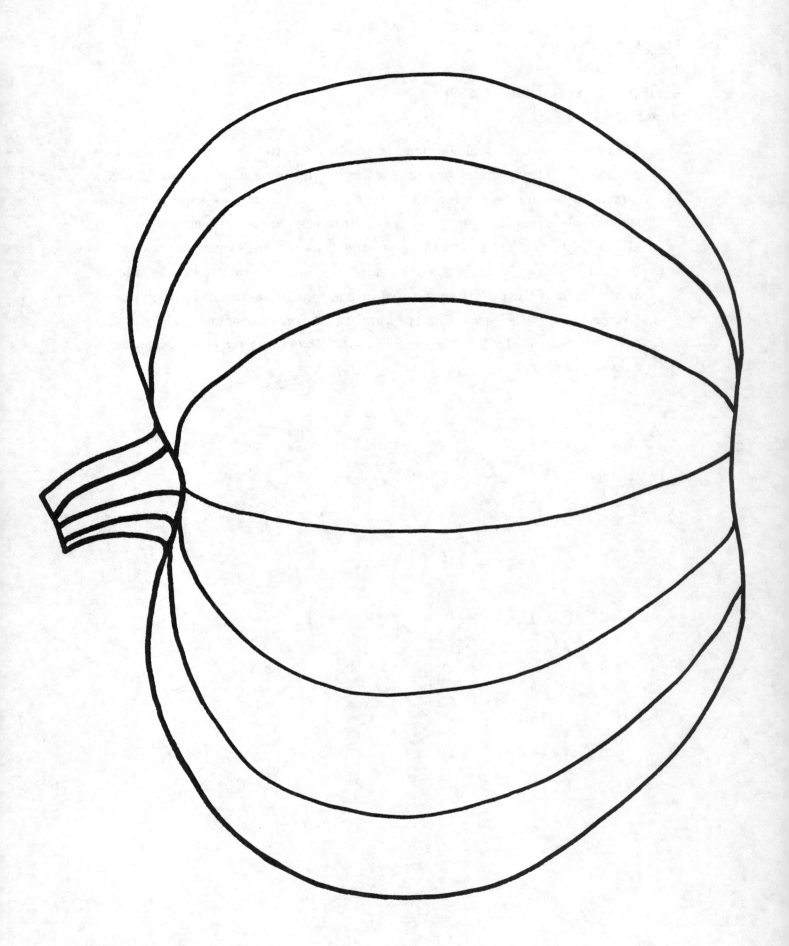

PATTERNS FOR PUMPKIN FACE

NOVEMBER

Dear Parents:

November is here and in November we will learn many things about Indians, Pilgrims and Thanksgiving!

BOOKS FROM LIBRARY

MATH COOKING
Celery Canoes and
Pilgrim Popcorn

ART
Make turkeys and
Indian necklaces

PHYSICAL EDUCATION
Gobble Walk and Paper Feather Hunt

SCIENCE
Winter feeding of birds
Changing of colors

LITERATURE
Pocahontas and Thanksgiving Poems

HAPPY NOVEMBER!

Week 1	Week 2	Week 3	Week 4
Parent Page ART – Paper Plate Turkey LITERATURE – FINGER PLAY – "Indian Child" PHYS. ED. – Exercises 1-2 BOOK – The Cookie House by Margaret Hillert	ART – Indian Head Dress LITERATURE – TRUE STORY – "Pocahontas" PHYS. ED. – Exercises 1-5 (do very slowly three times) BOOK – Cranberry Thanksgiving by Wende Devlin	ART – Indian Necklace LITERATURE – FINGER PLAY – "Little Indian" and "Pumpkin Pie" PHYS. ED. – Exercises 1-7 & E MATH COOKING – Nutritious Snack BOOK – Little Chief by Syd Hoff	ART – Tambourine LITERATURE – POEM – "Look Out Mr. Turkey" PHYS. ED. – Exercises 1-8 (do through very fast, do through very quietly) BOOK – Little Bear's Thanksgiving by Janice (pseud.)
ART – Scribble Turkey LITERATURE – POEM – "Mr. Turkey Gobble Gobble" PHYS. ED. – Exercises 1-3 MATH COOKING – Make A Turkey BOOK – Arthur's Thanksgiving by Marc Tolon Brown	ART – Decorated Indian Headband LITERATURE – Recall the story of "Pocahontas" SCIENCE – Activity B PHYS. ED. – Exercises 1-5 & C	ART – Indian Canoes LITERATURE – FINGER PLAY – "The Brave Little Indian" SOCIAL STUDIES – Pilgrims PHYS. ED. – Exercises 1-7 & E BOOK – Little Indian by Peggy Parish	ART – (Complete) Tambourine SOCIAL STUDIES – The Popcorn Treat PHYS. ED. – Exercises 1-8 & E MATH COOKING – A Pilgrim Popcorn Treat
ART – Hand Turkeys SOCIAL STUDIES – "The Thanksgiving Story" PHYS. ED. – Exercises 1-3 (five times) BOOK – Let's Find Out About Thanksgiving by Martha and Charles Shapp	ART – Indian Vest LITERATURE – FINGER PLAY "Marching Along" PHYS. ED. – Exercises 1-6 & D BOOK – Indian Two Feet and His Eagle Feather by Margaret Friskey	ART – (Complete) Indian Canoes LITERATURE – FINGER PLAY – "The Indian" SCIENCE – Activity D SOCIAL STUDIES – Pilgrims and Indians PHYS. ED. – Exercises 1-8 & E	ART – Thanksgiving Cornucopia LITERATURE – FINGER PLAY – "We Give Thanks" PHYS. ED. – Exercises 1-8 & E MATH COOKING – Pumpkin Pie BOOK – Over The River and Through the Wood by Lydia Maria Child
ART – Turkey Hand Print LITERATURE – FINGER PLAY – "Five Fat Turkeys" PHYS. ED. – Exercises 1 & B BOOK – The Thanksgiving Story by Alice Dalgliesh	ART – (Complete) Indian Vest MUSIC – "Mr. Turkey" SCIENCE – Activity C SOCIAL STUDIES – "The First Thanksgiving" PHYS. ED. – Exercises 1-6 (do five times very quickly)	ART – Musical Instruments LITERATURE – FINGER PLAY – "Five Little Turkeys" SCIENCE – Activity E PHYS. ED. – Exercises 1-8 & F BOOK – Running Owl The Hunter by Nathaniel Benchley	ART – (Complete) Thanksgiving Cornucopia SCIENCE – Activity F SOCIAL STUDIES – Thanksgiving Becomes A Holiday PHYS. ED. – Exercises 1-8 (but do them backwards)
ART – (Complete) Turkey Hand Print LITERATURE – POEM – "We Are Thankful For Our Land" SCIENCE – Activity A PHYS. ED. – Exercises 1-4 & B	ART – (Complete) Indian Vest LITERATURE – NURSERY RYHME – "Diddle Diddle Dumpling My Son John" PHYS. ED. – Exercises 1-6 (do twice as slowly as possible) MATH COOKING – Indian Canoes BOOK – My First Thanksgiving by Jane Moncure	ART – Quick and Easy Rhythm Rattle LITERATURE – NURSERY RHYME – "Here Am I" PHYS. ED. – Exercises 1-8 & (MATH COOKING – Corn Muffins BOOK – The First Thanksgiving by Lou Rogers	ART – Two Little Indian Wigwams LITERATURE – FINGER PLAY – "The New PHYS. ED. – Exercises 1-8 & B BOOK – Little Runner of the Longhouse by Betty Baker

I. ART
Children will develop skills in:
Organization
Sequence
Use of small muscles (small motor)

A. PAPER PLATE TURKEY
Cut colored construction paper (orange, red, brown and purple) in 2" x 6" strips. Taper one end of each strip to make a feather shape. Paste feathers under a small paper plate to make a turkey tail. Cut 2" x 3" strips of the same colored construction as listed above to paste on top of the plate. Add a head made of brown construction paper. Make wattle under neck of red paper.

B. **SCRIBBLE TURKEY**

Cut a medium circle from brown construction paper. Paste the circle on 9" x 12" sheet of construction paper. With crayons, draw the legs and head. Using a variety of colors, scribble around the circle in a row. Make each scribbled row a different color.

C. **HAND TURKEYS**

On a sheet of paper have the child trace their own hand. Give help if necessary. Color in the feathers and body and add legs. For a different texture, glue corn, rice or macaroni to turkey to make feathers.

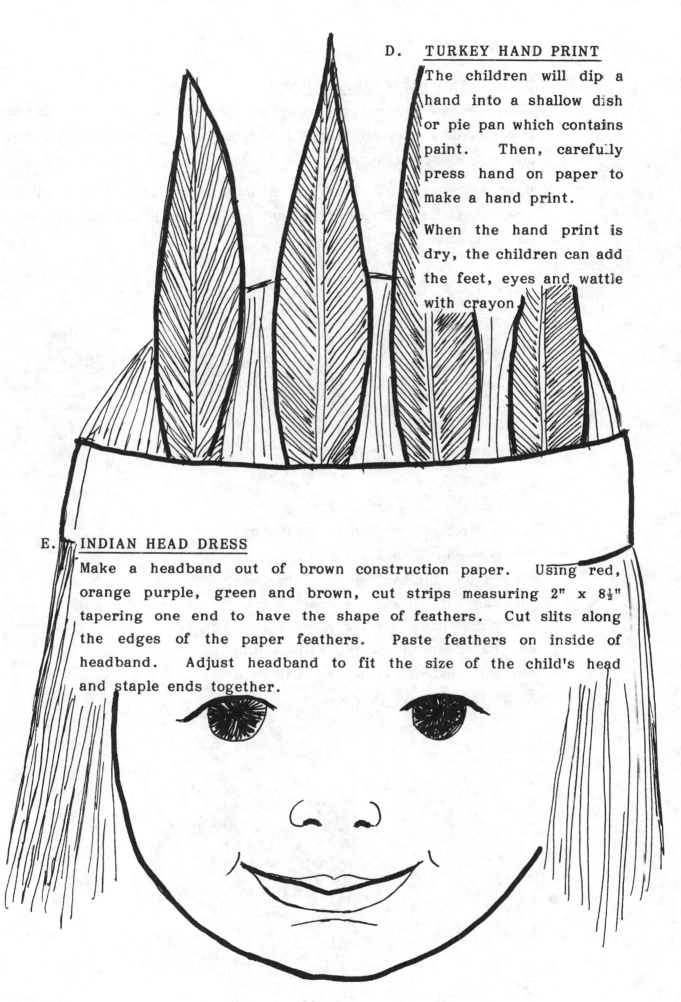

D. TURKEY HAND PRINT

The children will dip a hand into a shallow dish or pie pan which contains paint. Then, carefully press hand on paper to make a hand print.

When the hand print is dry, the children can add the feet, eyes and wattle with crayon.

E. INDIAN HEAD DRESS

Make a headband out of brown construction paper. Using red, orange purple, green and brown, cut strips measuring 2" x 8½" tapering one end to have the shape of feathers. Cut slits along the edges of the paper feathers. Paste feathers on inside of headband. Adjust headband to fit the size of the child's head and staple ends together.

F. __DECORATED INDIAN HEAD BAND__

Make a headband out of brown construction paper. Cut circles, triangles and diamond shapes out of orange, yellow, purple, green and red construction paper.

Have children paste these shapes in a design along the headband. When it is dry, fit the headband on the child's head and staple ends together.

G. __INDIAN VEST__

Cut front of a bag for the vest opening. Cut a circle in the bottom of the bag for the child's head. Cut holes in the sides of the bag for arms. Decorate the bag with Indian symbols. Rows of fringe may be used also. They can be added by cutting and pasting fringed construction paper. Use yarn to tie the front of the vest.

H. INDIAN NECKLACE

Make a tip on the end of the yarn or string by wrapping a piece of tape around the end. String macaroni and straws cut into pieces until the length of the desired necklace is achieved. Be sure to leave enough string or yarn at the ends so they can be tied together.

FOR ADDED FUN: Color the macaroni by dipping it into a small dish of water and food coloring the day before you make the necklaces so it has time to dry. Use tongs or slotted spoon to remove macaroni from food coloring and dry on waxed paper.

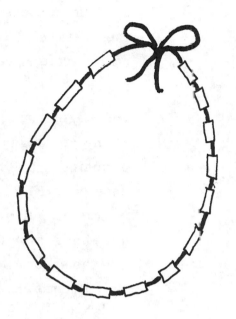

I. INDIAN CANOES

Fold a 9"x12" sheet of brown construction paper in half. Trace the outline of a canoe and have the children cut along this line. With paper punch, punch holes along curved edge of canoe. Tape one end of a strand of yarn. With the taped end of the yarn, have the children string the yarn through the holes. Decorate the outside of the canoe. If desired, put an Indian inside.

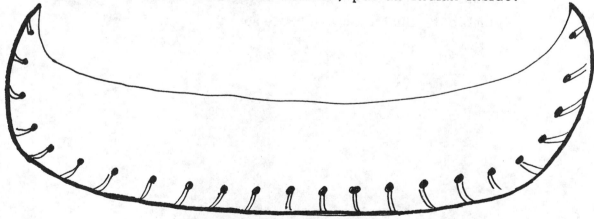

J. MUSICAL INSTRUMENTS

Decorate paper in Indian symbols and designs. Cover the oatmeal, salt box or empty coffee can with the paper.

For marching: Put yarn or string through the top by punching holes. Allow enough string or yarn so it can be put over the head and hang around the neck. Use the spoon, pencil or stick as a drumstick.

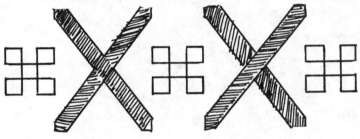

K. QUICK AND EASY RHYTHM RATTLE

Punch two holes on bottom of a plastic margarine tub. Thread elastic or bias tape through the holes and tie or staple the ends together. Place beans or rice inside tub and put lid securely on the tub. Child will slip hand under the elastic or tape, leaving the thumb out. Shake to make rattle sound.

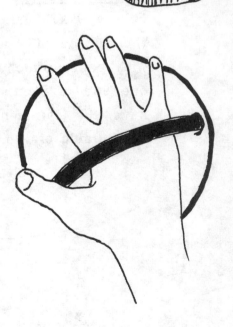

L. TAMBOURINE

Decorate the paper plate (of heavy cardboard) with Indian symbols. Hammer 10 bottle caps flat. With a hammer and a nail, pound a hole in the middle of each cap. Put five holes around the edge of the carboard plate. Thread the heavy cord from the bottom through the hole in the plate, through two bottle caps, through a bead, then back through the same holes in the bottle caps and back through the same hole in the plate. Repeat for the remaining four holes. When you reach the place where you started, tie the ends of the cord securely together. Shake the tambourine for noise.

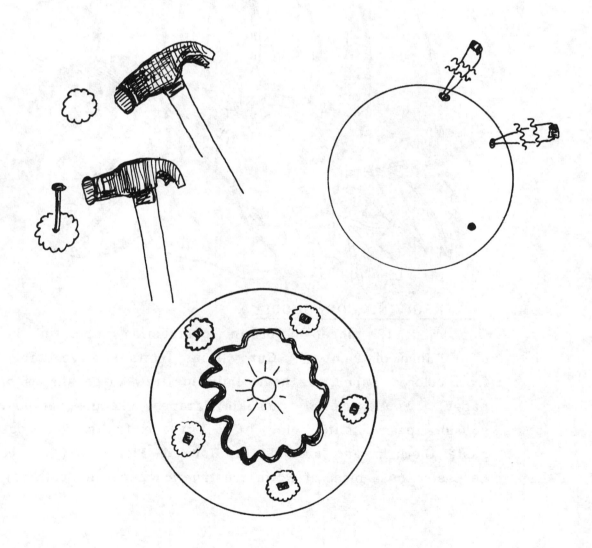

M. **THANKSGIVING CORNUCOPIA**

Cut 9" x 12" sheet of brown construction paper in the shape of a "Horn of Plenty." Cut various fruits and vegetable shapes from colored paper, or have children draw these shapes on white paper. For example: pumpkin, grapes, oranges, apples, corn, squash, pears, nuts, etc. Cut out the fruits and vegetables, paste them in and around the Horn of Plenty. (This could all be pasted on a piece of white construction paper if desired.)

N. TWO LITTLE INDIAN WIGWAMS

Cut a triangle from a piece of white construction paper. Cut a small triangle door. Decorate with Indian designs. Cut three small feather shaped pieces and paste at the top of the wigwam.

Another variation: Measure and cut from the directions below wigwams from a sheet of 9" x 12" brown construction paper. Make a small opening at the top and tape the overlap piece with a triangle opening at the bottom for the door. Make three feather-shaped pieces and tape at the top of the wigwam.

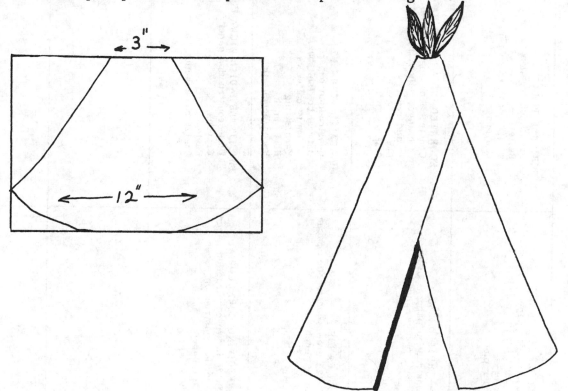

MATERIALS CHART

NOVEMBER

A. PAPER PLATE TURKEY
Construction paper - orange,
red, brown, purple
Paste
Paper plate

B. SCRIBBLE TURKEY
Brown construction paper
Paste
9"x12" construction paper
Crayons

C. HAND TURKEYS
Black paper
Crayons
Glue
Corn
Rice
Macaroni

D. TURKEY HAND PRINT
Shallow dish/pie pan
Paint
Blank Paper
Crayons

E. INDIAN HEAD DRESS
Construction paper - brown,
red, orange, purple
Paste
Staple

F. DECORATED INDIAN HEAD BAND
Construction paper - brown,
orange, yellow, purple,
and red
Paste
Staple

G. INDIAN VEST
Large bag
Construction paper
Yarn

H. INDIAN NECKLACE
Yarn/string
Tape
Macaroni
Straws
Food coloring
Tongs/slotted spoon
Waxed paper

I. INDIAN CANOES
9"x12" brown construction paper
Paper punch
Yarn
Tape

J. MUSICAL INSTRUMENT
Construction paper
Oatmeal box/salt box/
empty coffee can
Yarn/string
Hole punch
Spoon/pencil/stick

K. QUICK EASY RYTHM RATTLE
Hole punch
Plastic margarine tub
Elastic/bias tape
Staple
Beans/rice

L. TAMBOURINE
Paper plate/heavy cardboard
Bottle caps
Hammer
Nail
Cord

M. THANKSGIVING CORNUCOPIA
9"x12" brown construction paper
Assorted construction paper
White paper
Paste

N. TWO LITTLE INDIAN WIGWAMS
White construction paper
Crayons
Paste
9"x12" construction paper

II. LITERATURE

Children will develop the ability to identify and enjoy:

Characters

Main ideas

Details

Sequence of events

A. POCAHONTAS

When Pocahontas was approximately twelve years old, about one hundred strange white men came to live near her village.

She was an Eastern Woodlands Indian and the daughter of Chief Powhaton.

She learned to speak English and she taught John Smith, one of the settlers, to speak her language. She also watched John Smith and his friends build their homes and cook their food.

Pocahontas was impressed by the settlers fine clothing, but she could see that they did not know how to farm or fish in the "new land."

By the end of the summer of 1607, many settlers had died and Pocahontas knew that the others would need help to live through the winter. She talked her family and a nearby village of Indians into sharing food with the settlers.

The Indians and the settlers did not always get along. The settlers were on Indian land and they did not always bargain fairly with the Indians.

John Smith and a small group of settlers were captured when they were exploring a river to see if it would take them across the "new land." Captain Smith's friends were killed but Pocahontas begged her father to spare John Smith's life. Captain Smith was allowed to return to the settlement with his new Indian name -- Nataquod.

POEMS/FINGER PLAYS/NURSERY RHYMES

Children will develop the ability to participate in and enjoy:

Rythm

Poetry

Sequence

Characters

B. POEMS

1. MR. TURKEY GOBBLE, GOBBLE

Mr. Turkey with your gobble, gobble, gobble,
I hope you're having fun.
Mr. Turkey, how you waddle, waddle, waddle,
Your days will soon be done.
(Children strut around the room with hands on hips as they
say this poem.)

2. LOOK OUT, MR. TURKEY

Look out Mr. Turkey,
We've made you nice and fat.
You're going to be our dinner,
What do you think of that?

3. WE'RE THANKFUL FOR OUR LAND

Many years ago, the Pilgrim found our land.
We thank them for discovering this country so grand.
We're thankful as can be,
For this land where we are free.

C. FINGER PLAYS

1. INDIAN CHILD

If I were an Indian child,

This is what I would do,

I'd shoot my bow and arrow, (Aim bow and arrow.)

And paddle in my canoe. (Paddle with arms.)

2. FIVE FAT TURKEYS

Five fat turkeys were sitting on a fence. (One hand up.)

The first one said, "I'm so immense." (Point to thumb.)

The second one said, "I can gobble at you."

(Pointer finger.)

The third one said, "I can gobble too." (Middle finger.)

The fourth one said, "I can spread my tail." (Ring finger.)

The fifth one said, "Don't catch it on a nail." (Little finger.)

A farmer came along and stopped to say,

(Pointer finger of other hand.)

"Turkeys look best on Thanksgiving Day."

3. PUMPKIN PIE)

I am a pumpkin big and round.

(Make a large circle with your arms, just touching your

finger tips together.)

Grandpa came and picked me from the ground.

(Stoop over as if picking something up.)

Grandma cut and chopped - oh my!

(Make cutting and chopping motions.)

Now I am Thanksgiving pie!

(Pat your stomach and lick your lips.)

4. LITTLE INDIAN

(Action game - children chant with the action - children form a circle.)

Little Indian, little Indian, playing on your little drum.
Rum-a-tum-tum, Rum-a-tum-tum.
This is how you run, run, run.

Little Indian, little Indian,
What'll you do when you hear this sound?
Skipping, skipping, skipping, skipping,
Skipping, skipping all around.

Little Indian, little Indian,
Hopping, hopping, hop, hop, hop.
Little Indian, little Indian, now it's time to stop.

5. WE GIVE THANKS

We give thanks for all good things.
    (Stand with hands like a prayer.)
For turkey and stuffing and pumpkin pie.   (Action of eating.)
And when our tummies are stuffed so full, (Puff out tummy.)
We say, "Oh, me! Oh, my!"
    (Place hands on tummies, roll eyes.)

6. FIVE LITTLE TURKEYS

Five little turkeys flew up in a tree, (One hand up.)

The first one said, "There's a man I see." (Point to thumb.)

The second one said, "He's coming this way." (Pointer finger.)

The third one said, "It's Thanksgiving Day." (Middle finger.)

The fourth one said, "What's he going to do?" (Ring finger.)

The fifth one said, "He's coming after you." (Little finger.)

Chop went the axe before they flew away.

    (Clap hands to chop.)

They all were on the table on Thanksgiving Day.

    (Make table of one hand for "turkeys" of other hand
    to sit.)

7. THE BRAVE LITTLE INDIAN

Little Scout was an Indian boy.

    (Hold two fingers at back of head.)

He was so brave (Fold arms across chest.) and strong. (Show arm muscles.)

He took his bow and arrow, (Hands holding bow and arrow.)

And hunted all day long. (Shade eyes.)

He wanted to catch the grizzly,

A great e-NORMOUS bear -- GRR-rrr (Hold up arms, spread fingers, growl.)

He took his bow and arrow, (Holding bow and arrow.)

And hunted everywhere. (Shade eyes.)

He looked along the river,

As he paddled his canoe. (Paddling with hands.)

He climbed up on the hill, (Moving arms and feet like climbing.)

To get a better view. (Shade eyes like looking all around.)

He saw a furry rabbit,

With his cottontail

    (Both hands wiggle behind.)

and tall ears.

    (Hands make tall ears.)

And there, with great huge antlers,

    (Spread fingers on either side of head.)

He could see a pretty deer.

And suddenly from behind a rock, came Mr. Grizzly Bear.

    (Growl and raise hands, look mean.)

Little Scout took one look and ran away from there.

    (Turn and run).

8. THE NEW LAND

The Pilgrims sailed the stormy sea   (Wave hand like water.)

To start a country new and free.

They met other people already there,

(Index and middle fingers of left hand "meet" index and
middle fingers of right hand.)

And they had a great party on the land they would share.

(Spread arms wide.)

9. THE INDIAN

This is how the Indian brave paddles his canoe,

Splash, splash, splash, splash.

(Hands holding a paddle, two strokes on the right side,
two on the left.)

See how he hunts with his bow and arrow, too.

Zip, zip, zip, zip.   (Action of shooting a bow and arrow.)

Hear how he beats upon his drum.

Boom, boom, boom, boom.

(Action of holding a drum in the left hand and beating
with the right hand.)

This is how he dances when day is done.

Woo, woo, woo, woo.

Woo, woo, woo, woo.

(Hopping twice on right foot and two times on the left,
moving head up and down while tapping mouth to make
the Indian sound.)

D. NURSERY RHYMES

1. DIDDLE DIDDLE DUMPLING MY SON JOHN

Diddle diddle dumpling my son John,
Went to bed with his trousers on,
One shoe off and one shoe on,
Diddle diddle dumpling my son John.

2. HERE AM I

Here am I,
Little Jumping Jane.
When no one's with me,
I'm all alone.

III. MUSIC

Children will develop the ability to participate in and enjoy music.

A. **MR. TURKEY**

(Tune: London Bridge Is Falling Down)

Mr. Turkey, here we come. Here we come, here we come.

Listen here, you'd better run. Or you'll be dinner.

We'll eat you up with pumpkin pie, pumpkin pie, pumpkin pie.

We'll eat you up so don't you cry.

You'll taste delicious.

IV. SCIENCE
Children will develop skills in:
   Distinguishing differences
   Similarities of attributes

A. Watch and feed winter birds. Discuss how much easier it is for them to find food in the summer.

B. Discuss the squirrels and birds. Where are they in the winter?

C. Bring an empty branch indoors. Put the empty branch and an evergreen side by side. How are they the same? How are they different?

D. Discuss places where plants grow all year. How is the weather different than the locations where there is ice and snow?

E. Decorate with evergreens. Discuss why the name is so appropriate.

F. Watch a certain non-evergreen tree. Discuss what will happen to it as the weather gets colder and colder. How will it change as the weather warms up in the spring? Have the children draw it as changes occur.

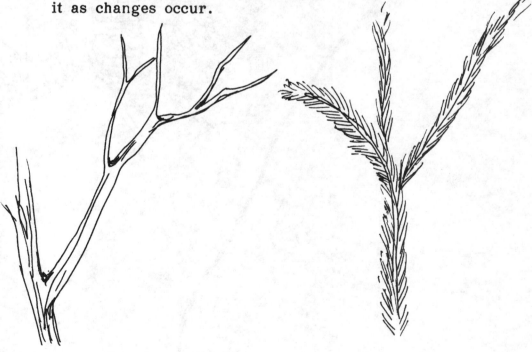

V. SOCIAL STUDIES

Children will develop an awareness of:

Holidays

Traditions

Seasonal changes

A. THE THANKSGIVING STORY

Many, many years ago, in a land across the Atlantic Ocean, a group of people had become very unhappy with the rules they were forced to obey. They had no freedom of religion. They weren't allowed to have a religious choice. They wanted to try for a new life in a new land. So, when they heard a ship called the Mayflower would be sailing to a new land, these brave people decided they would leave their homes and journey to this new land and start a new way of life.

The Mayflower left Southampton, England in August of 1620 with 102 people. The ship was crowded and it was a difficult trip for the adults and particularly for the children. It was hard for the children because there was very little space on the ship for them to play. The ocean voyage took 65 days, or two months, to complete. By the time the Mayflower reached America, they had very little food left. Also, it was the beginning of winter and the weather was very cold.

The Pilgrims met some friendly Indians who helped them build houses and hunt for food. The Pilgrims were curious about these Indians; their red skin and their clothing made of buckskin. They noticed the shoes they wore were made of deerskin and were called moccasins. The Indians were likewise curious about these light-skinned people who came in a big boat. They looked at the strange clothes the Pilgrims wore. They looked at their buckled shoes and the tools they had brought with them.

The winter was very hard and only half of the Pilgrims were strong enough to survive. They were happy and grateful when spring finally arrived. The weather became warm and the Indians helped the Pilgrims plant crops. The Indians taught the new settlers to fertilize the land by putting a fish in the ground with the seeds they had brought to America.

All summer the sun and the rain helped the crops grow. The plants grew strong and healthy. Then, in the fall, it was time to harvest the crops. They gathered the fruits and vegetables they had planted. They had enough food to store for their use during the coming winter.

The Pilgrims were so thankful to have such a bountiful crop, they decided to have a feast. "Let us have a celebration and give thanks for the food, our homes, our Indian friends and all of our blessings. We will have a big feast and invite our Indian friends to share in our happiness."

The Pilgrims set out the food on tables outside as there was no house big enough for all the Pilgrims and their Indian friends. Chief Massasoit came with 90 Indians to join in the celebration. The Indians brought turkeys to be shared on the special occasion. Long ago there were wild turkeys all over American and so we say that the turkey is the real American bird. Perhaps this is why we think of turkey as being the traditional meal for Thanksgiving Day.

As the Pilgrims and Indians gathered for their feast, they all bowed their heads to offer a prayer of thanks to God. They thanked God for keeping them safe, for giving them a bountiful crop and for all their blessings. Thus, they called this "Thanksgiving Day."

That was the first Thanksgiving Day. It took place many years ago. Now Thanksgiving has been made a legal holiday and throughout America, as we remember the Pilgrims and their bravery and struggle in establishing this land for us, we give thanks for all our blessings.

B. <u>PILGRIMS</u>

Many years ago, in September of the year 1620, a ship called the Mayflower sailed from England. The Mayflower carried 102 people even though it was only 90 feet long. It took 65 days, or two months, to make this ocean voyage. The Pilgrims sailed for a month looking for a good place to land. Finally, in December, they landed in Plymouth, Massachusetts.

Today there is a huge rock, called the Plymouth Rock, which is believed to be near the spot where the Pilgrims landed. The first winter was very hard on the people. They struggled with little food, and insufficient housing against the bitter winter. Only half of the colonists survived the difficult experience.

C. <u>THE PILGRIMS AND THE INDIANS</u>

The Pilgrims were very curious about the Indians and the Indians were equally curious about the Pilgrims. The Indians lived in wigwams, long log houses, teepees, adobe houses, hogans and chickees, depending on their environment and the various parts of the country where they roamed.

The Indians wore buckskin clothes and shoes which were called moccasins. The Indians made jewelry, pottery, baskets, rugs, their leather clothes and they did beautiful beadwork.

The Indians were very kind to the Pilgrims and taught them how to grow and use many foods. Among these were: corn, berries, squash, pumpkins, sweet potatoes, apples, beans and maple sugar.

Massasoit was the name of the leader of the Wampanoag Indians. They were friendly toward the Pilgrims and even helped protect them against less friendly Indian tribes. The Indians were curious about these people who came to their country in a big ship. They were interested in the different looking clothes they wore, the tools they used and the log cabins they constructed for their homes.

D. ## THE FIRST THANKSGIVING
   The Pilgrims struggled through the first winter in their new land. When the summer came, the Indians taught the Pilgrims how to plant crops. Squanto was the Indian who showed the Pilgrims how to make corn, pumpkins and beans grow by using fish to fertilize the soil.

   They all worked hard and by the time the summer was over, the Pilgrims realized they would have bountiful harvest. They decided to celebrate by having a feast. Thus, in the fall of 1621, the first Thanksgiving was celebrated in the new world.

   Edward Winslow, a friend of Governor William Bradford's, tells in his journal how the Governor, because of his gratitude to the Indian leader Massasoit, invited him to the feast. Massasoit gladly accepted and brought ninety fellow tribesmen with him. Massasoit realized that the Pilgrims would need more food to feed so many people, so he sent his men to hunt for game. They returned with five deer to add to the Thanksgiving feast.

   The Thanksgiving meal consisted of venison, wild turkey, geese, clams, boiled eels, bass, cornbread, gooseberries, straw-berries, cherries and plums. In later years, cranberries, sweet potatoes and pumpkin pie were added to the menu. The feast was eaten outside on log tables, as there was no building large enough to hold 142 people.

   Forks were not available at that time. Knives were sometimes used for cutting meat and wooden spoons were used for stirring. Wood spoons, bowls and mugs were likely used and the people probably ate with their hands.

E. ## THE INDIANS POPCORN TREAT
   The Indians heated corn in earthen jars over a fire until

the kernels burst in white puffs. Maple syrup was poured on the popped corn to make a special treat for the delighted Pilgrim children. They spent three days feasting, praying in thanks for their bountiful harvest, and in singing before returning to their daily tasks.

F.   THANKSGIVING BECOMES A HOLIDAY

On November 26, 1789, the first president of the United States, George Washington, declared we would have a national day of thanks. However, for many years there was no regular national Thanksgiving Day. Some states had a holiday and others didn't. Finally, in 1863, President Lincoln set aside the last Thursday of November as a day of Thanksgiving and praise. This continued for many years until 1939, when President Roosevelt proclaimed that Thanksgiving Day would be celebrated one week earlier. Finally, in 1941, Congress ruled that the fourth Thursday of November would be observed as Thanksgiving Day and it would be a legal holiday.

Thus, since 1941, we have celebrated Thanksgiving on the fourth Thursday of November. Many people gather with their families to feast on turkey and dressing, cranberries, sweet potatoes and pumpkin pie. Some people attend a church service to pray and sing to express their thankfulness for all their blessings. Some people go to watch a Thanksgiving Day parade with their families, as this is a signal of the coming Christmas season.

In whatever manner people choose to celebrate this special day, the fact remains that the people of the United States of American are grateful and thankful to be living in this land of the free. They are thankful they are able to make a choice of religion. After all, pursuing the opportunity of worshipping in their own way was the reason the Pilgrims braved the long and dangerous ocean voyage and struggled to make a home for themselves and future generations in a new land.

VI. NOVEMBER PHYSICAL EDUCATION FUN

Children will develop skills in:

Rhythm

Imaging

Use of large and small muscles

Good sports conduct

A. MOVE AS IF YOU ARE:

1. Leaves fluttering down to the ground.
2. Raking and bagging leaves.
3. Walking to school.
4. A squirrel digging a hole to bury a nut.
5. A wind blowing softly . . . more . . . more . . . less.
6. A tree swaying in the wind.
7. A bird flying south for the winter.
8. Growing from small to tall.

B. PILGRIM SEVEN UP

Seven children stand up in a line shoulder to shoulder facing the other children. The other children cover their eyes with their hands so they cannot see. Each of the seven tiptoe around the other children, taps one on the head and returns to the line. When all seven have tapped a child and returned to the line, the signal is given to uncover eyes. Each child is given a turn to guess which Pilgrim tapped him/her. The first seven to guess replace the seven in line. Process is repeated.

C. PAPER FEATHER HUNT

Cut feathers out of various colors. Hide these all around the room. Have the children hunt for the feathers and see how many each child has found. This is good for counting and also for identifying the different colors.

D. **PASS THE BALL**

The children will sit in a circle. One child will sit in the center beating his tom-tom while the children pass the ball. When the tom-tom stops, the child holding the ball takes the drummer's place in the center of the circle.

E. **WHAT FEATHER IS MISSING?**

Cut Indian feathers from assorted colors, using one of each color. Place four feathers in the middle of the circle. One child hides his eyes and another takes a feather away. The other child will try to guess which color is missing. Then, he will try to guess which child took it. Play this until each child has a chance to guess the missing color.

F. **PLAY THE GOBBLE WALK**

Chose one child to be the turkey. The group of children will walk around the room in the same direction and, with their hands on their hips, will strut like turkeys. When the "turkey" gobbles, the group must turn around and walk in the opposite direction.

VII. MATH COOKING

Children will develop skills in:

    Number awareness

    Counting

    Measuring

A.   <u>A PILGRIM POPCORN TREAT</u>

    Popcorn: Follow directions on package

Show the children how the corn kernels look before popping. Then pop the corn. Just as the Indians did for the Pilgrims, pour maple syrup over the corn to make a tasty treat.

Math: Is popped corn larger or smaller or equal to the unpopped corn?

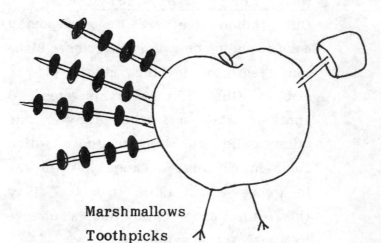

B.   <u>MAKE A TURKEY</u>

    Apple   Marshmallows

    Raisins   Toothpicks

The apple is the body, put the marshmallow head on with a toothpick. Use three or four toothpicks to make the tail. Put raisins on the toothpicks to make the turkey's tail. Now Mr. Turkey is all set to be eaten.

Math: Count toothpicks, raisins, apples and marshmallows.

C. INDIAN CANOES

    Celery   Cream cheese

    Cheese Whiz®   Peanut butter

Clean celery and cut into 3" lengths and 5" lengths. Fill the "canoes" with cream cheese, Cheese Whiz® or peanut butter.

Math: Are some celery sticks longer or shorter than others? Are some celery sticks equal to others?

D. NUTRITIOUS SNACK

    Raisins   Nuts

    Dried apricots   Pieces of apple

    Golden Graham cereal®

Combine above ingredients.

Math: Count pieces of apple and dried apricots. Are there more nuts than pieces of apple?

E. CORN MUFFINS

    Corn muffin mix (follow directions on box)

Use corn muffin mix and make muffins or corn bread.

Math: Count muffins or weigh corn bread.

F. PUMPKIN PIE

Bake a pumpkin pie. Look for canned pumpkin which has all the ingredients included. Then pour into a frozen pie shell. Bake and enjoy.

Math: Discuss fractions $\frac{1}{2}$, $\frac{1}{4}$, etc. as you cut the pie.

READ ALOUD BOOKS FROM THE LIBRARY

NOVEMBER

Books

Children will develop the ability to enjoy and gain knowledge from books.

1. **Little Runner of the Long House**
    Baker, Betty
    Illustrated by Arnold Lobel
    Harper, New York, 1962
    63 pages, color illustrations

    > This "I Can Read Book" has multi-colored drawings of brown, black and yellow. Its vocabulary is very simple. The story tells about Indian customs and Little Runner, who thinks he has tricked his mother into giving him all the maple sugar that he and his brother can eat.

2. **Running Owl The Hunter**
    Benchley, Nathaniel (1915)
    Illustrated by Memoru Funai
    Harper and Row, New York, 1979
    64 pages, illustrated
    (An I Can Read book)

    > His father told Running Owl that he was not old enough to go with him on the buffalo hunt. Running Owl decided he would go on his own hunting trip and get some eagle feathers to prove his hunting prowess. After many adventures, he builds a trap and catches an eagle who takes him up to her nest. She gives him a feather and he walks home to tell his father.

3. **Arthur's Thanksgiving**

Brown, Marc Tolon

1st edition, Little Brown, Boston, 1983

Unpaged, color illustrations

> Arthur directs the school play. No matter what he does, no one will agree to play the Turkey. Finally, Arthur surprises everyone by playing the Turkey himself and doing a very good job.

4. **Over The River and Through The Woods**

Child, Lydia Maria (1802-1880)

Illustrated by Brinton Turkle

Coward, McCann, 1974

Unpaged, partially colored illustrations

> Pictures show family life in the 1800's as a family goes over the river and through the woods. The pictures illustrate the words of "Over The River and Through The Woods" song. A good way to teach children the song. The music is included at the end.

5. **The Thanksgiving Story**

Dalgliesh, Alice

Illustrations by Helen Sewell Scribner

1954

Unpaged, illustrations, map

> This story of the first Thanksgiving comes in five brief chapters, one of which could be read each day. The chapters are titled: "Two Ships and a Big Adventure," "A Ship Sails Alone," "The New Land," "New Homes in a New Land" and "A Time of Thanksgiving."

6. **Cranberry Thanksgiving**
   Devlin, Wende and Harry
   Parents Magazine Press, 1971
   Unpaged, color illustrations

   > Maggie and her grandmother are helped by "Mr. Wishers" when an unscrupulous bakery owner tries to steal grandmother's secret cranberry bread recipe. The "secret recipe" is included at the end of the lively story.

7. **Indian Two Feet and His Eagle Feather**
   Friskey, Margaret, (1901)
   Illustrated by John and Lucy Hawkinson
   Childrens, Chicago, 1967
   Unpaged, color illustrations

   > Indian Two Feet is a young Indian boy who tries very hard to be brave enough to earn eagle feathers. After he helps save his village from flood waters and has earned his feathers, he thinks "to the beat of his heart" -- "I'm an **In**-di-an, **In**-di-an, **In**-di-an. **Proud** of it, **Proud** of it, **Proud** of it."

8. **The Cookie House**
   Hillert, Margaret
   Illustrated by Kinuko Craft
   Follett, Chicago, 1978
   28 pages, color illustrations
   (A Follett Just Beginning To Read book)

   > A very simple vocabulary and illustrations reminiscent of nineteenth century illustrations tell the story which is very much like Hansel and Gretel. A witch in a cookie house imprisons two children who push her in the oven and escape to return to their father.

9. Little Chief
   Hoff, Syd (1912)
   Harper, New York, 1961
   64 pages, color illustrations

   Little Chief helped his mother, and after the work was done he decided to play hunter. As he saw each animal in the woods, he asked them for their coat but the animals would not cooperate. Other animals offered to play with Little Chief, but he wanted children to play with him. Soon he saw a wagon train with lots of children. He played with them and saved them from a charging buffalo herd. They decided to stay in the valley and Little Chief was very happy to have friends.

10. Little Bear's Thanksgiving
    Janice (pseud.)
    Illustrated by Mariana
    Lothrop, New York, 1967
    Unpaged, partially color illustrated

    Little Bear was invited to Goldies' for Thanksgiving Dinner. He got tired and began his winter sleep with a planned nap. He woke up Thanksgiving afternoon just in time for the big dinner and then he went back to sleep until spring.

11. My First Thanksgiving
    Moncure, Jane Berk
    Illustrated by Gwen Connelly
    Children's Press, Chicago, 1984
    Unpaged

    A colorful collection of poems about Thanksgiving. Some of the titles are "Popcorn," "Being Thankful" and "Indian Ways."

12. Little Indian
    Parish, Peggy
    Illustrations by John E. Johnson
    Simon and Schuster, 1968
    Unpaged, illustrations

    Little Indian needed a name. His father told him that Indians
    must find an appropriate name for themselves. After a series
    of adventures in the woods with birds, skunks, rabbits and porcupines
    a snapping turtle saved the day in a humorous way and Little
    Indian became Snapping Turtle.

13. The First Thanksgiving
    Rogers, Lou
    Fillett, Chicago, 1962
    29 pages, illustrations

    Large print and simple vocabulary are used to tell the story of
    the Pilgrims trip to American and the first Thanksgiving feast.
    Captain Miles Standish, Squanto and Governor Bradford are a few
    of the historical figures named in the book, which ends after
    mentioning that Abraham Lincoln was the president who "set a
    special day for Thanksgiving," and said "it should be held each
    year."

14. Let's Find Out About Thanksgiving
    Shapp, Martha and Charles
    Illustrated by Gloria Gaulke
    Watts, New York, 1964
    41 pages, color illustrations

    Orange, black and white drawings illustrate this very simple explana-
    tion of the history of Thanksgiving. There is a vocabulary list
    at the back of the book for beginning readers.

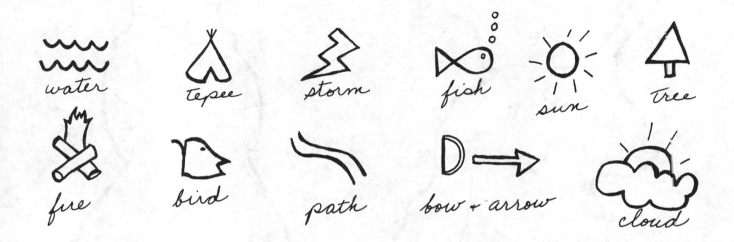

water · tepee · storm · fish · sun · tree

fire · bird · path · bow + arrow · cloud

INDIAN DESIGNS

INDIAN HEADBAND

DECEMBER

Dear Parents:

This month, of course, the focus is on holidays and good food!

ART
Santa's Reindeer and
Christmas Trees

MATH COOKING
Christmas Finger Jello and
Ornaments You Can Eat

SOCIAL STUDIES
Facts about Christmas

LITERATURE
Christmas Is A Time Of Giving
Poems for Hanukkah

SCIENCE
Animals In Winter
Plants In Winter

HAPPY DECEMBER!

BOOKS FROM THE LIBRARY

SUGGESTED DAILY LEARNING PLAN

DECEMBER

Parent Page ART - Paper Chains LITERATURE - POEM - "Christmas Is A Time For Giving" PHYS. ED. - Exercises 1-2 (five times) MATH COOKING - Christmas Finger Jello BOOK - Arthur's Christmas by Marc Tolon Brown	ART - Santa's Boot MUSIC - "Oh, Christmas Tree" PHYS. ED. - Exercises 1-3 (five times) SCIENCE - Discuss A "Animals in the Winter" BOOK - Miffy In The Snow by Dick Bruna	ART - Candy Canes SOCIAL STUDIES - Christmas PHYS. ED. - Exercises 1-4 (very slowly three times) MATH COOKING - Chocolate Fondue	ART - Christmas Ornaments To Lace NURSERY RHYME - "Twinkle, Twinkle Little Star" MUSIC - "Santa Will Be Coming" PHYS. ED. - Exercises 1-5 & B SCIENCE - Recall A BOOK - The Christmas Kitten by Ruth Carroll	ART - Christmas Placemats LITERATURE - POEM - "Menorah" PHYS. ED. - Exercises 1-5 (do very, very slowly) MATH COOKING - Christmas Ornaments You Can Eat BOOK - Island Winter by Charles E. Martin
ART - Wrapping Paper & Painting with Evergreen Sprigs LITERATURE - POEM - "Hanukkah" PHYS. ED. - Exercises 1-6 (do each three times) BOOK - The Winter Cat by Howard Knotts	ART - Christmas Color Finger Paints LITERATURE - POEM - "Hanukkah" SOCIAL STUDIES - Hanukkah PHYS. ED. - Exercises 1-6 & B MATH COOKING - Reindeer Sandwiches	ART - Dough Ornaments LITERATURE - POEM - "Candles" & "Hanukkah-Feast of Lights" PHYS. ED. - Exercises 1-7 (four times) SCIENCE - Discuss B "Plants in Winter" BOOK - The Christmas Box by Eve Merriam	ART (Complete) - Dough Ornaments; make Crayon Batik Christmas Cards SOCIAL STUDIES - Recall "Hanukkah" PHYS. ED. - Exercises 1-7 & B	ART - A Christmas Card With A Window LITERATURE - POEM - "Eight Little Reindeer" PHYS. ED. - Exercises 1-7 BOOK - The Christmas Train by Ivan Gantschev
ART - Santa's Reindeer LITERATURE - FINGER PLAY - "This Is The Way We Make The Toys" PHYS. ED. - Exercises 1-8 BOOK - Winter Is Here! by Jane Belk Moncure	ART - Red Felt Stocking and/or Red Felt Bells LITERATURE - POEM - "My Christmas Stocking" PHYS. ED. - Exercises 1-8 (how fast can you do them?) MATH COOKING - Jelly Twists BOOK - Nine Days To Christmas by Marie Hall Ets	ART - Christmas Candle LITERATURE - POEM - "The Candle" SOCIAL STUDIES - More Facts About Christmas PHYS. ED. - Exercises 1-8 (do fast and slow)	ART - Holly Leaf Man LITERATURE - FINGER PLAY - "Five Little Bells" PHYS. ED. - Exercises 1-8 & B MATH COOKING - Chocolate No Bake Cookies BOOK - Santa's Crash Bang Christmas by Steven Kroll	ART - Holly Leaf Wreath LITERATURE - FINGER PLAY - "Christmas" PHYS. ED. - Exercises 1-8 (and the one you like best) BOOK - White Snow, Bright Snow by Alvin R. Tresselt
ART - Santa Claus Face LITERATURE - POEM - "A Treat for Santa" PHYS. ED. - Exercises 1-8 (and the one you don't like) MATH COOKING - Candy Cane Cookies BOOK - The Polar Express by Chris Van Allsburg	ART - Two Easy Christmas Trees LITERATURE - POEM - "The Pretty Christmas Tree" PHYS. ED. - Exercises 1-8 (do very quickly)	ART - Fan Christmas Tree LITERATURE - POEM - "Menorah Your Lights We Will Light" PHYS. ED. - Exercises 1-8 (pick one and do it again) BOOK - The Night After Christmas by James Stevenson	ART - Two Easy Wreaths LITERATURE - FINGER PLAY - "Santa" PHYS. ED. - Exercises 1-8 & B MATH COOKING - Rice Krispie Christmas Wreaths BOOK - Claud The Dog, A Christmas Story by Dick Gackenbach	ART - Folded Christmas Wre[ath] NURSERY RHYME - "Star Light, Star Bright" PHYS. ED. - Exerc[ises] MATH COOKING - Sugar Co[okies] BOOK - O... An[...]

DECEMBER

...kills in:

...uscles (small motor)

...ER CHAINS

Cut various colors of construction paper. Cut paper into 1" x 4" strips. Take a strip of paper and form a ring. Paste ends together by over-lapping one end over the other. Take the next strip of paper, slip it through the ring, paste the ends together and now you have two rings. Continue adding more rings until your paper chain is as long as you want it. Children love to see how long they can make a chain. For Christmas, you may wish to make the chain out of red or green paper, as these are the colors of the Christmas season.

B. SANTA'S BOOT

Fold red paper (12" x 18" sheet) in half and lay a boot pattern on fold. Trace the outline on the red paper; cut out boot. Punch holes along front of boot. Use white yarn to lace the boot and tie a bow at the top. Put the child's name on a 1" x4½" strip of white paper. Paste the paper at the top of the boot.

C. CANDY CANES

Draw or trace candy canes on white construction paper. Draw diagonal lines on the canes. Fill in alternating sections by coloring with red crayon. Cut out candy canes.

Optional: Cut a bow from red paper or make a bow out of red ribbon. Paste on candy cane.

D. <u>CHRISTMAS ORNAMENTS TO LACE</u>

On colored construction paper, trace stars, bells, circles, etc. using patterns. Cut out shapes and punch holes around edges of each ornament. Try to make the holes an equal distance apart. Yarn will be needed to do the lacing. Put a knot in one end of the yarn and tape the other end for lacing through the holes.

E. ## TWO CHRISTMAS PLACEMATS

Using 12" x 18" sheets of construction paper (red, green or white), let children decorate their own placemat. They can draw Christmas pictures or they can trace around Christmas shapes: stars, bells, candy canes, trees, etc. Fringe the edges on two or four sides.

Use the placemat for party time.

Another placemat: Cut out pictures from used Christmas cards. Paste pictures on a piece of cardboard. Overlap the pictures so none of the cardboard is showing. Place transparent food wrap or contact paper over the cards. The food wrap may have to be taped to hold it onto the back. This is attractive and can be used over and over because it can be wiped clean.

F. **WRAPPING PAPER**

Cut a small sponge into a Christmas shape. Place poster paint in a shallow pan. Dampen sponge with water. Dip the sponge into the paint and press on the newsprint or butcher paper. Print a pattern on the paper. Allow paper to dry before using.

G. **PAINTING WITH EVERGREEN SPRIGS**

Have the children use evergreen sprigs as paint brushes. They should use white poster paint on the dark colored paper and the dark colored poster paint on white paper.

Using the evergreen sprigs creates a delicate look.

H. **CHRISTMAS COLOR FINGER PAINTS**

Children will cover a large sheet of finger paint paper with red and green finger paint. When the paint is dry, cut Christmas designs such as bells, trees, stars, etc.

Also, finger paintings may be matted by using the mat cut into a Christmas design.

I. **DOUGH ORNAMENTS**

1 cup flour	1/3 cup salt
½ cup water	Few drops of vegetable oil

Mix the flour and salt in a bowl. Slowly add the water and oil. Knead the dough well and shape into a ball. Have the children squeeze it and roll it, this is good for fine muscles.

When they are ready to make the ornaments, roll out the playdough. If it becomes sticky, add more flour. Using cookie cutters, cut out Christmas shapes. Make a hole in the top. Let it dry for a day, then turn over and dry the other side. Paint the ornaments, sprinkle with sparkle. Hang by putting yarn or string through top hole.

J. CRAYON BATIK CHRISTMAS CARDS

Fold wax paper in half. Put crayon shavings between halves. Place a sheet of newspaper or cloth over the wax paper and press with warm iron. Shavings will melt and the paper will stick together.

For another effect, use bits of tissue paper or colored cellophane paper and press between the layers of wax paper.

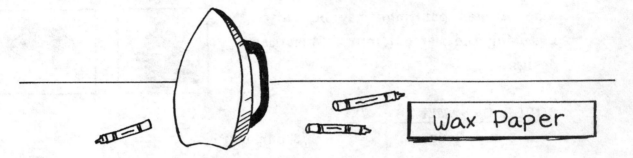

K. A CHRISTMAS CARD WITH A WINDOW

Fold the 6" x 9" sheet of black construction paper in half. Then fold the top cover in half. Using a light colored crayon, draw half of a church window. Keeping the paper folded, cut out the window.

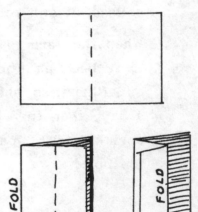

Glue over the opening either tissue paper, cellophane paper or the crayon shavings that were melted between wax paper.

Put a greeting inside the card.

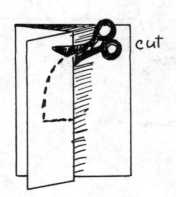

L. SANTA'S REINDEER

Fold paper (9" x 12" brown construction paper) diagonally making two triangles. Cut off excess on one side of paper. Fold black paper in half and trace the child's hand with fingers spread apart. Then, cut out the hand print and also cut two circles from the black paper. The hand prints will make the antlers. Paste on the antlers and the eyes. Cut a circle from red paper to make a nose. Paste on the red nose.

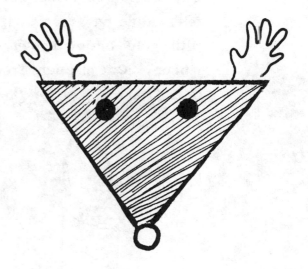

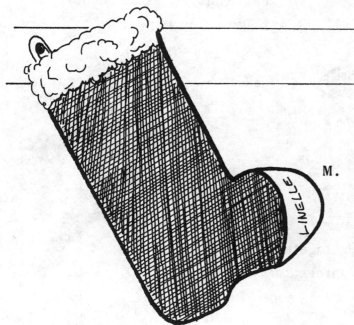

M. RED FELT STOCKING

Cut stocking shape out of red felt. Glue cotton around the top. Cut white felt in shape of toe part. Write child's name on white felt and paste on the toe of the stocking.

N. RED FELT CHRISTMAS BELLS

Cut Christmas bells out of red felt. Glue on green strip. Trim with gold braid, eyelet, lace or ribbon. Cut clappers from yellow felt. Make a bow for the top.

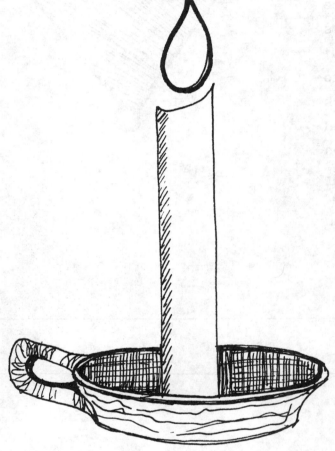

O. CHRISTMAS CANDLE

Cut candle from red construction paper - 1½" x 6". Cut flame out of yellow paper. Candle holder can be cut from black or brown construction paper. (Pre-cut pieces for children.) Paste candle on bright blue paper.

P. HOLLY LEAF MAN

Cut five green holly leaves, use pattern. Put holly leaves together to form a man. Cut a circle for the head. Use red for eyes and buttons.

Q. HOLLY LEAF WREATH

Make a circle of cardboard. Use holly leaf pattern, cut enough green leaves to cover the cardboard. Overlap the leaves. Cut small circles of red berries. Paste three circles in a group to form a triangle. Place group of berries at various places around the wreath. Make a red bow. Paste at top or bottom of wreath.

R. SANTA CLAUS FACE

Cut circle for face from manilla paper. Cut Santa's hat out of red paper. Cut small red circle for Santa's nose. Cut two circles for Santa's eyes. Use cotton for beard, eyebrows, mustache. Make a cotton ball for the hat and use cotton to trim the edge of hat. Paste on Santa's face.

S.   <u>TWO EASY CHRISTMAS TREES</u>

Draw or trace tree on green construction paper. Cut out and paste on black or white paper. Cut out ornaments using different colors or draw and color ornaments. Paste ornaments on the tree. Put a star at the top.

Another tree: Fold green construction paper in half. Trace or draw Christmas tree. Cut out trees and staple along middle crease. Put ornaments on, if desired. Fan open tree. It should stand by itself. To hang put hole in top, string through hole.

T. FAN CHRISTMAS TREE

Fold a sheet of 9" x 12" green construction paper like a fan. Grasp one end and staple all layers together.

staple after folding

Place on black construction paper. Staple to hold in place. Use yarn for trim. Make colored ornaments. Paste these on tree and paste a star on top.

Optional: Draw packages, cut out and paste under the tree.

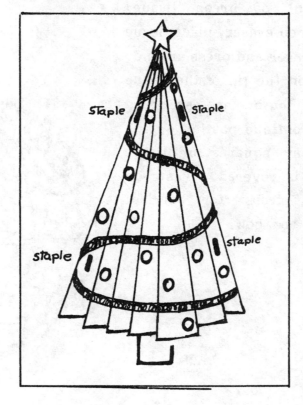

U. <u>TWO EASY WREATHS</u>

Paint or color a paper plate green.
Cut a circle out of the middle
of the plate. Paste on small red
circles for berries. Paste on a
red bow.

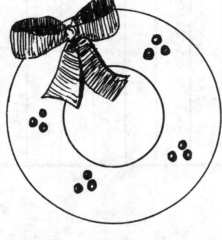

Another variation: Draw the outline of a wreath on cardboard
or paper. Cut small tissue paper
squares out of green tissue.
Using a pencil eraser, place tissue
over the eraser and press around.
Put paste on the tip of the tissue
and press onto the cardboard
wreath. Continue pasting on the
tissue paper squares until the
cardboard is covered. Paste on
small red circles for berries.
Paste on a red bow.

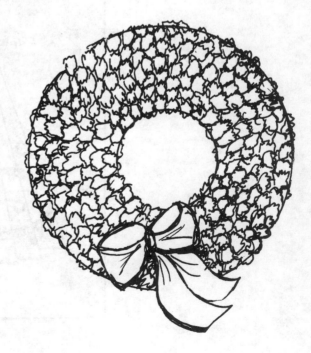

V. FOLDED CHRISTMAS WREATH

Fold green 9" x 18" sheet of construction paper in half, lengthwise, then fold under 1½".

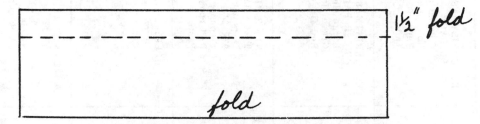

Cut from the fold to the fold line in a wavy line.

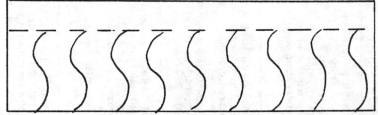

Paste along the 1½" fold. Place folds together, forming a circle. Staple ends of circle to hold in place. Decorate with red circles for berries. Paste on a red construction paper bow.

MATERIALS CHART

DECEMBER

A. PAPER CHAINS
- Assorted construction paper
- Paste

B. SANTA'S BOOT
- 12"x18" red construction paper
- Hole punch
- White yarn
- Paste

C. CANDY CANES
- White construction paper
- Red crayon
- Red paper/ribbon

D. CHRISTMAS ORNAMENTS TO LACE
- Colored construction paper
- Hole punch
- Yarn
- Tape

E. TWO CHRISTMAS PLACEMATS
- 12"x18" construction paper - red, green or white
- Used Christmas cards
- Paste
- Cardboard
- Transparent food wrap
- Tape

F. WRAPPING PAPER
- Small sponge
- Poster paint
- Shallow pan
- Newsprint/butcher paper

G. PAINTING WITH EVERGREEN SPRIGS
- Evergreen sprigs
- White poster paint
- Dark poster paint
- White construction paper
- Dark construction paper

H. CHRISTMAS COLOR FINGER PAINTS
- Large finger paint paper
- Green finger paint
- Red finger paint

I. DOUGH ORNAMENTS
- Flour
- Water
- Salt
- Paint
- Sparkle
- Yarn/string
- Cookie cutters
- Vegetable oil

J. CRAYON BATIK CHRISTMAS CARDS
- Wax paper
- Crayons
- Newspaper/cloth
- Iron
- Tissue paper/colored cellophane

K. A CHRISTMAS CARD WITH A WINDOW
- 6"x9" black construction paper
- Light colored crayons
- Glue
- Tissue paper/cellophane/melted crayon shavings (in waxed paper)

L. SANTA'S REINDEER
- 9"x12" brown construction paper
- 9"x12" black construction paper
- Red construction paper
- Paste

M. RED FELT STOCKING
- Red felt
- Glue
- Cotton
- White felt

N. RED FELT CHRISTMAS BELLS
- Red felt
- Glue
- Green felt
- Gold braid/eyelet ribbon
- Yellow felt
- Ribbon

O. CHRISTMAS CANDLE
- Red construction paper
- Yellow construction paper
- Black/brown construction paper
- Paste
- Blue construction paper

P. HOLLY LEAF MAN
- Green construction paper
- Red construction paper
- Paste

Q. HOLLY LEAF WREATH
- Cardboard
- Green construction paper
- Red construction paper
- Red ribbon
- Paste

R. SANTA CLAUS FACE
- Manilla paper
- Red construction paper
- Cotton
- Black construction paper

S. TWO EASY CHRISTMAS TREES
- Green construction paper
- Black/white construction paper
- Assorted construction paper
- Crayons
- Paste
- Staple
- String

T. FAN CHRISTMAS TREE
- 9"x12" green construction paper
- Staple
- Black construction paper
- Yarn
- Assorted construction paper
- Paste

U. TWO EASY WREATHS
- Paint/crayons
- Paper plate
- Paste
- Red construction paper
- Red ribbon
- Cardboard
- Green tissue paper

V. FOLDED CHRISTMAS WREATH
- 9"x12" green construction paper
- Paste
- Staple
- Red construction paper
- Red ribbon

II. LITERATURE

Children will develop the ability to identify and enjoy:

Characters

Main ideas

Details

Sequence of events

POEMS/FINGER PLAYS/NURSERY RHYMES

Children will develop the ability to participate in and enjoy:

Rhythm

Poetry

Sequence

Characters

A. POEMS FOR CHRISTMAS AND HANUKKAH

1. **CHRISTMAS IS A TIME OF GIVING**

   Christmas time is a happy time,

   For every girl and boy.

   We learn to share,

   We learn to care,

   And giving brings us joy.

2. **THE PRETTY CHRISTMAS TREE**

   See the pretty Christmas tree,

   It stands there for you and me,

   When Mom or Dad turn on the lights,

   Our Christmas tree will shine so bright.

3. **A TREAT FOR SANTA**

   Remember to leave Santa a treat,

   'Cause Santa likes a snack to eat.

   He doesn't have much time to stay,

   He leaves his gifts - then he's on his way.

4. **MY CHRISTMAS STOCKING**

Here's my stocking,
It's quite small, you see.
But Santa will know,
This stocking's for me.

5. **CANDLES**

We light the candles one by one,
Until at last all eight are done.
These candles we dedicate,
As Hanukkah we celebrate.

6. **MENORAH**

Menorah, Menorah,
Your candles burn so bright,
As we celebrate Hanukkah tonight.

7. **HANUKKAH**

We light a candle every night,
Until eight candles burn so bright.
For this is Hanukkah, a special
time, you see.
A time of dedication and faithful
we will be.

8. **HANUKKAH - FEAST OF LIGHTS**

Hanukkah is the Feast of Lights.
It's a time we dedicate.
We light the candles,
And exchange our gifts.
As Hanukkah we celebrate.

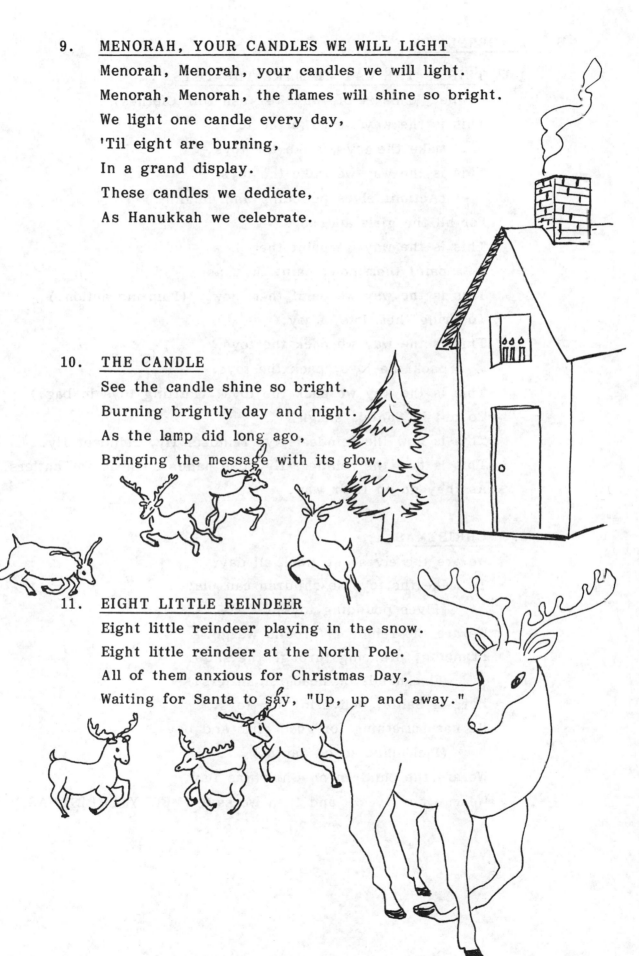

9. <u>MENORAH, YOUR CANDLES WE WILL LIGHT</u>

Menorah, Menorah, your candles we will light.

Menorah, Menorah, the flames will shine so bright.

We light one candle every day,

'Til eight are burning,

In a grand display.

These candles we dedicate,

As Hanukkah we celebrate.

10. <u>THE CANDLE</u>

See the candle shine so bright.

Burning brightly day and night.

As the lamp did long ago,

Bringing the message with its glow.

11. <u>EIGHT LITTLE REINDEER</u>

Eight little reindeer playing in the snow.

Eight little reindeer at the North Pole.

All of them anxious for Christmas Day,

Waiting for Santa to say, "Up, up and away."

B. FINGERPLAYS

1. THIS IS THE WAY WE MAKE THE TOYS
   (Tune: This is the Way We Wash Our Clothes)
   This is the way we make the toys,
        make the toys, make the toys.
   This is the way we make the toys
        (Action: elves pounding and singing.)
   For all the girls and boys.
   This is the way we paint them now,
        paint them now, paint them now.
   This is the way we paint them now. (Painting action.)
   To bring them lots of joy.
   This is the way we pack the toys,
        pack the toys, pack the toys.
   This is the way we pack the toys. (Putting toys in bag.)
   To put in Santa's sleigh.
   This is how the reindeer fly, reindeer fly, reindeer fly.
   This is how the reindeer fly (Use hands on head for antlers.)
   As they go on their way.

2. CHRISTMAS
   We are the elves. We work all day.
   To make the toys so children can play.
        (Elves pounding toys.)
   We are the reindeer, around we go.
   Prancing, prancing through the snow.
        (Use hands on head for antlers.)
   Here is Santa, delivering the toys,
   He has something for good girls and boys.
        (Pick child to be Santa.)
   We are the children on Christmas Day.
   We rub our eyes - and then we say, "MERRY CHRISTMAS."

3. **FIVE LITTLE BELLS**

Five little bells hanging in a row. (Hold up hand.)

The first one said, "Ring me slow." (Point to thumb.)

The second one said, "Ring me fast." (Pointer finger.)

The third one said, "Ring me last." (Middle finger.)

The fourth one said, "I'm like a chime." (Ring finger.)

The fifth one said, "Ring me at Christmas time."

    (Little finger.)

4. **SANTA**

When Santa come down the chimney

    (Downward motion with hands.)

I should like to peek. (Peek through fingers.)

But he'll never come, no never (Shake head.)

Until I'm fast asleep. (Palms together beside head.)

C. NURSERY RHYMES

1. **STAR LIGHT, STAR BRIGHT**
   Star light, star bright,
   First star I see tonight,
   I wish I may, I wish I might,
   Have the wish I wish tonight.

2. **TWINKLE, TWINKLE LITTLE STAR**
   Twinkle, twinkle little star,
   How I wonder what you are!
   Up above the world so high,
   Like a diamond in the sky.

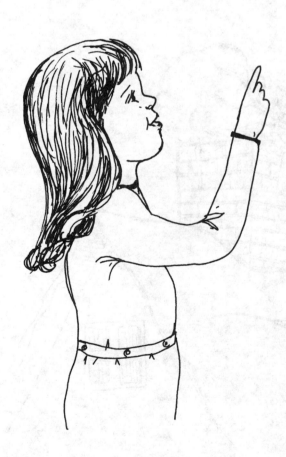

III. MUSIC

Children will develop the ability to participate in and enjoy music.

A. OH, CHRISTMAS TREE

(Tune: Oh, Christmas Tree)

Oh, Christmas tree. Oh, Christmas tree.
We'll decorate your branches.
Oh, Christmas tree. Oh, Christmas tree.
We'll decorate your branches.
Here's a star. And here's a ball.
A candle shines over all.
Oh, Christmas tree. Oh, Christmas tree.
How beautiful you are.

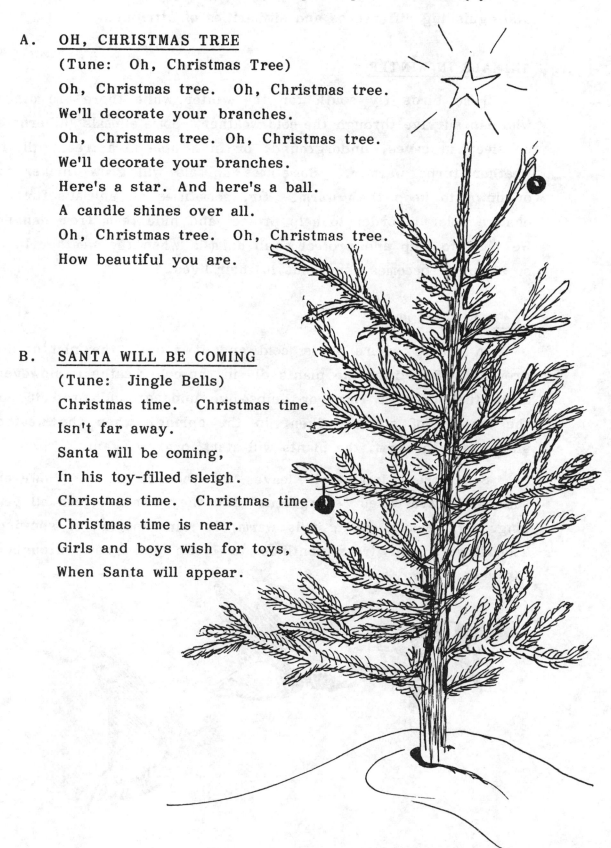

B. SANTA WILL BE COMING

(Tune: Jingle Bells)

Christmas time. Christmas time.
Isn't far away.
Santa will be coming,
In his toy-filled sleigh.
Christmas time. Christmas time.
Christmas time is near.
Girls and boys wish for toys,
When Santa will appear.

IV. SCIENCE

Children will develop skills in:

Distinguishing differences and similarities of attributes

A. ANIMALS IN WINTER

Some birds fly south for the winter while there are others who can survive through the cold weather. Some animals "hibernate" or sleep in caves, underground, or in a hole in a tree until the weather turns warmer. Sometimes animals will grow thicker fur or down to keep them warm. Or, sometimes an animal's fur will change color in order to help protect and hide them from danger. We need to help and protect small animals when the weather turns so severe it becomes dangerous to their lives.

B. PLANTS IN WINTER

In places where it is cold and it snows, the plants stop growing. Sometimes the plants die in the cold weather. However, often the seeds or roots or bulbs live underground protected by the blanket of snow. Then, in the spring, when the weather starts to turn warm, the plants will start to grow again.

Some trees lose their leaves and become bare. However, some trees are called "evergreens" and they remain green all year long. In places where it is warm, it rains instead of snowing. The flowers and trees continue to bloom and grow throughout the year.

V. SOCIAL STUDIES

Children will develop an awareness of:

Holidays

Traditions

Seasonal changes

A. HANUKKAH

During the month of December, the Jewish people celebrate Hanukkah (sometimes called Chanukah). This is the Jewish Feast of Lights or Feast of Dedication and it lasts for eight days. The story of this celebration goes back in history to 165 B.C. when the Jews in Judea, defeated the Syrian ruler. They cleaned out the Temple in Jerusalem of Syrian idols and rededicated it to God. They found only one small cruse of oil with which to light their holy lamps. This small cruse of oil miraculously provided enough oil for the lamps to burn for eight days. Thus, Hanukkah was declared a festival.

Now the Jewish people celebrate Hanukkah by lighting a candle each evening and by the last evening, all eight candles are burning together. The special candle holder which holds all eight candles is called a Menorah. Also, during this festival gifts are exchanged.

B. CHRISTMAS

Christmas is a special time of the year. It is a time of gift giving and sharing. It is a time for family get togethers, attending church services and singing Christmas Carols. The word Christmas comes from the early English phrase "Christes Masse" which means Christ's Mass. It is a happy time for children as they anticipate the coming of Christmas and Santa Claus.

Christmas Day is always celebrated on December 25th and is a national holiday in the United States. Christmas is a Christian holiday and celebrates the birth of the Christ child named Jesus. The idea of giving gifts for Christmas goes back to the gifts that were brought to the Christ child by the three wise men.

In some countries the children believe in St. Nicholas. This originated many years ago when a real St. Nicholas, who was a kind bishop and the patron saint of school boys, became famous for his generosity and his habit of giving gifts. People came to believe that any surprise gift came from St. Nicholas.

One legend that comes to us through the years is about the beginning of the Christmas tree. Martin Luther, a German clergyman, found a beautiful little fir tree in the forest and took it home for his children. Because the tree had been just freshly cut, he was able to place many lighted candles on its branches. The glow of the candles was to represent the beauty of the stars over Bethlehem on the night when Christ was born.

C. MORE ABOUT CHRISTMAS

Santa Claus is a very real part of Christmas for young children. Small children believe that Santa will bring them toys on Christmas morning. They also believe that Santa and his wife live at the North Pole and spend the year making toys. Then, on Christmas Eve, Santa loads his sleigh which is pulled by eight reindeer. They fly from housetop to housetop delivering toys to boys and girls who have been good.

Children often hang up stockings on Christmas Eve which they hope will be filled with treats when they awake on Christmas morning. Some children may leave a treat for "Santa" - perhaps a glass of milk and some cookies.

One of the most delightful stories of Christmas is "A Visit From St. Nicholas" by Clement C. Moore. He wrote this in 1822 for his children. A friend persuaded him to publish it and the story became an immediate success. Boys and girls are still enjoying this wonderful Christmas story.

Christmas is one of the most exciting and joyful times of

the year. Children love to believe in Santa Claus. However, as children grow and mature they soon learn that Santa Claus is really the wonderful spirit of Christmas that should be in the hearts of everyone. It is necessary for children to be taught the importance of giving and sharing. They need to learn the real pleasure is not in what they receive, but like St. Nicholas, there is true joy in giving.

VI. DECEMBER PHYSICAL EDUCATION FUN

Children will develop skills in:

Rhythm

Imaging

Use of large and small muscles

Good sports conduct

A. MOVE AS IF YOU ARE:

1. Wrapping a huge present.
2. Wrapping a very tiny small present.
3. Putting up a Christmas tree.
4. Trimming a Christmas tree.
5. Hanging stockings for Santa.
6. Putting on your snow suit, gloves, scarf and boots.
7. Taking off your snow suit, gloves, scarf and boots.
8. Shoveling snow.

B. WALK, SKIP, HOP RELAY

Stand (as few as two or as many as six) children in a line. The first turn through the line is "walk." Have each student walk to a designated place (or tape line on the floor) and return as fast as possible (but still walking not running). The second turn through the line is to skip to the line. Third turn is to hop to the line. Which group finished first? (Care must be taken so that each person returns to the group before the next person starts his/her turn.)

VII. MATH COOKING

Children will develop skills in:

Number awareness

Counting

Measuring

A. CHRISTMAS FINGER JELLO

4 envelopes Knox® unflavored gelatin

3 packages (3 oz.) flavored gelatin

4 cups of boiling water

Combine unflavored and flavored gelatin in a large bowl; add boiling water. Sitr until gelatin is dissolved. Pour in 9" x 12" baking pan. Chill. When firm, cut into squares to serve. For Christmas, make red jello and green jello.

Math: Discuss and count measurement of ingredients. Discuss cube. How many red cubes are there? How many green cubes are there?

B. CHOCOLATE FONDUE

6 milk chocolate bars (melted)

½ cup milk (stir in with above)

-or-

1 stick margarine (melted)

1 pkg. chocolate chips

1 can condensed milk

When chocolate is melted, dip in pieces of fruit. (Keep chocolate warm to keep it soft.)

Math: Count chocolate bars - break each one in "half." Break each bar in "fourths." How many pieces are there when a bar is broken in half - in fourths?

C. **CHRISTMAS ORNAMENTS YOU CAN EAT**

Dissolve dry yeast in 1½ cups warm water.

Mix in: 1 egg

           ½ cup honey

           ½ cup shortening

           1 tsp. salt

Stir in: flour - a little at a time until dough isn't too sticky. Knead about five minutes on waxed paper. Cover and let rise in a warm place about 25 minutes. Fashion into Christmas shapes: bell, tree, star, Santa, etc. Bake in 350° oven for 20 minutes or until golden brown.

If you don't want to eat your ornaments and would rather hang them on the tree, put a hole in the top before baking. Bake and cool. To preserve the ornaments, shellac when cooled.

Math: Time kneading for five minutes. Discuss time and relationship to cooking. Count the number of bells, trees, stars, Santas, etc. Which shape has the largest (greater) number? Which has the smallest (least) number?

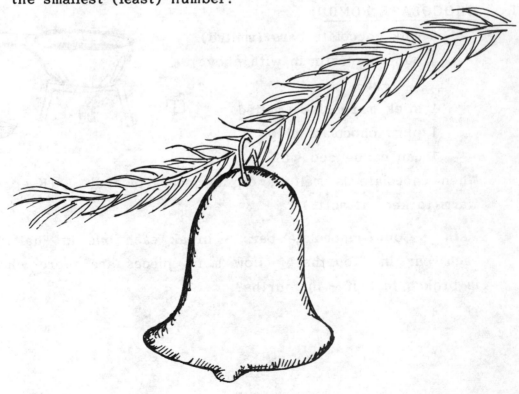

D. REINDEER SANDWICHES

Bread   1 tsp. sugar (optional)
1 egg   Drop of vanilla (optional)
½ cup milk   Nutmeg (optional)

Cut the bread diagonally to form triangles. Lightly whip an egg in a bowl. Add other ingredients. Brown on greased griddle. When serving, add raisin eyes, cherry nose, pretzel antlers.

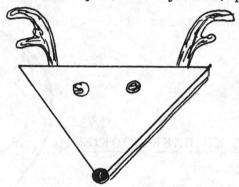

Math: Discuss triangle - how is it different from a circle and a square?

E. RICE KRISPY CHRISTMAS WREATHS

¼ cup margarine or butter   5 cups Rice Krispie cereal
40 regular marshmallows   Red and green food coloring

-or-

4 cups miniature marshmallows

Melt margarine in saucepan over low heat. Add marshmallows and stir until completely melted. Cook 3-4 minutes longer, stirring constantly. Remove ¼ cup of mixture and add red food coloring. Add green food coloring to the other portion. Remove from heat. Add Rice Krispie cereal and stir until well coated. Give each child a heaping tablespoon of mixture to shape. They should have well-greased hands. Shape a wreath. Add dots of red mixture. Cook on waxed paper. Yields: 24-30 wreaths.

Math: Discuss and count measurements of ingredients. Guess how many wreaths will result. Count how many wreaths were made. Is it less or more?

F.   JELLY TWISTS

Can of refrigerator biscuits

Favorite jelly (grape, strawberry, etc.)

Flatten each biscuit. Hold in both hands, stretch slightly and twist to make a figure eight. Place on ungreased baking sheet. Work a hollow in each side by pressing with thumb. Fill depressions with jam. Brush with melted butter. Bake.

Math: Discuss number "8".

G.   CHOCOLATE NO BAKE-COOKIES

Boil together:

½ cup butter (1 stick)

2 cups sugar

½ cup milk

Take off stove; add:

4 T. cocoa

1 cup coconut

3 cups oatmeal

(Or, eliminate coconut; add 4 cups oatmeal)

Mix thoroughly. Drop by teaspoonful on waxed paper. Eat when cool.

Math: Discuss and count ingredients. Count cookies. Are some larger than others? Are some smaller? Are some equal?

H. CANDY CANE COOKIES

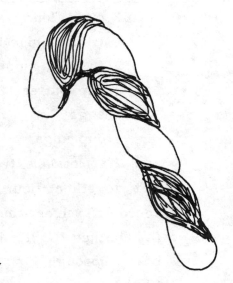

½ cup butter, softened

½ cup shortening

1 cup confectioners sugar

1 egg

1½ t. almond extract

1 t. salt

1 t. vanilla

2½ cups flour

½ t. red food coloring

½ cup crushed peppermint candy

½ cup granulated sugar

Mix thoroughly butter, shortening, confectioners sugar, egg and flavoring. Blend in flour and salt. Divide dough in half; blend food color in one half. Shape 1 t. dough from each half into a 4" rope. For smooth, even dough, roll back and forth on a lightly floured board. Place ropes side by side; press together lightly and twist. Place on ungreased baking sheet. Curve top down to form handle of cane. Bake about nine minutes or until very light brown. Mix candy and sugar. Immediately sprinkle cookies with mixture; remove from baking sheet.

Yield: Approximately four dozen cookies.

Math: Count and discuss ingredients. Discuss nine minutes. Set timer. What would happen if we didn't time cookies?

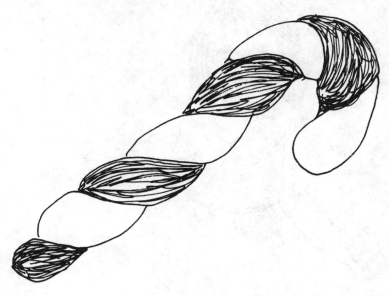

I. <u>OLD FASHIONED SUGAR COOKIES</u>

   3 cups flour

   ½ t. baking soda

   ½ t. baking powder

   1 cup butter (2 sticks)

   2 eggs

   1 cup sugar

   1 t. lemon extract or 1 t. grated lemon peel

Sift together flour, baking soda and baking powder. On low speed of mixer, cut in butter until mixture resembles cornmeal. In another bowl, beat egg; add sugar and lemon extract and beat thoroughly. Blend egg mixture into flour-butter mixture. Chill.

On lightly floured surface, roll dough 1/8 inch thich. Cut cookie shapes with floured cookie cutters. Sprinkle with colored sugar or candies. Bake in preheated oven, 375° for 6-8 minutes, or until lightly browned. Decorate with frosting, if desired.

Yield: Six dozen.

Math: Discuss and measure ingredients. Discuss cookies 1/8 inch thick. How many cookies would have to be stacked to make a stack 1" high? Are baked cookies thinner or thicker than uncooked cookies?

READ ALOUD BOOKS FROM THE LIBRARY

DECEMBER

Children will develop the ability to enjoy and gain knowledge from books.

1. **Arthur's Christmas**
   Brown, Marc Talon
   1st edition, Little Brown, Boston
   31 pages, color illustrations

   Arthur lives in a delightful world peopled by people and animals. He takes great care to make a present which he is certain Santa will like. After seeing it, others are not so certain that Santa will really appreciate it. After being helped by his sister, D.W., Arthur is happy to receive a thank you note from Santa.

2. **Miffy In The Snow**
   Bruna, Dick
   Illustrated by A.W. Bruna and Zoon
   Methuen, New York, 1975
   30 pages, illustrations

   A small book with bright, bold, colorful pictures. The gentle story of little Miffy Rabbit who puts on her snow suit, hat, boots and gloves and plays in the snow. She builds snowmen, skates, sleds and saves a little bird who is half frozen. In the end, Miffy and the bird are happy and Miffy is tired so she goes into the house and mother tells her it's time for bed.

3. The Christmas Kitten
    Carroll, Ruth and Labrobe
    Walck, 1970
    Unpaged, illustrations

    > No words are necessary to tell how a small kitten finally gets
    > a home for Christmas. Drawings are green, orange, black and
    > white.

4. Nine Days to Christmas
    Ets, Marie Hall (1895) and Labastida, Aurora
    Illustrated by Maria Hall Ets
    Viking Press, New York, 1959

    > This Caldecott Award winner tells the story of a small Mexican
    > girl who is finally five and old enough to have her own pinata.
    > It tells of her life as she waits each passing day until Christmas.

5. Claud The Dog: A Christmas Story
    Gackenback, Dick
    Illustrated by author
    Seabury Press, 1974
    Unpaged, illustrations

    > Generous Claud the dog gives his Christmas gift to his homeless
    > friend, Bummer. Very few words and large charming drawings
    > tell this inspiring Christmas story.

6. The Christmas Train
    Gantschev, Ivan (Weihnachtszug, English)
    Translated from the German by Karen M. Klockner
    Little Brown, Boston, 1984
    26 pages, color illustrations

    > A young girl sets her Christmas tree on fire, decorations and
    > all. The fire was to signal a train that a rock slide has blocked
    > the tracks on Christmas eve day. Muted dream-like paintings
    > illustrate this beautiful book.

7. **One Luminaria for Antonio**
Hood, Flora Mae
Illustrated by Ann Kir
Putnam, New York, 1966, 1957

> Antonio worries because he does not have even one luminaria to light the Christ Child's way as He walks through the village to bless the lighted houses. Tempted to steal a broken candle, he asks and is given it by an understanding shopkeeper. On Christmas eve, the flickering luminaria attracts a frightened, hurt red squirrel which Antonio adopts until it is healed.

8. **The Winter Cat**
Knotts, Howard
Illustrations by author
Harper and Row, New York, 1972
32 pages, illustrations

> Homer, a wild field cat, who was born in the summer, watches in wonder as the fall changes to winter. He runs away when children try to befriend him. After being cold and hungry, Homer decides to let himself be carried into the warm house. He settles down to becoming a house cat until summer returns.

9. **Santa's Crash Bang Christmas**
Kroll, Steven
Illustrated by Tomie DePaola
Holiday House, New York, 1977
Unpaged, partially color illustrations

> Santa begins Christmas Eve by falling right out of his sleigh and the evening progresses from one mishap to another. But, things are all as they should be when the happy family comes downstairs Christmas morning to get their gifts.

10. Island Winter

Martin, Charles E. (1910)

Greenwillow Books, New York, 1984

32 pages, colored illustrations

> Heather found that life on an island is very full, even after the summer people have gone home. She attended a one room schoolhouse, played bikes with her friends and helped paint bouys. She celebrated Halloween, Thanksgiving and Christmas. She went lobstering, greeted the migrating ducks and the warm spring weather. She was busy all winter and didn't worry the next year when one of the arriving summer people asked her, "What do you do here all winter?"

11. The Christmas Box

Merriam, Eve

Illustrated by David Small

William Morrow, New York, 1985

Unpaged, color illustrations

> The whole family rushes down Christmas morning to find only one long, thin present under the tree. Out of the box, connected by fishing line, came a wonderful present for each pleased family member, including the cat.

12. Winter Is Here!

Moncure, Jane Belk

Illustrated by Frances Hook

Child's World, Elgin, IL, 1975

Unpaged, color llustrations

> Bright, multi-colored illustrations help explain the wonderful sing-song words of this story in verse. The first page is a words and picture page and the last page contains the music and words for a song called "Winter." This is the type of book children love to hear over and over, and soon they will start saying it as you read it.

13. White Snow, Bright Snow

Tresselt, Alvin R.

Illustrations by Roger Duvoisin

Lothrop, 1947

33 pages, illustrations

> This 1948 Caldecott Medal winner is a word on picture story of adults, children and animals coping with and enjoying the snow. Soon the snow melts and everyone enjoys the signs of spring.

14. The Night After Christmas

Stevenson, James

1st edition, Greenwillow Books, New York, 1981

32 pages, color illustrations

> Chauncey, the dog, helps a Teddy Bear and Annie, the doll, who have been thrown in the trash after being replaced by new toys at Christmas. Annie and Teddy become sadder and sadder. Finally, the dog solves their problems by taking them to a public school where students adopt them and take them home.

15. The Polar Express

Van Allsburg

Illustrated by author

Houghton Mifflin, Boston, 1985

Unpaged, color illustrations

> Beautiful full-color pastel drawings illustrate this story of a young boy's trip to the North Pole on the Polar Express Train. The lovely story and drawings are of equally high quality, making this one of the best Christmas books available.

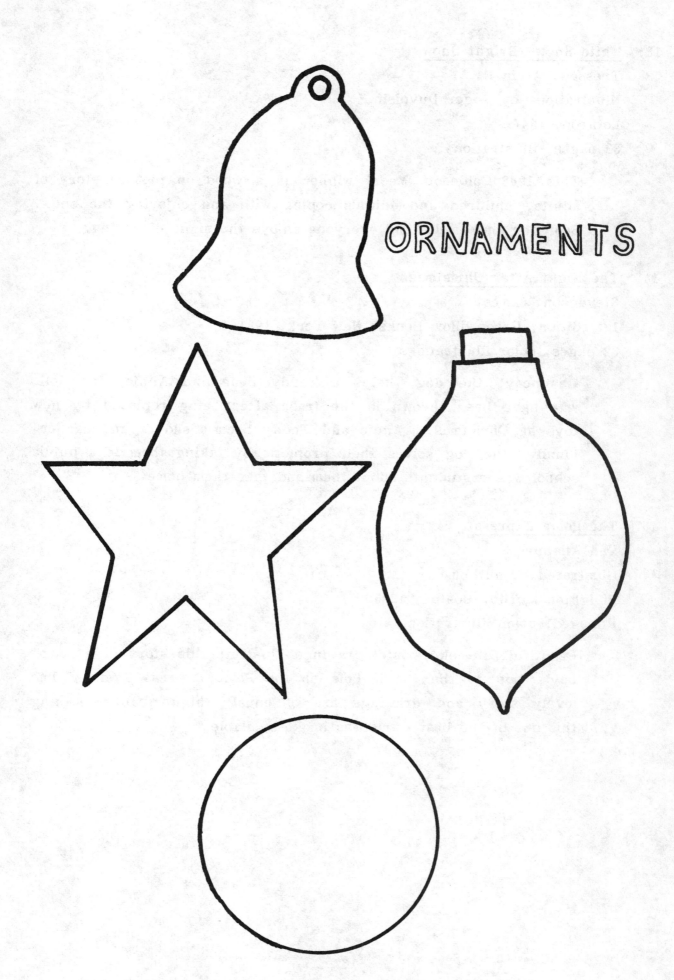

ORNAMENTS

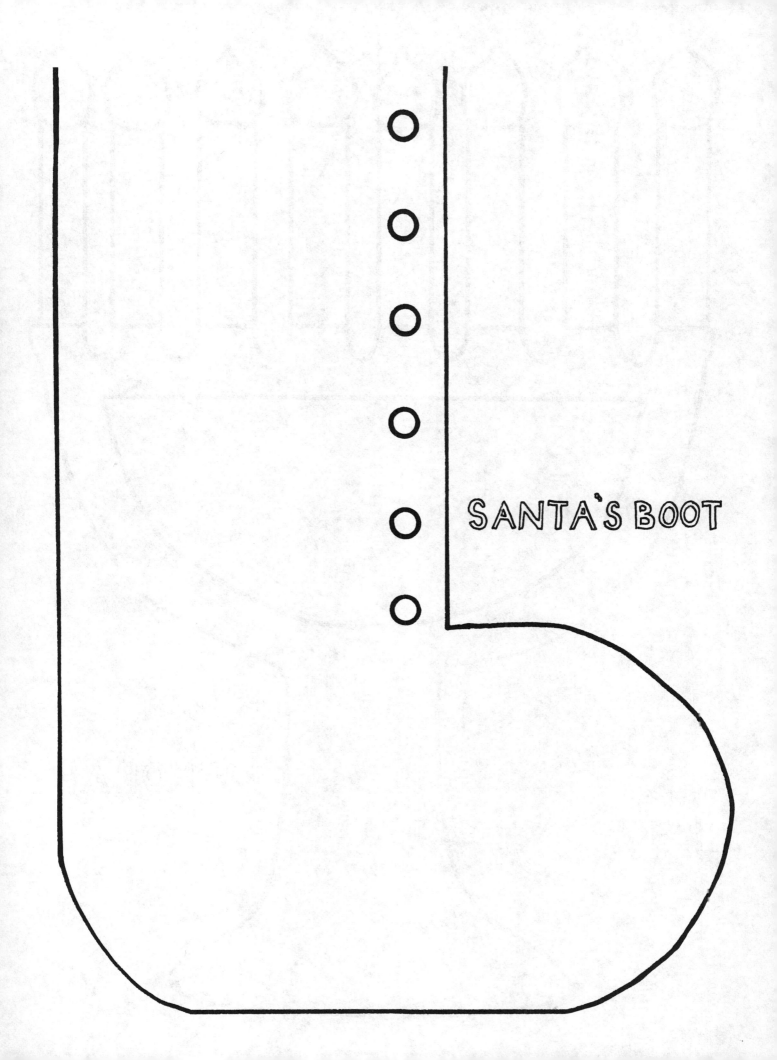

SANTA'S BOOT

MENORAH

CHRISTMAS CANDLE

HOLLY LEAF MAN

CANDY CANE

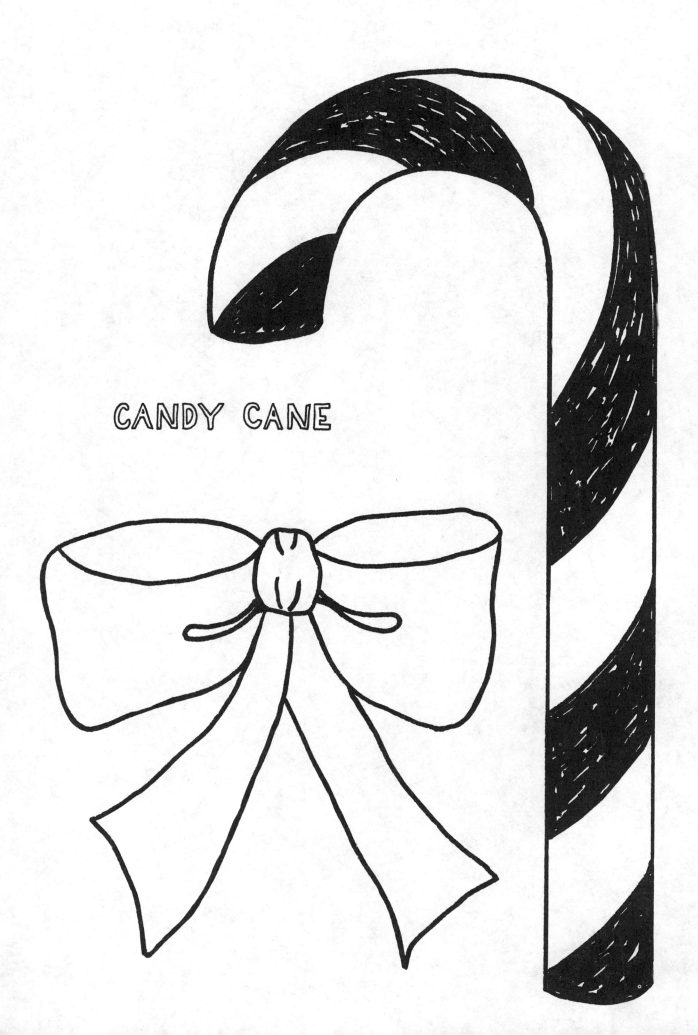

JANUARY

Dear Parents:

We learn more about snow and cold weather during January!

LITERATURE
Winter poetry, stories and finger plays

ART
Making snow flakes
Winter scenes

SCIENCE
Exploring winter wonderland

BOOKS FROM THE LIBRARY

MATH COOKING
Snow Cones

HAPPY JANUARY!

SUGGESTED DAILY LEARNING PLAN

JANUARY

Parent Page ART - Snowflakes SOCIAL STUDIES - Discuss "Interesting Facts About Winter" PHYS. ED. - Exercises 1-2 & B BOOK - Hold My Hand by Charlotte Zolotow	ART - Circle Snowman LITERATURE - ACTION POEM - "Mr. Snowman" SCIENCE - Activity 1 PHYS. ED. - Exercises 1-3 (five times) BOOK - The Snowman Who Went For A Walk by Mira Lobe	ART - Fluffy Snowman MUSIC - "Snow Flakes, Snow Flakes" MATH COOKING - Snow Cones PHYS. ED. - Exercises 1-3 & C BOOK - Winter Noisy Book by Margaret Wise Brown	ART - White Chalk Snow Picture and/or White Chalk Design LITERATURE - POEM - "The Snow" PHYS. ED. - Exercises 1-3 & B BOOK - The Biggest Snowstorm Ever by Diane Paterson	ART - Frosty Winter Scene LITERATURE - POEM - "The Snowflake" PHYS. ED. - Exercises 1-4 (very slowly) BOOK - Good Morning Baby Bear by Eric Hill
ART - Green Pepper Star Painting LITERATURE - FINGER PLAY - "Baby" PHYS. ED. - Exercises 1-4 (very fast, very slowly) BOOK - The Snow by John Burningham	ART - Snow Picture with Whipped Soap LITERATURE - POEM - "Winter Time is Great" PHYS. ED. - Exercises 1-5 & D MATH COOKING - Frozen Juice Popsicles	ART - Triangle Snow Trees LITERATURE - FINGER PLAY - "The Baby" PHYS. ED. - Exercises 1-6 BOOK - Hamilton Duck by Arthur Getz	ART - Snowman Stick Puppets LITERATURE - ACTION POEM - "Making A Snowman" SOCIAL STUDIES - "Winter Problems" PHYS. ED. - Exercises 1-6 & D BOOK - The Snow Party by Beatrice Schenk DeRegniers	ART - Colorful Mittens LITERATURE - STORY "A Winter Story" and NURSERY RHYME - "Three Little Kittens" SCIENCE - Activity 2 PHYS. ED. - Exercises 1-7
ART - Dress A Child For Winter LITERATURE - STORY - Recall "A Winter Story" PHYS. ED. - Exercises 1-7 & E	ART - (Complete) Dress A Child for Winter LITERATURE - FINGER PLAY - "Dressing For Winter" SCIENCE - Activity 3 & 4 PHYS. ED. - Exercises 1-8 BOOK - A Walk On a Snowy Night by Judy Delton	ART - Food For The Birds LITERATURE - POEM - "Snowflake, Snowflake" PHYS. ED. - Exercises 1-8 & F	ART - Winter Bird Picture LITERATURE - FINGER PLAY - "Baby" SCIENCE - Activity 5 & 6 PHYS. ED. - Exercises 1-8 & F MATH COOKING - Cupcake Cones BOOK - The Big Snow by Berta Hader (Hoerner)	ART - Paper Bag Eskimo LITERATURE - FINGER PLAY "The Snow" MUSIC - "A Snowy Winter Day" PHYS. ED. - Exercises 1-8 (very slowly three times) BOOK - The Snowy Day by Ezra Jack Keats
ART - Make A Penguin SCIENCE - Activity 7 & 8 PHYS. ED. - Exercises 1-8 & E BOOK - Walt Disney's "The Penguin That Hated The Cold" by Barbara Brenner	ART - (Complete) Make A Penguin MUSIC - "A Sledding We Will Go" SOCIAL STUDIES - (Recall) "Winter Problems" PHYS. ED. - Exercises 1-8 & C	ART - Torn Paper Snowman LITERATURE - FINGER PLAY - "The Snowman" PHYS. ED. - Exercises 1-8 & B BOOK - Summer Snowman by Gene Zion	ART - Winter Trees PHYS. ED. - Exercises 1-8 & D BOOK - Sleepy Bear by Linda Dabcovich	ART - Winter Scene LITERATURE - ACTION POEM - "A Snowy" PHYS. ED. - Exercises 1-8 & E MATH COOKING - Jack Wax BOOK - The Self-Made Snowman by Fernando Krahn

I. ART

Children will develop skills in:

Organization

Sequence

Use of small muscles (small motor)

A. SNOWFLAKES

Fold a square white sheet of paper several times.
(Make sure the paper is in the shape of a square.)

Tear or use scissors to cut on folded sides. Open the snowflake.
Paste on black or blue paper. Or, hang the snowflake with a
string to give it a floating effect.

FOUR POINTED SNOWFLAKE

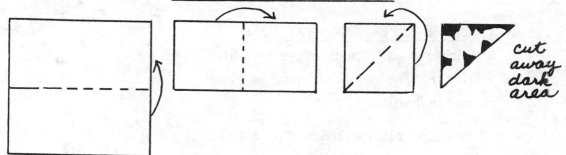

cut away dark area

SIX POINTED SNOWFLAKE

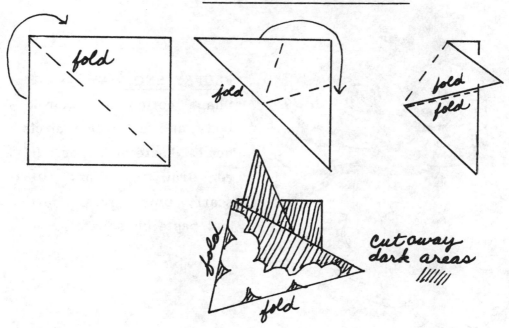

fold

fold

fold

fold

cut away dark areas

fold

fold

B. **CIRCLE SNOWMAN**

Draw a small, medium and a large circle from white paper.

Cut out circles and paste on a sheet of colored construction paper. Stress the difference in sizes (small, medium and large).

Use a crayon to add facial features and hats, buttons, arms, scarf, etc.

C. <u>TORN PAPER SNOWMAN</u>

Children will tear edges of white paper to make a snowman's head and a body.

Paste on black construction paper.

Tear black scraps to make eyes, nose and buttons.

D. <u>FLUFFY SNOWMAN</u>

Shape cotton in a circle for the body and a smaller circle for the head. Paste on paper. Have children draw, color and cut out hat, scarf, pipe, eyes, buttons, etc. and paste on snowman.

E. <u>WINTER SCENE</u>

Children will draw a winter scene on a gray or blue piece of paper.

Use cotton for snow and snow flakes. Paste on cotton to make a snow scene.

F. <u>WHITE CHALK SNOW PICTURE</u>

Children will draw a winter scene with white chalk on the colored paper.

For example: A snowman drawn with white chalk on black paper turns out very attractive.

G. <u>WHITE CHALK DESIGN</u>

Draw wavy lines with loops on dark colored paper with the white chalk.

Children will color in the loops with the white chalk.

H. **FROSTY WINTER SCENE**

Have children draw a picture or design on a 9" x 12" sheet of white construction paper.

Advise them to press hard on crayons and color in all areas with bright colors. When the picture is finished, paint over the entire picture with white paint.

The paint won't stick where the crayon has been heavily used, but will collect in some areas to give the picture a frosty look.

I. **GREEN PEPPER STAR PAINTING**

Cut a green pepper in half. Point out to the children the star shape in the middle of the green pepper.

Dip the green pepper star into white paint that has been placed in a shallow dish. Print the star or snowflake pattern on the colored construction paper you have selected for this project.

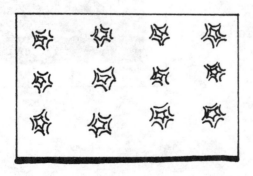

J. **SNOW PICTURES WITH WHIPPED SOAP**

Empty two to three cups of Ivory soap flakes in a large bowl. Gradually, pour the boiling water in the bowl while beating rapidly. Use just enough water to make the mixture thick and creamy. Use immediately. Make a picture using the whipped soap.

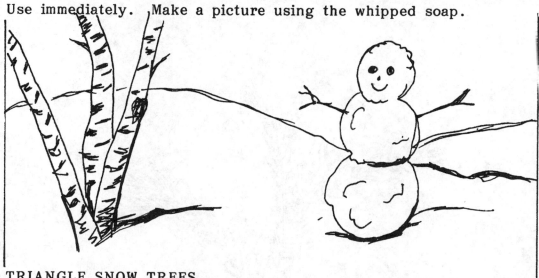

K. **TRIANGLE SNOW TREES**

Using whipped soap (see direction above) and green triangle shapes already cut out, spread the soap on the triangle trees. After completing this procedure, place the trees on a larger piece of paper.

L. WINTER TREES
Place whipped soap (see directions on previous page) on small evergreen branches. Shake some silver glitter on the wet mixture. Place the branch in a cup filled with sand.

M.   SNOWMAN STICK PUPPETS

Cut circles from a piece of 9" x 12" white construction paper for the snowman's head and body.

Draw in the facial features.

Add buttons, scarf and triangle hat. When puppet is finished, glue the tongue depressor to the back of snowman.

N. **COLORFUL MITTENS**

Help each child trace around his right and left hand.

Color the mittens in bright colors.

Cut mittens out and punch a hole in each one. Attach a mitten at each end of the yarn.

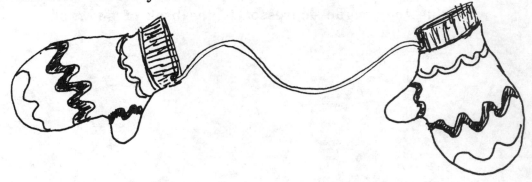

O. Another idea using mittens:

Have children trace their hands on colored paper. Then, cut out mittens.

On newsprint (large) have children draw a picture of themselves.

Paste the mittens where they belong.

P. **DRESS A CHILD FOR WINTER**

Draw an outline of a child or trace pattern. Have children draw
and cut out winter clothes and paste them on the pattern.

Discuss winter clothes with the children. For example: snow
jacket and snow pants, hat scarf, boots and mittens.

Q. <u>FOOD FOR THE BIRDS</u>

Have the children string the cereal until the string is adequately filled. Use cereals that are shaped so there is a hole in the middle, for example: Cheerios®, Fruit Loops®, etc. Then, tie the ends of the string together.

Discuss how hard it is for the birds to find food when the ground is covered with snow. Tell the chilren to put these cereal loops on a bush or tree to feed the birds. Birds that stay in the north instead of migrating to warmer climates are Sparrows, Cardinals, Blue Jays, Woodpeckers and Chickadees.

R. WINTER BIRD PICTURE

From colored 9" x 12" red, blue or brown construction paper, cut a small and medium circle.

Also, from colored paper, cut a tiny and a medium triangle.

Paste the small and medium circle on the white paper. The medium circle is the body and the small circle is the head. Paste the tiny triangle on the bird's head for the beak. Paste the larger triangle on the body for the tail.

Children will draw in the bird's eye and legs.

S.   A PAPER BAG ESKIMO

Cut off the bottom of a small brown paper bag. Cut a circle
of brown for the face. Draw facial features with crayons. Cut
brown arms and mittens.   Cut white paper to make fur trim.
You may also use cotton balls or rolled cotton for the fur trim.
Cut black boots.

Paste the eskimo together.   Use a black crayon to draw in front
laces.

T.   MAKE A PENQUIN

Round off the corners of one sheet of 9" x 12" black construction paper for the body.   Cut two flippers (arms) from another sheet of black construction paper.   Cut a white front from white construction paper (or use cotton balls or rolled cotton).   Cut feet from orange paper.   Cut two eyes from a scrap of yellow paper.   Cut diamond-shaped beak from orange paper.

Paste the "tummy" on the penquin.   Paste the two flippers onto the back and paste the orange feet onto the back of the body. Paste on the yellow eyes and cut pupils from black scraps.

Fold the diamond-shaped mouth in half and paste only the bottom half so the top half sticks out.

MATERIALS CHART

JANUARY

A. SNOWFLAKES
White construction paper
Paste
Black construction paper
Blue construction paper
String

B. CIRCLE SNOWMAN
White paper
Paste
Colored construction paper
Crayons

C. TORN PAPER SNOWMAN
White paper
Paste
Black construction paper

D. FLUFFY SNOWMAN
Cotton
Paste
Paper
Crayons

E. WINTER SCENE
Crayons
Gray paper/blue paper
Cotton
Paste

F. WHITE CHALK SNOW PICTURES
White chalk
Colored paper

G. WHITE CHALK DESIGN
White chalk
Dark paper

H. FROSTY WINTER SCENE
Crayons
9"x12" white construction paper
White paint

I. GREEN PEPPER STAR PAINTING
Green pepper
White paint
Shallow dish
Colored construction paper

J. SNOW PICTURES WITH WHIPPED SOAP
Ivory soap flakes
Large bowl
Boiling water
Beater
Construction paper

K. TRIANGLE SNOW TREES
Whipped soap (See "J")
Green construction paper
Colored construction paper

L. WINTER TREES
Whipped soap (See "J")
Evergreen branches
Silver glitter
Cup
Sand

M. SNOWMAN STICK PUPPETS
9"x12" white construction paper
Crayons
Glue
Tongue depressor

N. COLORFUL MITTENS
Construction paper
Crayons
Hole punch
Yarn
Large newsprint
Paste

O. MORE COLORFUL MITTENS
Colored paper
Newsprint
Paste

P. DRESS A CHILD FOR WINTER
Large paper
Crayons
Paste

Q. FOOD FOR THE BIRDS
String
Cereal - Cheerios
Fruit Loops

R. WINTER BIRD PICTURE
9"x12" red construction paper
9"x12" blue construction paper
9"x12" brown construction paper
White paper
Crayons

S. A PAPER BAG ESKIMO
Small brown paper bag
Brown construction paper
Crayons
White paper/cotton
Black construction paper

T. MAKE A MENGUIN
9"x12" black construction paper
White construction paper/cotton
Orange construction paper
Yellow construction paper
Paste

II. LITERATURE

Children will develop the ability to identify and enjoy:

Characters

Main ideas

Details

Sequence of events

A. A WINTER STORY

Amy and Tommy loved to visit Grandmother and Grandfather on the farm. In the summer there were so many interesting things to see and do. They could help feed the animals, they could take long walks, and even have a picnic. But, now it was the middle of winter. The ground was covered with snow. They would probably have a boring time because they would have to play indoors. For two active children, the thought of having to stay inside and be content with working puzzles or drawing and coloring made them feel rather unhappy.

However, after they had eaten a delicious breakfast of pancakes and cocoa (Grandmother made the best pancakes and cocoa in the whole world.), Grandfather said, "Now, let's take a walk."

Quickly Amy and Tommy ran for their snowsuits. They zipped up their suits, put on their fur-lined snow boots, their warm wool hats and their lined mittens. Last of all they put a scarf around their neck and pulled it over their noses, in case the air would be too cold to breathe. Finally, they were ready.

"All set?" asked Grandfather.

"Ready," they both shouted happily.

Out the door they went, down the steps, along the path. They passed the barn and the orchard and soon they were walking along the stream. The snow was white and clean. Not a mark could be seen except the footprints of some little forest animals.

"Look here," said Grandfather. "Who do you think was here?"

They studied the footprints that made a path through the bushes and trees. "What animal made that kind of footprint?"

Amy and Tommy looked carefully at the little prints in the snow. Finally, they looked at Grandfather and shook their heads. They just didn't know.

"It was a rabbit," said Grandfather. "A little cotton tail rabbit, probably looking for something to eat."

Amy and Tommy studied the rabbit prints. Now they would always know this is the kind of footprint a rabbit makes.

They walked a little farther and they spotted more footprints. But, these were different.

"What animal made these footprints, Grandfather?"

"Why, that's the hoof print of a deer. See how the tracks go down to the stream? The deer probably wanted a drink of water."

"Let's go to the place where the water current is so swift the water can't freeze," said Grandfather.

This was getting exciting. It was almost like being detectives. They followed the tracks and, as they got closer to the running water, there were many different kinds of tracks all mixed together. Many different animals had come to the stream for a drink of water. They spotted some very unusual tracks in the snow.

"Grandfather! Grandfather! Look at these tracks! Who made these tracks?"

Grandfather looked at the spider-like tracks that led off the path into the underbrush. Amy and Tommy wondered what little creature could have made such feather-like tracks in the cold,

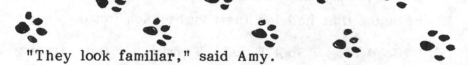

white snow.

"Why, those are the tracks of a little field mouse," said Grandfather. "See how they lead into the thick brushes. He probably has a sung little home in there."

Amy and Tommy had been so interested in studying the footprints, they had forgotten all about being bored.

"Look at this print, Grandfather." Tommy was peering at another set of prints in the snow.

"They look familiar," said Amy.

"Let's follow these prints and see where they go," said Tommy, who was always ready for adventure.

"Yes, let's do it," agreed Amy.

The children were so eager that Grandfather quickly agreed. The tracks led up the hill, through the underbrush and over to a large tree. They followed the tracks around the tree and saw that they led across the field. The children were moving along so fast in their eagerness to find where the tracks were leading that Grandfather had to scramble in order to keep up with them.

The tracks were leading the children through the orchard and past the barn. To the amazement of Amy and Tommy, the tracks led right up to the back steps to Grandmother and Grandfather's house.

"Oh, my gosh," said Amy. "Look Grandfather, these footprints go right up the steps and into the house."

Sure enough, the prints clearly went right into the house. Amy and Tommy ran up the steps and knocked at the door. Grandmother opened the door, and with a big smile on her face, she said, "Well, how did you like your walk this morning?"

Both children tried to talk at once. They wanted to tell Grandmother all about the footprints they had found and now they were anxious to find out who they had tracked to the house and, most of all, who or what had come right into the house.

Grandmother laughed at the serious look on their faces. At that moment, Spot came running into the room wagging his tail with delight at seeing the children.

Then, Amy and Tommy knew whose tracks they had followed in the snow that had led them right back home.

"Good dog, Spot," said Tommy. "Your tracks led us back home just in time for lunch."

They all laughed together, for they knew Tommy was always hungry.

POEMS/FINGER PLAYS/NURSERY RHYMES

Children will develop the ability to participate in and enjoy:

    Rhythm

    Poetry

    Sequence

    Characters

B.   **POEMS**

    1.   **A SNOWY DAY**

        See us play,

        On a snowy day.

        We all know,

        It's fun to play in snow.

    2.   **WINTER TIME IS GREAT**

        Winter time is fun, you know.

        We love to play out in the snow.

        We run and slide and ski and skate.

        Winter time is really great!

    3.   **SNOWFLAKE, SNOWFLAKE**

        Snowflake, snowflake,

        How pretty you are.

        So sparkly and white,

        You shine like a star.

4. **THE SNOW**

See the snow come floating down,
Softly, silently, without a sound.
But feel the snow on a windy day,
It stings us and bites us,
When we're at play.

5. **THE SNOWFLAKES**

Snowflakes, snowflakes, sailing down,
Falling, falling, on the ground.
Covering everything in sight,
Until the world is a snowy white.

C. ACTION POEMS

1. MR. SNOWMAN

See Mr. Snowman on a cold winter day,
He's smiling and happy
While we're at play.
(Children stand straight and tall,
arms level with shoulders.)

But look at Mr. Snowman,
When the sun shines bright,
He starts to melt
Right out of sight.
(Children start to sag;
slowly lay on floor.)

2. ## A SNOWY DAY

   Let's go out on a snowy day,
   'Cause when it's snowing,
   It's fun to play.
   Put on a snowsuit, some boots,
   And a hat,
   Some mittens, a muffler,
   I feel kind of fat.
   (Children will act out putting on each item of clothing
   as it is mentioned.)

   But when the wind begins to blow,
   I'll be nice and warm, you know.
   (Cross arms in front like a hug.)

3. ### MAKING A SNOWMAN

To make a snowman, pick some snow up from the ground.
Pack a little snowball and then roll it around.

When the ball gets too big, just let it be,
Then roll a smaller one for the head, you see.

Put the head on top and then make a face,
Put the eyes and then the mouth in place.

If you have a carrot, that'll be the nose,
See how funny Mr. Snowman grows?

Use sticks for arms and then find a hat,
Mr. Snowman is pretty fat.

His buttons can be stones from the ground.
Now wrap a fancy scarf around.

And now our snowman is all done.
Didn't we have lots of fun?

D. FINGER PLAYS

1. BABY

Here's a ball for baby (Make circle with thumb and pointer.)

Big and soft and round.

Here is baby's hammer. (Make hammer with fist.)

Oh, how he can pound!

Here is baby's music. (Hold up hands facing each other.)

Clapping, clapping, so. (Clap hands.)

Here are baby's soldiers. (Hold fingers upright.)

Standing in a row.

Here is baby's trumpet. Toot-too, too-too, too.

        (Two fists, one atop the other before mouth.)

Here's the way that baby

Plays at peek-a-boo.

        (Fingers of both hands spread before eyes.)

Here's a big umbrella

        (Bring fingertips together in peak over head.)

To keep the baby dry.

Here is baby's cradle.

        (Make peak of pointers and little fingers and rock.)

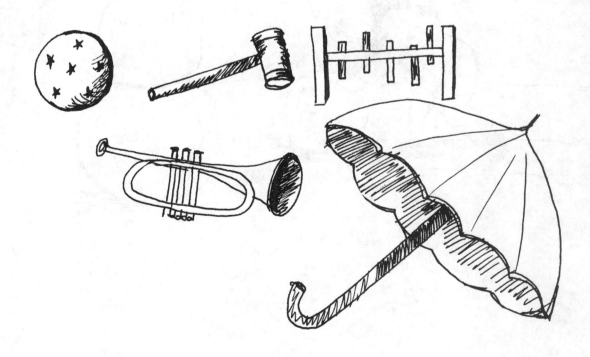

2. THE BABY

Sh! Be quiet! (Finger over lips.)
The baby is sleeping. (Arms like cradle rocking baby.)
Sh! Be quiet! (Finger over lips.)
The baby is sleeping. (Arms lile cradle rocking baby.)
Sh! Be quiet! (Finger over lips.)
The baby is sleeping. (Arms like cradle; rocking baby.)
We don't want to wake it up.

Walk on tiptoe, (Walking on tiptoe.)
So we don't make a sound.
Walk on tiptoe,
So we don't make a sound.
Walk on tiptoe,
So we don't make a sound.
Or the baby will start to cry.

The baby woke up,
And is crying waa-waa. (Rub eyes as if crying.)
The baby woke up,
And is crying WAA-WAA.
The baby woke up,
And is crying W A A - W A A!
See all the tears on its face.
        (Use pointer fingers to make tears running down face.)

We'll tickle the baby,
Under the chin. (Tickle self under chin.)
We'll tickle the baby,
Under the chin.
We'll tickle the baby,
Under the chin.
Maybe the baby will smile.

See how the baby,
Starts to grin. (Smile.)
See how the baby,
Starts to grin.
See how the baby,
Starts to grin.
Now we are happy again!

3. BABY

Here is baby's tousled head. (Make a fist.)
He nods and nods. (Bend first back and forth.)
Let's put him to bed.

    (Bend other arm; tuck fist into crook of elbow.)

4. THE SNOW

This is how the snow comes floating softly down.

    (Children raise and lower arms while wiggling fingers.)

In a little while it covers all the ground.

    (Arms outstretched.)

Then I'll make some snowballs, more than one or two.

    (Making snowballs.)

Are you ready? Are you set?
I'll throw them all at you. (Throwing snowballs.)

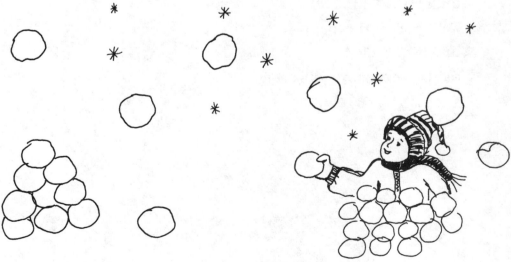

5. THE SNOWMAN

This s how the snowman stands out in the snow.

(Children stand up.)

He's happy, even though it's cold,

And the wind begins to blow.

But look at Mr. Snowman on a sunny day.

He starts to sag, and then falls down,

(Children start to slowly sag until they are on floor.)

And he melts away.

6. DRESSING FOR WINTER

This is how we dress on a cold winter's day.

We put on our snowsuits to go out to play.

(Putting on snowsuit.)

Then we put our boots on for walking in the snow.

(Putting on boots.)

Next, our hats and mittens,

'Cause the wind begins the blow.

(Put on hats and mittens.)

And now we're all ready to go out and play.

We'll stay nice and warm on this cold winter day.

(Clap hands together.)

E. NURSERY RHYMES

1. <u>THREE LITTLE KITTENS</u>

Three little kittens, lost their mittens
And they began to cry.
"Oh mother dear, we greatly fear,
That we have lost our mittens."
"What, lost your mittens, you naughty kittens,
Then you shall have no pie."
Mee-ow, mee-ow, mee-ow.
"Then we shall have no pie."
The three little kittens found their mittens
And they began to cry,
"Oh mother dear, see here, see here
Our mittens we have found."
"What! Found your mittens
You silly kittens,
Then you shall have some pie."
Purr-rr, purr-rr, purr-rr,
"Oh, let us have some pie."

III. MUSIC

Children will develop the ability to participate in and enjoy music.

A. <u>A-SLEDDING WE WILL GO</u>

(Tune: The Farmer In The Dell)

Oh, a-sledding we will go, a-sledding we will go.

We'll run and slide,

Down the hill we'll glide,

As a-sledding we will go.

B. <u>A SNOWY WINTER DAY</u>

(Tune: Here We Go Round the Mulberry Bush)

Look at the snow come sailing down,

Sailing down, sailing down.

Look at the snow come sailing down,

On a winter day.

Let's make a snowball, or two, or three,

Two or three, two or three,

Let's make a snowball, or two, or three,

On this snowy day.

Throw the snowballs, zing, zing, zing,

Zing, zing, zing,

Zing, zing, zing.

Throw the snowballs,

Zing, zing, zing,

As we play in the snow.

C. __SNOWFLAKES, SNOWFLAKES__

(Tune: Twinkle, Twinkle Little Star)

Snowflakes, snowflakes, soft and white,

Falling gently through the night.

While the children sleep for hours,

You will cover trees and flowers,

When they 'wake they'll rub their eyes,

A land so white is a big surprise.

IV. SCIENCE

Children will develop skills in:

Distinguishing differeces

Similarities of attributes

A. WINTER WONDERLAND!

1. Go outside on a very cold day. Have the children observe the water vapor when they breathe and talk.

2. Look for animal or bird tracks in the snow.

3. When the snow is falling, have the children look closely at the individual flakes. Catch some on dark cloth and use a magnifying glass for a closer inspection.

4. Bring some snow inside for measuring and exploring.

5. Let the children mix food coloring with the snow.

6. Store some snowballs in the deep freeze so the children can observe they are still frozen in the spring when the snow has melted and completely disappeared outside.

7. Take a pan of water outside when the temperature is below freezing. Have the children observe what happens to the water. After it has frozen, bring the pan inside again. Have the children observe what happens again. Discuss it.

8. Fill a juice can and a cardboard milk container with water. Take both outside in freezing weather and observe what happens. For a frozen treat, place a small carton of milk or cream outside when the temperature is below freezing. When it has frozen, give the chilren a spoonful to observe and taste.

V. SOCIAL STUDIES
Children will develop an awareness of:
    Holidays
    Traditions
    Seasonal changes

A. WINTER PROBLEMS

Although playing in the snow can be fun, it does create some problems. The animals and birds have a difficult time finding food when the ground is covered with snow. People can help these animals survive the winter by putting out seeds and bread crumbs. Also, specially prepared seed and suet bells can be purchased at the store and put out to help the animals get through the winter.

Adults who have to drive in ice and snow learn to drive very carefully. Snow can make the streets very slippery and can be the cause of automobile accidents. Drivers will often use snow tires and chains to help make driving safer. They also have to put antifreeze in their cars to keep radiators from freezing. Also, although walking in the snow can be very enjoyable, especially if it is very cold and you can hear the crunch of the snow every time you take a step, it can be slippery and dangerous.

People have to dress warmer in winter. Coats and jackets that are lined help keep our bodies warm. Also, hats, mittens, and boots keep our head, hands and feet warm and dry. We try to keep our bodies well protected.

Some places in the world stay warm all winter. They never have snow or ice storms. The people who live in these places dress in lightweight clothes. Instead of snow, they will usually have a rainy season.

B. INTERESTING FACTS ABOUT WINTER

> Winter is a time of ice and snow.
>
> Snow is frozen crystals of winter.
>
> Sleet is frozen raindrops.
>
> Ice is a frozen area of water.

Many people like the winter weather even though it is very cold. Winter has some sports that are very popular. People love to get out in the brisk, fresh air to ski or skate or go sledding or tobogganing.

Snow can fall in beautiful crystal flakes sailing lazily out of the sky, floating down, landing softly and silently as it changes the world to a colorless, white land. However, sometimes the snow can be so icy, it seems like grains of sand and when it is driven by the wind, it can sting and hurt when it hits our cheeks and nose.

Children, especially, love the winter weather. It's fun to play in the snow. They love to jump and roll around in it because even though snow is cold, it is light and airy and can be soft and fluffy.

Children also like to make a snowman. This can be a very creative experience. Children also like to make snow forts.

VI. JANUARY PHYSICAL EDUCATION FUN

Children will develop skills in:

Rhythm

Imaging

Use of large and small muscles

Good sports conduct

A. <u>MOVE AS IF YOU ARE</u>:
1. A big fluffy snowflake softly twirling toward the ground.
2. A little wet snowflake swiftly moving down to the ground.
3. Shoveling snow.
4. Walking through very deep snow.
5. Ice skating.
6. Making angels in the snow.
7. Making a snowman.
8. A polar bear.

B. <u>ICE TOWER</u>

Groups of as few as one child and as many as four can play this game.

Pretend the blocks are pieces of ice. How tall can you (your group) build an ice tower and have it still standing? Which group has built the tallest tower?

C. <u>MAKE A MATCH</u>

Hold up a hat. Say, "This hat is blue. Find me something that is blue." Children will name things that are blue. Or, show the children a ball. Say, "This ball is round. Find me something that is round." Continue using colors and shapes to describe.

D. **MATCH MITTENS**

Scramble several pairs of mittens in a pile. Have children take turns matching the pairs.

E. **WHAT'S MISSING**

Gather the following items that represent winter: knit hat, pair of mittens, scarf, picture of a snowman, styrofoam snowball, and a plastic or paper snowflake. Place these items on the floor. Have one child hide their eyes. Remove one winter item and then have child open their eyes and see if they can guess what is missing. Give each child a turn.

F. **MAKE AN INSIDE SNOWMAN**

Have children help make a snowman by stuffing a pillowcase with crumpled newspaper. Tie the pillowcase at the top and in the middle. Have children make "snowballs" from crumpled paper. Set up the "snowman" and have the children try to hit him with their snowballs. This is a great group and gross motor activity.

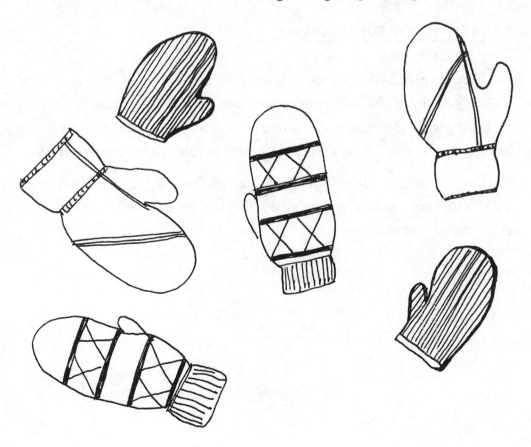

VII. MATH COOKING

Children will develop skills in:

Number awareness

Counting

Measuring

A. SNOW CONES

Crushed ice

Flavored syrup/fruit flavored gelatin powder

Paper cups

Pack clean crushed ice in paper cups with an ice cream scoop. Pour flavored syrup or fruit flavored gelatin powder or fruit juice over the ice. Children will love it.

Math: Count the cups - is there one for each child?

B. FROZEN JUICE POPSICLES

Fruit juice

Toothpicks/tongue depressors

Make popsicles in the refrigerator by using fruit juices. Place a toothpick, or tongue depressors cut in half, in each ice cube container to use as a handle when the juice has frozen solid.

Math: Discuss the cube shape of popsicle. Count popsicles. Can children guess how many sticks there will be if there are that many popsicles? Count sticks.

C. **CUPCAKE CONES**

       Cake mix   Frostings

       Ice cream cones   Chocolate chips/M&M®candies

       Sugar crystals

Use prepared cake mix. Prepare according to directions on the package. Fill cones with the cake mixture and bake until done. Frost with desired frosting and sprinkle sugar crystals or use chocolate chips or M&M®candies.

Math: Count ingredients and discuss **measurements**. Count chocolate chips or M&M®candies.

  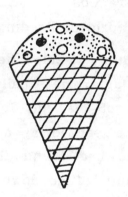 

D. **JACK WAX**

       Maple syrup

       Crushed ice

Pour two cups of maple syrup in a saucepan and boil until the softball stage is reached. Next, pour the hot syrup over crushed ice in a large bowl. Twirl the wax onto forks for a sweet treat.

Math: Discuss measurement of two cups. Discuss more and less. Do some students have more and some less on their forks? Or are they all equal?

READ ALOUD BOOKS FROM THE LIBRARY
JANUARY

BOOKS

Children will develop the ability to enjoy and gain knowledge from books.

1. Walt Disney's "The Penguin That Hated The Cold"
    Brenner, Barbara
    Random House, New York, 1973
    42 pages, color illustrations
    (Disney's Wonderful World of Reading)

    Pablo, the penquin, decided he had enough of cold weather. After several false starts, he finally sailed into warm waters, but his boat was made of ice and it melted. Luckily, he jumped into a bathtub which served as a boat until he landed on a tropical island where he had found the place of his dreams. He built a straw house and settled down.

2. Winter Noisy Book
    Brown, Margaret Wise (1910-1952)
    Illustrated by Charles G. Shaw
    Harper, New York, 1947
    Unpaged, illustrations

    Muffin, the dog, hears the inside and outside noises and sees the inside and outside sights of winter. There are also some things Muffin can not hear, like the cat lying on the fur rug and frost forming on the window. He sees and hears and feels a lot of interesting things.

3. The Snow

Burningham, John

Designed by Jan Pienkowski

Thomas Y. Crowell, New York, 1975

Unpaged, color illustrations

A very little boy makes a big snowball and rides on a sled pulled by his mother. He loses his mitten and gets cold. He snuggles into bed with his teddy bear and hopes that the snow is still there tomorrow. This book contains very simple vocabulary and pastel drawings.

4. Sleepy Bear

Dabcovich, Lydia

E.P. Dutton, New York, 1982

A very few words and many clever pictures tell the story of a brown bear who becomes sleepy, finds a cave and sleeps until the snow begins to melt. The birds and bugs return to wake him and remind him of honey.

5. The Snow Party

DeRegniers, Beatrice Schenk

Illustrated by Reiner Zimmik

Patheon, New York, 1959

Unpaged, illustrations

A lovely old lady wishes that she and her husband could give a party. Soon a snowstorm forces people to seek shelter and a bus, cars and bakery trucks bring men, women, children and trays of fresh rolls and a cake. A stranded accordian player plays and the people dance and have a fine time. Soon, the storm is over, the road cleared and all the "company" goes home.

6. A Walk On A Snowy Night
    Delton, Judy
    Illustration by Ruth Rosner
    Harper and Row Publishers, New York, 1982

    Father and daughter enjoy a nighttime walk during a snow
    storm. They appreciate the unfamiliar snow covered look
    of familiar landmarks.

7. Hamilton Duck
    Getz, Arthur
    Illustrated by author
    Golden Press, Western Publishing Company, New York
    Racine, Wisconsin, 1972
    Unpaged, color illustrations

    Hamilton Duck observes the changes that take place as winter
    comes to the farm and the farm's pond. He returns to the
    warm barn and makes a snug bed in the hay. Very few
    words; the story is told with large multicolored pictures.

8. The Big Snow
    Hader, Berta (Hoerner) and Elmer
    Illustrated by authors
    MacMillan, New York, 1948, 1976
    Unpaged, color and black/white illustrations

    The book won the Caldecott Medal in 1949. Words and pictures
    work together to tell the story of animals and birds preparing
    and surviving the long cold winter. They were helped by
    the man and woman who live in a cottage in the woods.
    The man and woman shovel a path through the snow and
    sprinkle seeds, nuts and bread crumbs to help the hungry
    animals and birds.

9. Good Morning Baby Bear

    Hill, Eric

    Random House, New York, 1984

    > Colorful simple pictures and a few large print words tell about baby bear getting started on his day. He washes, eats breakfast, plays with his blocks and then goes out into the sunshine with his wagon.

10. The Snowy Day

    Keats, Ezra Jack

    Viking, New York, 1962

    33 pages, illustrated

    > This charming book won the Caldecott Medal in 1963. After breakfast, Peter put on his red snowsuit and went out to play in the snow. He knew he was too little to play with the big boys, so he made angels and a snowman. He put a snowball in his pocket and was disappointed when he found that it had melted after he had been inside the house for awhile. He went to bed and dreamed the snow melted but it was only a dream and the snow was still there in the morning.

11. The Self-Made Snowman

    Krahn, Fernando

    Illustrated by author

    Lippincott, New York, 1974

    32 pages, illustrations

    > This wordless book illustrates the saga of a ball of snow which is knocked off a mountain by a mountain goat. The snow rolls and scoots down the mountain, becoming a snowman complete with a camper's tent for a skirt and an abandoned farm wagon which provides transportation to a holiday parade in the city. The snowman becomes the center of attention in the town square.

12. The Snowman Who Went For A Walk

Lobe, Mira

Translated by Peter Carter

Illustrated by Winifred Openoorth

William Morrow Company, New York, 1984

24 pages

> After drinking a cup of tea given to him by a kind boy, the snowman takes a walk through the city and countryside. He has many adventures in the land of the "polar bears" where he lives. Detailed multicolored pictures and a simple vocabulary tell this charming story.

13. The Biggest Snowstorm Ever

Paterson, Diane (1946)

Illustrated by author

Dial Press, New York, 1974

Unpaged, illustrations

> The Bunch family played happily in the soft, white snow as the fat snowflakes kept coming down, down down. Soon only the tip of the roof of their house showed above the snow. Their dog, Califlower, tunneled them to the doorway and they went inside to sit by a roaring fire and drink chocolate while the heat from the house melted the snow that covered the house.

14. The Summer Snow Man

Zion, Gene

Illustrated by Marfaret Bloy Graham

Harper and Row Publishers, New York

> Henry's little brother, Pete, successfully secrets a small snowman in the refrigerator. Henry transfers it to the freezer without telling his brother. Henry's snowman becomes the surprise and the "**real** hit" of the Fourth of July celebration. Shows how a snowman melts in heat.

15. <u>Hold My Hand</u>
    Zolotow, Charlotte (1915)
    Illustrated by Thomas di Grazia
    1st edition, Harper and Row, New York, 1972
    24 pages, color illustrations

> This poetic story with beautiful illustrations shows two little
> girls enjoying a cold, cold snowy walk together. They notice
> the air, the snow and how bright and cold everything is.
> This book contains a few very simple words. The story
> is also told by the truly touching pictures.

SNOWMAN

SNOW WOMAN

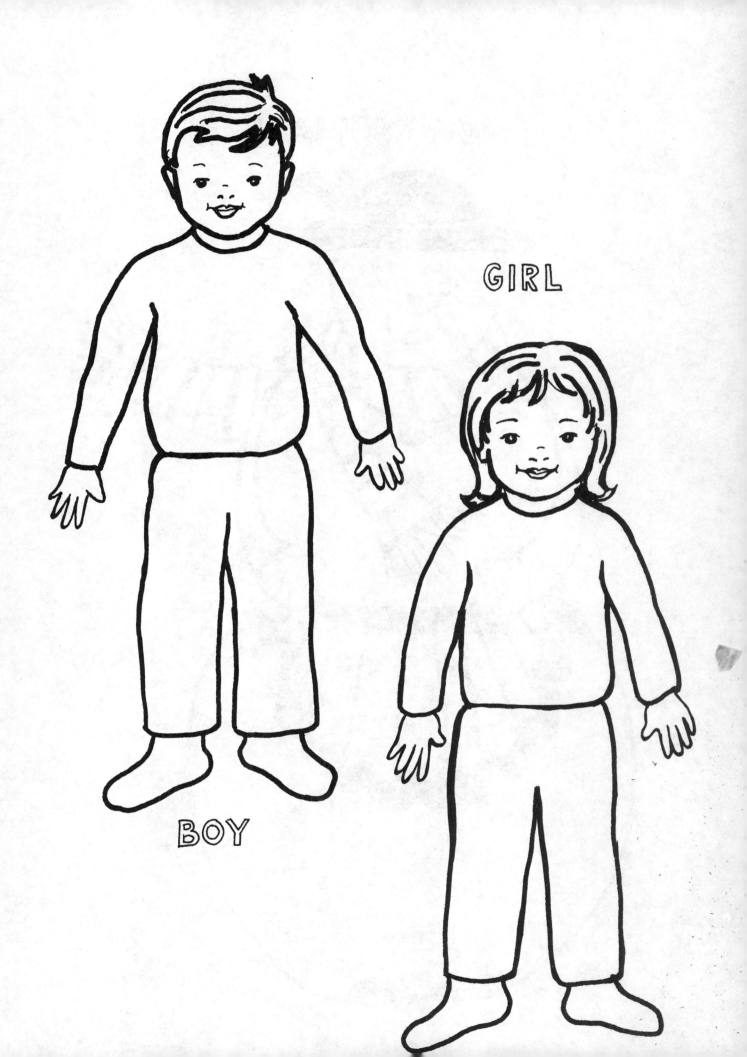

GIRL

BOY

WINTER CLOTHES
FOR BOY

WINTER
CLOTHES
FOR GIRL

FEBRUARY

Dear Parents:

February is the month for Valentine's Day, Presidents, health and safety!

ART
Valentine **Tree**
President silhouettes
and health

LITERATURE
A Valentine Story
Valentine Party

MATH COOKING
Valentine Cupcakes

BOOKS FROM THE LIBRARY

SOCIAL STUDIES
How did Valentine's Day start?

PHYSICAL EDUCATION
Chop down a cherry tree!

SCIENCE
Health and keeping clean

HAPPY FEBRUARY!

Day 1	Day 2	Day 3	Day 4	Day 5
Parent Page ART – Let's Trace Hearts and/or Heart Mobile LITERATURE – POEM – "A Valentine Message" PHYS. ED. – Exercises 1 & 2 BOOK – My First Valentine's Day by Mary Bennett	ART – Let's Make Valentines and/or Valentine Collage LITERATURE – FINGER PLAY – "Happy Valentines" MUSIC – Happy Valentines Day To You PHYS. ED. – Exercises 1-3 MATH COOKING – Jello Snack	ART – Heart Man and/or Heart Figures LITERATURE – "A Valentine Story" POEM – "A Pretty Valentine" PHYS. ED. – Exercises 3-2-1 & D BOOK – Arthur's Valentine by Marc Tolon Brown	ART – Valentine Bouquet SOCIAL STUDIES – Discuss C – Valentines Day PHYS. ED. – Exercises 1-3 (do three time each) MATH COOKING – Red Kool Aid	ART – Finger Paint A Heart LITERATURE – POEM "A Valentine For Mother" SOCIAL STUDIES – Recall C PHYS. ED. – Exercises 1-3 & B
ART – A Bag For Valentines and/or A Valentine Mailbag LITERATURE – FINGER PLAY "A Mail Box Valentine" PHYS. ED. – Exercises 1-4 & E	ART – Valentine Tree LITERATURE – POEM – "Roses Are Red" PHYS. ED. – Exercises 1-4 & B SOCIAL STUDIES – D – Getting Along BOOK – Valentine's Day by Gail Gibbons	ART – Valentine Card Container and/or A Valentine Basket MUSIC – Valentine's Day PHYS. ED. – Exercises 1-5 (two times) & D MATH COOKING – Cupcakes	ART – Heart Placemats LITERATURE – FINGER PLAY – "A Day For Love" SCIENCE – Discuss "Dressing For The Weather" PHYS. ED. – Exercises 1-5 & D BOOK – A Man Named Lincoln by Gertrude Norman	ART – Valentine Pocket LITERATURE – POEM – "Today Is Valentines Day" PHYS. ED. – Exercises 1-5 & E SOCIAL STUDIES – Discuss E – "No Stones" BOOK – Magic Monsters Learn About Health by Jane Belk Moncure
ART – Valentine Basket MUSIC – Sad Tooth, Happy Tooth PHYS. ED. – Exercises 1-6 BOOK – George Washington by Clara Judson	ART – Washington's Silhouette SOCIAL STUDIES – Discuss A – George Washington PHYS. ED. – Exercises 1-7 BOOK – George Washington by Ingri & Edgar D'Aulaire	ART – Lincoln Silhouette SOCIAL STUDIES – Discuss B – Abraham Lincoln PHYS. ED. – Exercise 1-7 & B MATH COOKING – Sugar Cookies BOOK – Abraham Lincoln by Ingri & Edgar D'Aulaire	ART – (Complete) Washington and Lincoln Silhouettes SCIENCE – Discuss B – "Healthy Diet" SOCIAL STUDIES – Recall A & B PHYS. ED. – Exercises 1-8 (do slowly) BOOK – Abraham Lincoln by Susan Lee	ART – Good Food Collage LITERATURE – NURSERY RHYME – "Two Birds" SCIENCE – C – "Balanced Diet" PHYS. ED. – Exercises 1-8 & B BOOK – The Berenstein Bears Go To The Doctor by Stan and Jan Berenstein
ART – Dressing For Weather MUSIC – This Is The Way We Put On Our Clothes SCIENCE – (Continue) Discuss "Balanced Diet 1, 2, 3 & 4 PHYS. ED. – Exercises 1-8 BOOK – Three Little Kittens Lost Their Mittens by Elaine Livermore	ART – (Complete) Dressing For The Weather PHYS. ED. – Exercises 1-8 & B SOCIAL STUDIES – Discuss F – "No To Strangers" BOOK – A Visit To The Sesame Street Hospital by Deborah Hautzig	ART – Good Food Mobile MUSIC – This Is The Way We Put On Our Clothes SCIENCE – Discuss D – "Keeping Clean" PHYS. ED. – Exercises 1-8 & B BOOK – I Wish I Was Sick Too! by Franz Brandenberg	ART – Kerchoo Picture LITERATURE – NURSERY RHYME "Good Night" PHYS. ED. – Exercises 1-8 & B BOOK – AhChoo by Mercer Mayer	ART – Sad Tooth, Happy Tooth MUSIC – Sad Tooth, Happy Tooth PHYS. ED. – Exercises 1-8 & B BOOK – Come To The Doctor, Harry by Mary Chalmers

I. ART

Children will develop skills in:

Organization

Sequence

Use of small muscles (small motor)

A. LET'S TRACE HEARTS

The chilren will trace heart patterns on pink and red construction paper and then cut them out. Allow them to do as many as they wish. Use these hearts to play the game "Hide the Hearts." Or, use these hearts to make a mobile.

B. HEART MOBILE

Cut paper hearts of various sizes. Attach the various lengths of string to the hanger. Glue two hearts together at the end of each piece of string with the string in the middle.

The hearts can be different colors and different sizes.

C.   LET'S MAKE VALENTINES

An easy way to make a heart: Fold colored paper in half. Hold
the paper on the fold, thumb on the top.   Cut on an angle from
the bottom of the fold, up and around the thumb, making the
shape of an ice cream cone.   When the fold is opened, you will
have a very nice heart shape.

Place the heart on the white paper, or on the paper doilie.

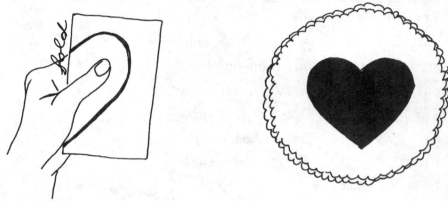

Another idea:

If you want the heart to have some dimension, cut two or three,
one inch strips and fold them back and forth in several small
folds.   Paste the folded strip on the back of the heart.   Attach
one end to the heart and the other end to the paper or doilie.
The heart will stand away from the paper.

D. **HEART MAN**
Fold red paper and cut out the large heart. Paste black strips on for arms and legs. Use the small hearts for the hands and feet. Draw a face on the heart man. Children can vary faces, making men, women or a whole family of heart people.

E. **HEART FIGURES**
Cut hearts of many different sizes. Paste or staple them together to make people, birds, butterflies, animals, etc. Use your imagination!

F. VALENTINE BOUQUET

Draw and color a vase on a sheet of 9" x 12" red, white or pink construction paper.

Use a brown or black crayon to make stems. Paste on tissue paper hearts. To give the project a three dimensional effect, you may fold each corner of the sheet of paper at a 45° angle.

To make a flat surface, fold the paper all the way around with a one inch border. To center the picture properly, the folding should be done before the vase and stems are drawn.

G. VALENTINE COLLAGE

Fold 9" x 12" red, white or pink construction paper in half. With the paint brush, "paint" glue on the cover of the card. Lay the tissue paper hearts on the glue, arranging them as you wish. Then, brush over the hearts again with the glue. The colors will run, giving a watery effect. A Valentine message can be printed inside.

H. FINGER PAINT A HEART

Cut finger paint paper into a heart shape. Use red finger paint. Paint the heart with fingers. Make sure entire area is covered.

I. VALENTINE TREE

Cover a tuna tin can -- contact paper that looks like a woven basket is great! If you use a foam cup, it isn't necessary to cover it with contact paper.

Anchor a twig in sand or clay in the can or cup.

Glue tissue paper hearts to the twig until it looks attractive.

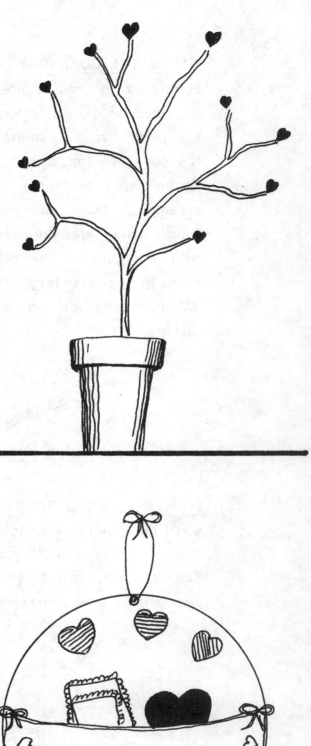

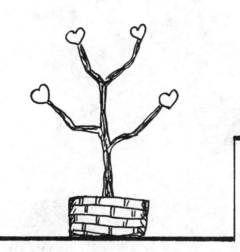

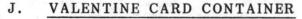

J. VALENTINE CARD CONTAINER

Cut a white paper plate in half. Place a full plate and the half plate together with the insides facing together. Staple to attach the half plate securely to the whole plate. Decorate with hearts. Punch a hole at the top. Put a ribbon or yarn through the hole and fasten in a loop. Now, it ready to receive lots of valentines.

K. A BAG FOR VALENTINES

Paint or color a lunch bag red.
Paste on white and pink hearts
to decorate. Punch holes on each
side of the bag. (It would be
a good idea to reinforce the holes.)
Attach the yarn at each side of
the bag.

It's ready for your valentines!

L. VALENTINE MAILBAG

Fold a 12" x 18" sheet of red,
white or pink paper in half. Punch
holes along the sides and across
the bottom. With yarn, lace the
bag together. Decorate the mailbag
with hearts. Put child's name on
the outside. Your valentine holder
is done!

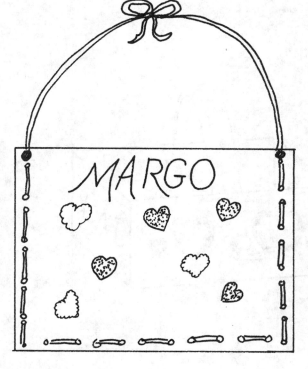

M. VALENTINE BASKET

Cut 9" x 12" red construction paper so it makes a square. Now, fold the paper in half and then in half again. Open the paper. Fold the paper in half the other way and fold it again. Now, cut the paper according to directions.

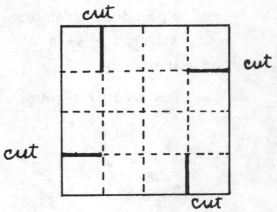

Paste the edges to make a basket. Paste or staple on a handle. Trim with hearts. Now it will hold your valentines treats!

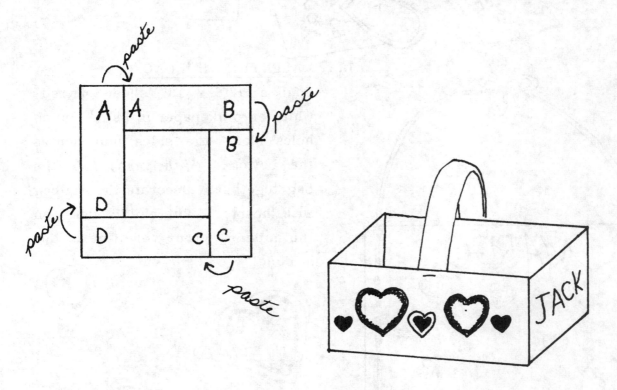

N. HEART PLACEMATS

Cut red and pink hearts and paste them on white paper. Make a design, or heart figure and use this placemat for a valentine treat.

Another placemat can be made by using 12" x 18" white construction paper for the placemat base. Fold the paper in half and cut from the fold to within an inch of the edge of the paper. Cut red and pink strips, ½ inch wide, 18 inches long. Weave the strips in and out of the cut sections, alternating under and over to create the pattern. When finished, paste the edges to hold in place. Cut out a large heart from red paper. Use the red outline and paste it over the weaving. What a nice heart placemat!

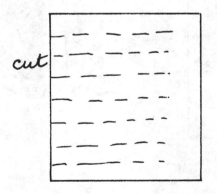

O. VALENTINE POCKET

Begin with a pocket from an old pair of jeans, or denim material for a pocket. If you like, you can draw a pocket from blue construction paper.

Staple pocket to tag board. (If denim material or blue paper is used, cut out a pocket and staple it to tag board.) Place valentine in pocket. Have children chant the following poem:

Here is my pocket,
I have something to hide.
It's a Valentine for you,
Just peek inside.

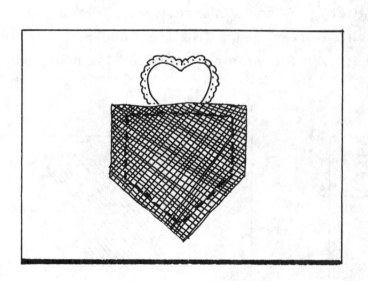

P.   WASHINGTON AND LINCOLN SILHOUETTES

Trace pattern of President Washington or Lincoln on white paper.
Cut out and paste the silhouette on blue paper.   Paste a red
strip on either side of profile.   Paste a star on each upper corner.

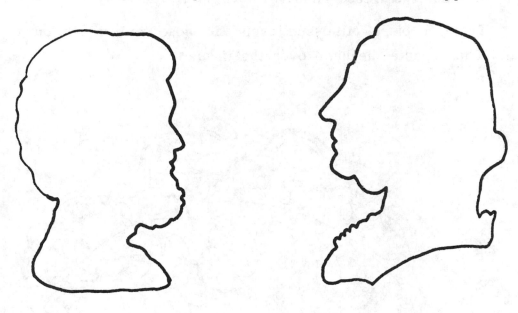

Optional activity -- check coins with Lincoln and Washington profile.
Look at the penny and the quarter.   Also, check a $1 bill for
Washington's picture and a $5 bill for Lincoln's picture.

Q. **KERCHOO PICTURE**

Draw a face on a paper plate. On a piece of construction paper, the child will trace his hand, fingers apart. (Give help if needed.)

Cut out the traced hand.

Paste a piece of tissue over the nose and mouth on the plate. Then, paste the hand over the tissue.

R.   SAD TOOTH - HAPPY TOOTH AND THE TOOTHBRUSH

Trace toothbrush pattern on paper.   Cut out.   Put child's name on the handle.   Punch a hole near the top.   Trace patterns of "Sad Tooth" and "Happy Tooth" on white paper.   Using crayons, draw in features on each tooth.   Cut out both teeth.   Using paper punch put a hole in the top of each tooth.   Put yarn through both teeth and the toothbrush, using enough yarn to go over the child's head.   Put the toothbrush near the happy tooth.

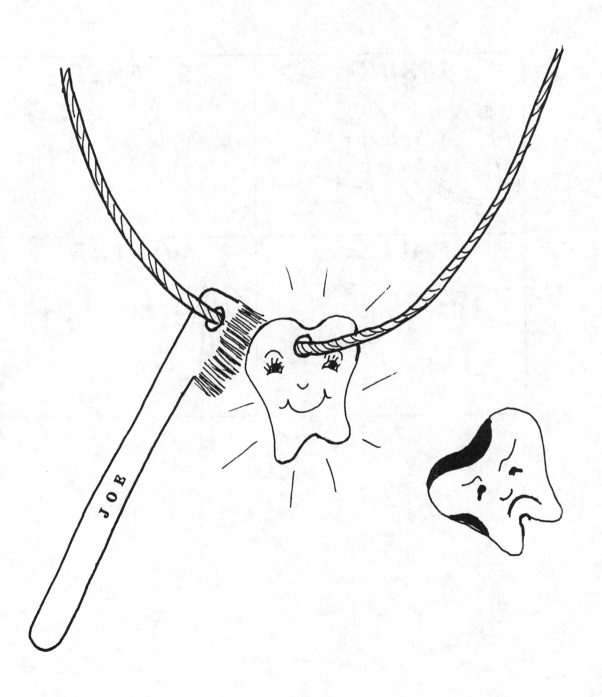

S. DRESSING FOR THE WEATHER

Mark 12" x 18" construction paper into four equal parts. Print the name of a season in each part (spring, summer, fall and winter). Children will draw or trace and color clothes for each season. Cut out clothing and paste in proper area.

Another idea: Use magazines and have children cut pictures of each season.

T. GOOD FOOD MOBILE

Draw pictures of foods that are good for our bodies. Cut out the pictures. Turn the pictures over and color the blank side so both sides have the picture. Cut various lengths of string or yarn. Punch a hole in the top of each picture and tie a knot with the string to the picture; attach the other end to the dowling. Use one piece of string tied to each end of the dowling to hang up the mobile.

Another idea: Use a hanger rather than wood dowling.

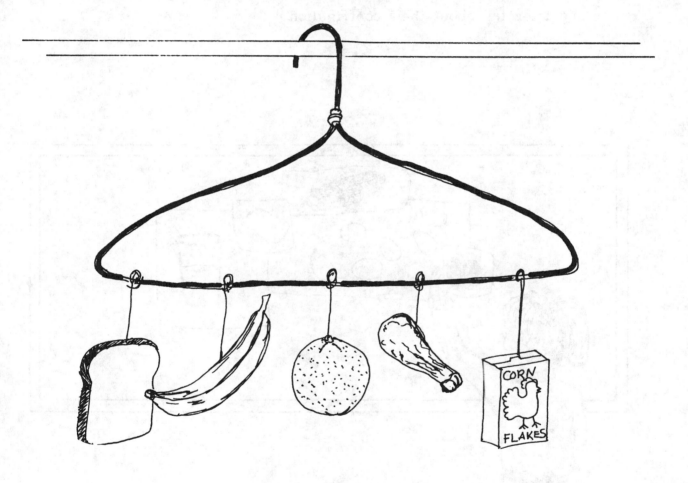

U. GOOD FOOD COLLAGE

Have children look through magazines for pictures of foods that are nutritious. Take a few minutes before they start to discuss the meaning of "nutritious." Have them give examples of foods that are good for their bodies.

Cut out pictures of foods. Paste them on the construction paper (12" x 18"), overlapping the pictures.

Another idea: Put a mural-sized paper on the wall and have all children contribute by pasting their pictures on the mural and later tell about their contribution.

A. LET'S TRACE HEARTS
Pink construction paper
Red construction paper

B. HEART MOBILE
Construction paper
String
Glue

C. LET'S MAKE VALENTINES
Colored construction paper
White paper/paper doilie

D. HEART MAN
Red construction paper
Paste
Black construction paper
Crayons

E. HEART FIGURES
Assorted construction paper
Paste/staple

F. VALENTINE BOUQUET
Crayons
9"x12" red/white/pink
  construction paper
Tissue paper

G. VALENTINE COLLAGE
9"x12" red/white/pink
  construction paper
Paint brush
Glue
Tissue paper

H. FINGER PAINT A HEART
Finger paint paper
Red finger paint

I. VALENTINE TREE
Tuna tin can/foam cup
Contact paper
Twig
Sand/clay
Tissue paper
Glue

J. VALENTINE CARD CONTAINER
Paper plates
Staple
Assorted construction paper
Hole punch
Ribbon/yarn

K. A BAG FOR VALENTINES
Lunch bag
Red crayon/red paint
Paste
White construction paper
Pink construction paper
Hole punch
Yarn

L. VALENTINE MAIL BAG
12"x 18" red/white/pink
  construction ppaer
Hole punch
Yarn
Assorted construction
  paper

M. VALENTINE BASKET
9"x12" red construction paper
Paste
Staple
Assorted construction paper

N. HEART PLACEMATS
Red construction paper
Pink construction paper
White construction paper
Paste

O. VALENTINE POCKET
Old jean pocket/denim material/
  blue construction paper
Staple
Tag board

**P. WASHINGTON/LINCOLN
SILHOUETTES**
White construction paper
Paste
Blue construction paper
Red construction paper

Q. KERCHOO PICTURE
Paper plate
Construction paper
Paste

R. SAD TOOTH – HAPPY TOOTH
White construction paper
Tooth pattern
Crayons
Scissors
Paper punch
Yarn

S. DRESSING FOR THE WEATHER
Construction paper
Manilla paper
Crayons
Scissors
Paste

T. GOOD FOOD MOBILE
White construction paper
Crayons
String/yarn
Wood dowling or
  thin metal hangers

U. GOOD FOOD COLLAGE
Construction paper
Magazines
Scissors
Paste

II. LITERATURE

Children will develop the ability to identify and enjoy:

Characters

Main ideas

Details

Sequence of events

A. A VALENTINE STORY

It was Valentine's Day at school and Penny wanted to stay home. She was in a new school and she hardly know any of the children. She had only been in this school two days -- just long enough to make a valentine bag with the boys and girls and decorate it with pink and red and white hearts. The teacher had talked about having a little party with a treat and exchanging valentines.

Penny thought about all the friends she had left behind at her other school. She would have had a good time with them. But at this new school she had only had a chance to meet one or two friends. It was just too hard to be in a new school and get to know everyone in such a short time.

Here was the day of the party and the valentine exchange. Everyone else would have a bag of valentines from their friends, but she would be lucky to have one or two. She hated to go to school, but she didn't want to tell her mother why.

"What's the matter, Penny," said her mother.

"Oh, nothing," Penny replied.

"You have a sad look on your face. This is Valentine's Day."

"I know it is," Penny said in a little sad voice.

"Come on," said Mother. "I have a treat for you to take to the party."

Penny thought of the heart cookies she had helped her mother bake last night. They were heart-shaped with pretty red crystals sprinkled on top. She and Mother had a good time baking this treat. She had been so excited thinking about the party. Mother had bought her valentines and, with a class list from the teacher, Penny and her mother had printed a valentine for each child in her room. Now it was time to leave for school and Penny started to worry. Maybe the class wouldn't like the cookies she was bringing. Probably no one would remember she was a new girl in the room.

Her mother called from the door. "Come on, Penny. It's time to leave for school. I have the cookies, do you have your bag of valentines?"

She really wanted to stay home, but Penny didn't want Mom to know how bad she felt.

"Come on, Penny," called her Mother. "We don't want to be late today."

Penny grabbed her bag of valentines and hurried to get in the car. Mom was driving her today because of the cookies and her bag of valentines. The drive to school only took a few minutes. Penny hopped out of the car. She took her bag of valentines and carefully carried the box of cookies into the school.

"Well," Penny thought, "here I am and I'll just have to make the best of it."

The day seemed long, but finally it was time to have the party. The children put their Valentine bags on their desks. They took turns passing out their Valentines. Then, the teacher had any children who had brought a treat come to the front of the room to pass it out. Each child passed out the treat they had brought. Then, it was Penny's turn. She was a little afraid, but she gave a cookie to each child, they smiled at her and said, "Thank you." At last she was finished and she went back to her desk.

She looked in her Valentine Bag. She could hardly believe her eyes. Her bag was full of Valentines. She was so happy. Now she felt she really belonged. It was nice to look at all the Valentines and know she had all these new friends.

POEMS/FINGER PLAYS/MURSERY RYHMES

Children will develop the ability to participate in and enjoy:

    Rhythm

    Poetry

    Sequence

    Characters

B.   VALENTINE POETRY

    1.   A VALENTINE MESSAGE
         Here's a Valentine,
         Guess what's in it?
         A little message,
         Small as a minute.
         But most of all,
         I want you to know,
         This Valentine means,
         I love you so.

    2.   TODAY IS VALENTINE'S DAY
         Today is Valentine's Day.
         Do you know what I will do?
         I'll make a pretty valentine,
         And give it right to you.

3.   A PRETTY VALENTINE

Oh, what a pretty Valentine,
Trimmed with ribbon and with lace.
I want to give it to you,
And see the smile on your face.

4.   A VALENTINE FOR MOTHER

I made a pretty Valentine,
'Cause I want you to know,
You're the best Mom in all the world,
And I love you so.

5.   ROSES ARE RED

Roses are red,
Violets are blue.
Sugar is sweet,
And so are you.

C. FINGER PLAYS

1. A MAILBOX VALENTINE

When you look in your mailbox,

What do you think you'll see?

    (Children pretend to look in mailbox.)

It might be a Valentine,

And it might be from me.

    (Children point to themselves.)

2. HAPPY VALENTINES

Five happy valentines (Hold up five fingers.)

From the ten cent store.

I sent one to Mother, (Bend down a finger.)

Now there are four.

Four happy valentines

Pretty ones to see?

I give one to Brother, (Bend down a finger.)

Now there are three.

Three happy valentines,

Yellow, red and blue?

I give one to Sister, (Bend down a finger.)

Now there are two.

Two happy valentines,

My, we have fun,

I give one to Daddy, (Bend down a finger.)

Now there is one.

One happy valentine,

The story is almost done.

I give it to Baby, (Bend down a finger.)

Now there are none.

3. <u>A DAY FOR LOVE</u>
Pretty red hearts,
   (Trace outline of heart in air with index fingers.)
And two by two,
   (Hold up two fingers of both hands.)
Holding hands,
   (Clasp hands together.)
And "I love you."
   (Clasp hands to heart.)
Scented flowers,
   (Hand "holds" flower to nose; sniff.)
From garden vines,
A day for love;   St. Valentine's.

D. NURSERY RHYMES

1. BIRDS

I had two birds, two birds I say,
They flew from me the other day.
What was the reason they did go?
I cannot tell for I do not know.

GOOD NIGHT

Good night
Sleep tight,
Get up bright,
In the morning light.

III. MUSIC

Children will develop the ability to participate in and enjoy music.

A. **HAPPY VALENTINE'S DAY TO YOU**

Happy Valentine's Day to you,
Happy Valentine's Day to you,
Happy Valentine's Day dear friends,
Happy Valentine's Day to you.

B. **VALENTINE'S DAY COMES ONCE A YEAR**

Valentine's Day comes once a year,
L - O - V - E
Brings us cards, candy and cheer,
L - O - V - E.

C. **SAD TOOTH, HAPPY TOOTH**

(Tune: Any slow, sad melody)
Sad, sad tooth, full of decay,
Sweets caused me to be this way.
(Tune: Any perky, happy tune)
Happy, happy tooth, shining bright,
Brushing keeps me beautiful and shining so white.

D. **THIS IS THE WAY WE PUT ON OUR CLOTHES**

(Tune: This Is The Way We Wash Our Clothes)
This is the way we put on our clothes,
    put on our clothes, put on our clothes.
This is the way we put on our clothes, so early in the morning.

IV. SCIENCE

Children will develop skills in:
Distinguishing differences
Similarities of attributes

A. DRESSING FOR THE WEATHER

It is important to wear proper clothing to keep well. It is always a good idea to check the weather report. If a cold temperature is predicted, you need to wear warm jackets, hats and mittens. If snow or rain is expected, boots should be worn to keep your feet dry. If the temperature is not too cold, but rain is expected that day, carry an umbrella and wear a raincoat to keep clothing dry.

When the weather turns warmer, wear a lighter weight jacket or sweater. When the temperature indicates a really warm day, light clothing with short sleeves will be cooler.

B. A HEALTHY DIET

Eating a proper diet helps give children strong muscles and bones, healthy skin and teeth, and a good blood supply. Good nutrition helps children have the pep and energy they need to do well in school and in their playtime activities.

Fresh air, sunshine, exercise and rest help boys and girls grow healthy and strong. One important health rule to follow is to drink plenty of water every day. Also, children need to eat a well-balanced diet.

HOW DO YOU WANT TO FEEL?

Like this   Or this

C. BALANCED DIET

1. MILK GROUP

This includes milk and milk products (cheese, ice cream, etc.). A child should have three to four cups of milk every day. Milk and cheese are valuable sources of calcium and help make strong teeth and bones.

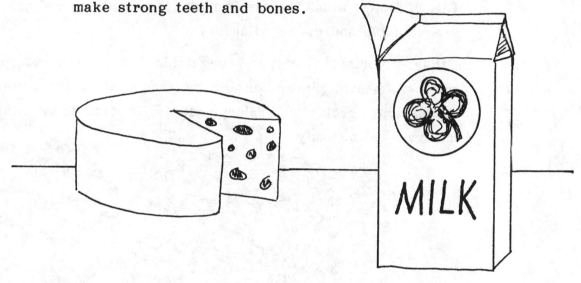

2. MEAT GROUP

This includes meat, fish, poultry, eggs and nuts. These supply protein and iron to the diet. It has been suggested that one to two daily servings in this meat group is recommended.

3. **VEGETABLE - FRUIT GROUP**

Green vegetables such as string beans, peas, broccoli and asparagus, provide vitamin A to the body. Also included in this group are carrots, squash, pumpkins, sweet potatoes and wax beans.

Citrus fruits, which include oranges, lemons, limes and grapefruit are valuable sources of vitamin C.

Other important fruits and vegetables are: apples, grapes, peaches, pears, pineapples and bananas. Also, corn, potatoes, cucumbers, beets and celery supply important vitamins and minerals to the body.

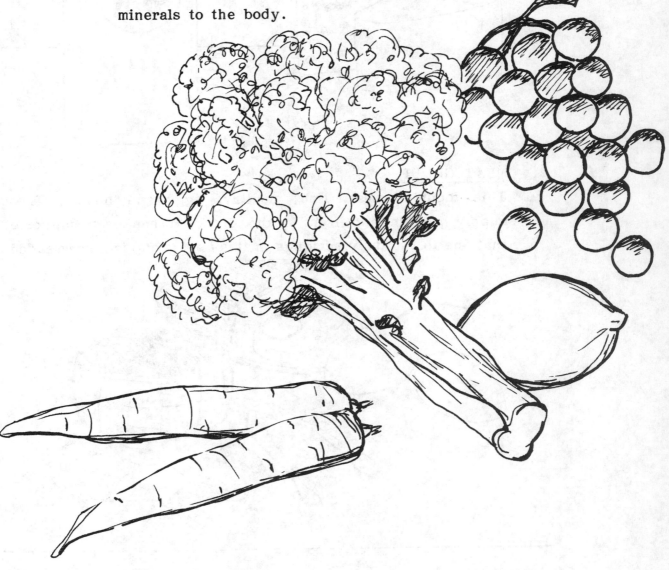

4. BREADS - CEREAL GROUP

Children should have at least two daily servings of bread or cereals. Bread should be made from whole grain or enriched flour. Cereals should be whole grain or natural and not have a high sugar content.

Spaghetti and macaroni are also a part of this group.

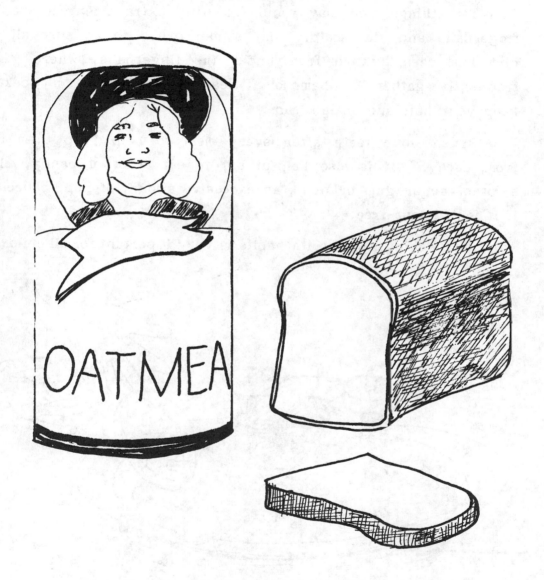

Proper food keeps the body healthy and strong and better protected against disease.

D. KEEPING CLEAN

An important health habit for everyone is to always wash your hands with soap and water before you eat. Germs can easily enter the body when food is eaten. It is wise to clean your hands before you eat. Keeping your body and hands clean can help keep the skin healthy and free from infection.

Two things that may require a little extra attention are the fingernails and the scalp. Use a nail brush to be sure all the dirt has been cleaned from under the fingernails, where germs frequently gather. Shampoo at least several times a week to keep your hair and scalp clean.

Brush your teeth after every meal to help keep them free from decay. It is also helpful not to eat a lot of candy, chew a lot of sugar gum or drink an excessive amount of pop, especially if it isn't sugar-free.

Establishing good health habits is very important for all children.

V. SOCIAL STUDIES

Children will develop an awareness of:

Holidays

Traditions

Seasonal changes

A. GEORGE WASHINGTON

Born: February 22, 1732   Died: December 14, 1799

George Washington was born in Westmoreland County, Virginia. As a boy, he was studious, quiet, patient and the normal hardships of colonial life helped him grow up sturdy and strong.

When he was a young man, he joined the military service and he became a Major. Later, when the colonists became angry about paying taxes to Great Britain, Washington commanded the Continental Army that won America her independence from Great Britain. It was on July 4, 1776, that our country signed the Declaration of Independence. The Fourth of July is a national holiday that all Americans celebrate.

George Washington helped write the Constitution of the United States. He was the first man ever to be elected president and this happened in the year 1789. Our American flag at this time only had 13 stars, one for each state in the Union. He was president for eight years and was lovingly called the "Father of Our Country."

George Washington loved horses and fox hunting. He was a very sociable person who loved people, parties and dancing.

Our nation's capitol, Washington, D.C., was named to honor him. He chose the spot for our capitol on the Potomac River. In 1880, after his death, work was begun on the huge monument to honor him. Four years later, in 1884, the Washington Monument was completed and it still stands today to honor this special man.

The State of Washington is the only state named after a

president. Many cities, streets, bridges, parks and schools bear his name. His picture has appeared on postage stamps, coins and is also on the $1 bill. His birthday is a national legal holiday. We honor George Washington because he was a great president. He was honest, had great courage in battles and, above all, he loved his country.

B. ABRAHAM LINCOLN

Born: February 12, 1809   Died: April 15, 1865

Abraham Lincoln was born in a log cabin in Kentucky. When he was a child he often hiked four miles to go to school. He loved to read and, by the time he was fourteen years old, he read at night by the light of the fire in the fireplace.

When Abe Lincoln became a young man, he studied law. He became a lawyer in 1836. He worked hard as a lawyer and became interested in the affairs of the government.

He was elected 16th President of the United States in the year 1860. He was a patient, strong president. Unfortunately, Lincoln was president during a time of great unrest. The Civil War split the nation in 1861. The southern states wanted to keep their slaves, but Lincoln knew in his heart that since the United States was founded on the principle of liberty and civil rights for all, the slavery problem had to be settled. So, on January 1, 1863, he signed the Emancipation Proclamation which freed the slaves.

On November 19, 1863 Lincoln was invited to say a few words at Gettysburg where the battlefield was to be dedicated as a national cemetary. Lincoln spoke briefly, but his noble speech has endured the years. The Gettysburg Address has become famous for its declaration that "government of the people, by the people and for the people shall not perish from the earth."

One of Lincoln's pleasures was to attend the theatre. So,

on the night of April 14th, Lincoln took his wife, Mary, and two guests to the Ford Theatre. On that fateful night, John Wilkes Booth, an actor, shot and killed President Lincoln.

After his death, the world began to realize the greatness of this kind and patient man. He has been called the "Great Emancipator." A magnificient memorial of white and pink marble was built in Washington, D.C. to honor this great man.

C. VALENTINE'S DAY

Valentine's Day is always celebrated on February 14th. It is believed that this day originally came from an ancient Roman festival called Lupercalia. The festival honored Juno, the Roman goddess of women and marriage, and Pan, the god of nature. It was a festival of love for young people.

Years ago in Europe, young people would meet on St. Valentine's Eve. Each young person drew the name of a friend from the Valentine Box. This became their special friend or "valentine."

Also, many years ago a Roman priest and a Bishop of Terni were important saints named Valentine. Both were executed. However, historians believe it is just a coincidence that their feast day is the day that once was set aside for lovers.

Valentine's Day became popular in the United States in the 1800's, which is about the time of the Civil War. Valentines at that time were very fancy. Often they were trimmed in lace, satin ribbon, feathers or tassels.

On Valentine's Day, sweethearts exchange messages of love. Gifts of candy, flowers or Valentine's with a special message are given. School children decorate their rooms and make valentines to give to their mother and father and also to their friends.

Candy producers and commercial paper products businesses have helped to promote this day and to continue its popularity with the people. Thousands of heart-shaped boxes of candy and millions of printed valentines are sold each year to be given as a sign of love and affection for Valentine's Day.

D.   SAFETY RULES -- GETTING ALONG

Discuss with children the importance of getting along with each other. They have to remember that biting or hitting each other isn't allowed. They need to learn to have self-control. Respecting one another and not hurting one another is important.

E.   SAFETY RULES -- NO STONES

Another important rule for children to remember is that throwing stones can be very dangerous. Stones that are thrown and hit someone can be very painful. Also, stones can tear the skin or may cause serious damage to the eyes. Children always need to remember this important rule -- DO NOT THROW STONES.

SAFETY POEM

Don't hit your playmates,
Don't throw stones,
Dont' hurt one another,
Children have tender bones.

F. <u>SAFETY RULES -- SAY "NO" TO STRANGERS</u>

Children should be cautioned not to go with stangers. If someone tries to entice them into a car by promising them candy, they need to run home as fast as they can.

VI. FEBRUARY PHYSICAL EDUCATION FUN

Children will develop skills in:

    Rhythm

    Imaging

    Use of large and small muscles

    Good sports conduct

A. **MOVE AS IF YOU ARE:**

    1. Cutting out a valentine for a giant.

    2. Chopping down a cherry tree.

    3. Making a cherry pie.

    4. Rocking a baby.

    5. Washing your face, arms, legs, neck, back, hair, etc.

    6. Combing your hair.

    7. Brushing your hair.

    8. Brushing your teeth.

B. **OVER THE ROPES**

Tie different colored string, crepe paper or yarn along each of **three to six different** ropes. Tell children the red rope is for running over, the blue rope is for crawling over, the green rope is for hopping over, etc. Each rope is to have a different exercise designation. Lay ropes around the room. Children walk around the room and follow the directions when they get to each rope.

The next step is to use the ropes as a game. Each child has a turn. If they forget the directions given for that colored rope, they must sit down.

Another idea -- the ropes may also be used as a relay.

C. THE MAILMAN

Children sit in a circle with their eyes covered. The child who is the Mailman carries a red heart and walks around the circle while the children chant the poem. The child who finds the heart when their eyes are opened is the next mailman.

Here comes the mailman,
With a Valentine.
Where will he leave it?
Will it be mine?

D. HIDE THE HEARTS

(Use the hearts the children made when they worked on tracing.)
Before the children arrive, hide the hearts all around the room.
When they are all ready to start, have them try to see how many they can find. Then have each child count how many they have found.

E. MUSICAL HEARTS

Use posterboard or tag board to make a heart for each child.
Place these on the floor in a circle. Have each child stand on a heart. As the music starts, have the children start to move in one direction, stepping over the hearts. Remove one heart and when the music stops, each child should stand on the heart nearest to them. The child without a heart to stand on is "out."
Continue removing a heart each time the music plays until only one heart is left. The child who gets on the heart first is the winner. (Keep the circle "big" until the end of the game.)

VII. MATH COOKING

Children will develop skills in:
Number awareness
Counting
Measuring

A. JELLO SNACK

Make red jello in a heart shape mold or red finger jello.

Math: Count cups of water.

B. RED KOOL-AID

Prepare Kool-Aid as directed on package. Also, fruit punch would be a red drink for a Valentine celebration.

Math: Count cups of water before and after making Kool-Aid. Fruit punch - pour into paper cups. Is there one for each child?

C. CUPCAKES

Make cupcakes according to directions on package. Frost with prepared frosting and trim with heart-shaped candies. Children might like frosting and trimming their own cupcakes.

Math: Count cupcakes. Is there one for each child? Is there more than one for each child? Count heart-shaped candies. How many did each child use?

D.   SUGAR COOKIES KIDS CAN MAKE

1 cup margarine	1 cup shortening
1 cup confectioner's sugar	1 cup granulated sugar
2 eggs	1 t. vanilla

Cream above ingredients thoroughly.

Mix together:

   1 t. soda

   1 t. cream of tartar

   5 cups flour

Add flour mixture to the creamed ingredients a little at a time. (Dough may be refrigerated, if desired.)   Mix well.   Roll out. Cut into shapes.   Bake approximately 12 minutes at 350°.   Decorate with icing and candy hearts.

Math: Count ingredients, count hearts.   Are all the hearts the same size?   Are some of them larger or smaller?

READ ALOUD BOOKS FROM THE LIBRARY

FEBRUARY

Children will develop the ability to enjoy and gain knowledge from books.

1. My First Valentine's Day Book
    Bennett, Mary
    Illustrated by Pam Peltier
    Children's Press, Chicago, 1985
    31 pages, color illustrations

    Valentine's Day parties, sample of Valentine's poetry and suggestions for appropriate Valentine's activities for young children are included in this brightly illustrated book. Valentine's gifts, candy and family activities are pictured as part of this special day.

2. The Berenstein Bears Go To The Doctor
    Berenstein, Stan and Jan (1923)
    Random Hosue, New York, 1981
    Unpaged, color illustrations

    The bear family gets a physical and each phase of the check-up is described. Father Bear, who has been protesting that he doesn't need check-ups anymore, is the only member of the family who is really sick and he is treated for a cold.

3. **I Wish I Was Sick Too!**
Brandenberg, Franz
Illustrated by Aliki
Greenwillow Books/Division of Morrow, New York, 1976
Unpaged, color illustrations

>Elizabeth was very jealous of her sick brother, Edward, because of all the special treatment that he got. But, her attitude changed when Edward recovered and she "caught" the illness. She felt so very bad that she didn't enjoy all the attention. Finally, she felt better and began doing her housework grateful that she had recovered.

4. **Arthur's Valentine**
Brown, Marc Tolon
Little, Brown, Boston, 1980
Unpaged, color illustrations

>Arthur tries to guess who is sending him Valentine's signed "your secret admirer." His friends found the valentines when they fell out of his pocket, and had a great time reading them aloud and laughing. After receiving many poems and notes, Arthur discovers that his secret admirer is his old friend, Francine, who always teases him. He leaves her candy kisses after he tells her to close her eyes and he will kiss her.

5. Come To The Doctor, Harry

Chalmers, Mary (1927)

Illustrated by author

Harper and Row, New York, 1981

32 pages, illustrations

> Gentle story about Harry the cat who gets his tail caught in the door and reluctantly goes to the doctor. Harry regains his bravery during the visit and proudly displays his bandaged tail to all of his friends. A very small book, it measures 4" x 6", but it's message of the prompt need for health care is a big one.

6. Abraham Lincoln

D'Aulair, Ingri and Edgar

Illustrated by authors

Doubleday, Garden City, NY, 1957, 1939

Unpaged, color illustrations

> Most copies of this book are a completely redrawn edition of the 1940 winner of the Caldecott Medal. This book is too long for very young listeners, but the pictures give a good view of Abe's "growing up" years in the very early 1800's. There are many selections which young children will enjoy, such as Abe reluctantly sharing a gingerbread cookie with a fat little boy, Abe learning to write by the fireplace, and Abe fighting off pirates near the Mississippi River.

7. George Washington

D'Aulair, Ingri and Edgar

Illustrated by authors

Doubleday, Garden City, NY 1936

Unpaged, color illustrations

> This book is much too long for very young listeners but the pictures and some of the selections are very appropriate. It shows young George Washington growing up in colonial America. The book ends with a page about Washington as the "Father of our Country."

8. Valentine's Day

Gibbons, Gail

Illustrated by author

Holiday House, New York, 1986

Unpaged, color illustrations

Very few simple sentences and strong bright illustrations make this one of the best books published to show young cnildren the history and current practices of Valentine's Day. Everything is covered including St. Valentine and Cupid. The last two pages are excellent "how to" directions for making Valentines and a Valentine's Box. The pictures are so well done that children will not have to know how to read to successfully follow these five and six step procedures.

9. A Visit To The Sesame Street Hospital

Hautzig, Deborah

Illustrated by Joe Mathiew

Random House, New York, 1985

Unpaged, illustrations

A book which will help prepare children for a trip to the hospital. Grover visits the hospital in preparation for the overnight stay he will have when he gets his tonsils out. He finds out about ordering food, how the doctors and nurses work and sees the playroom. He sees the hospital name bracelets, the x-ray machine and the scrub room. He visits the operating and recovery room and the medical library. He ends his visit by seeing the new babies and the gift shop.

10. George Washington

Judson, Clara (Ingram - 1879)

Illustrated by Bob Patterson

Follett, Chicago, 1961

29 pages, color illustrations

(Beginning To Read Series)

Biography of George Washington is somewhat simple vocabulary (378) words. Parts of this book could be read to very young children. Included are most of the traditional incidents about Washington including Valley Forge. Washington the farmer, politician and surveyor are also included, but the famous (probably untrue) chopping down the cherry tree story has been omitted.

11. Abraham Lincoln

Lee, Susan

Illustrated by Ralph Canoday

Children's Press, Chicago, 1978

47 pages, color illustrations

A brief biography of Abraham Lincoln. It is too long for young readers, but selections may be read and it is good background information for discussing the pictures.

12. Three Little Kittens Lost Their Mittens

Livermore, Elaine

Illustrated by author

Houghton Mifflin, Boston, 1979

30 pages, illustrated

The three little kittens have a big day. They eat ice cream, go to the library and then play on the snow covered playground. They visit a farm, grocery shop and go sledding. On their way home, they discover their mittens are missing. The mystery is solved by the readers who must go back through the pictures to find the missing mittens which are hidden in the drawings.

13. **Ah-choo**

Mayer, Mercer (1943)

Dial Press, New York, 1976

Unpaged, illustrations

What happens when an elephant sneezes? This almost wordless books shows how sniffing a bunch of flowers causes the elephant to sneeze and blow a house down. He is arrested and taken to court where he sneezes again and blows the court room away. He ends up in jail where a final mighty sneeze blows the jail away. All's well that ends well and he meets a charming lady hippo who also has a powerful sneeze. After he supplies her with a handkerchief, they walk off happily together.

14. **Magic Monsters Learn About Health**

Moncure, Jane Belk

Illustrated by Helen Endres

Child's World, Elgin, IL 1980

31 pages, color illustrations

There are a variety of monsters who have very unhealthy practices described in this book. They are contrasted to the Magic Monsters who know very healthy practices and the good they can do each of us. The healthy monster eats three balanced meals a day, exercises and plays, sleeps at night and plays with healthy kids. This is a story in rhyme and it has many interesting, colorful characters in it.

15. **A Man Named Lincoln**

Norman, Gertrude

Illustrated by Joseph Cellini

Putnam, 1960

Unapged, illustrations

This biography of Abraham Lincoln is written in "easy to read" style. It will probably not hold the interest of very young children, but some of it could be read in sections or used as the basis for discussion.

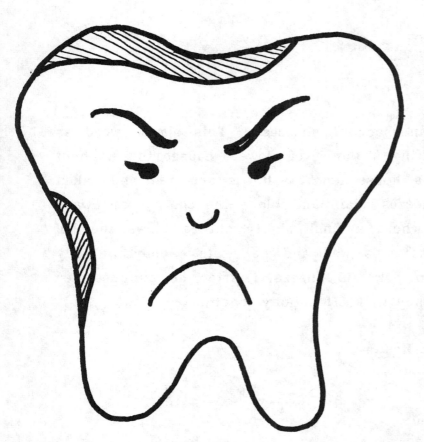

HAPPY TOOTH   SAD TOOTH

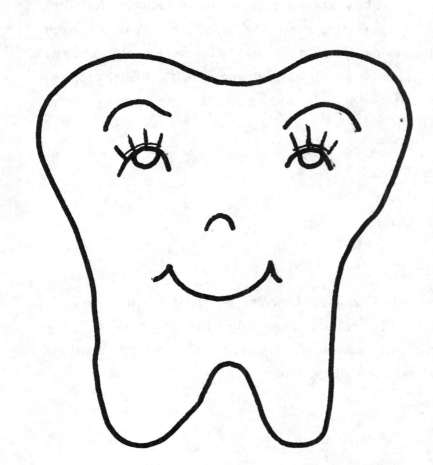

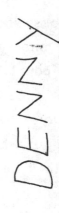

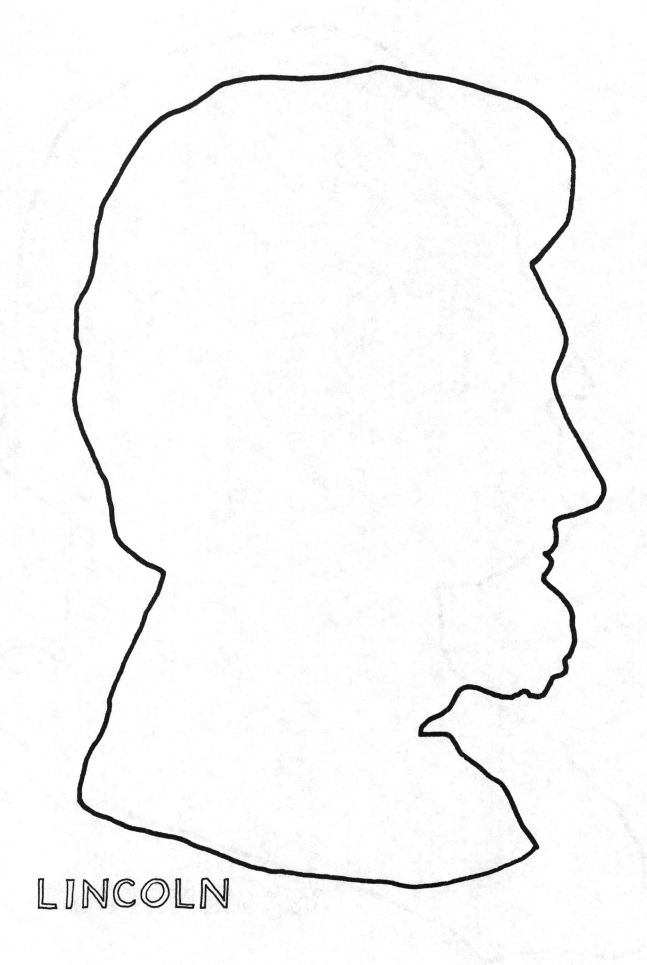

LINCOLN

WASHINGTON

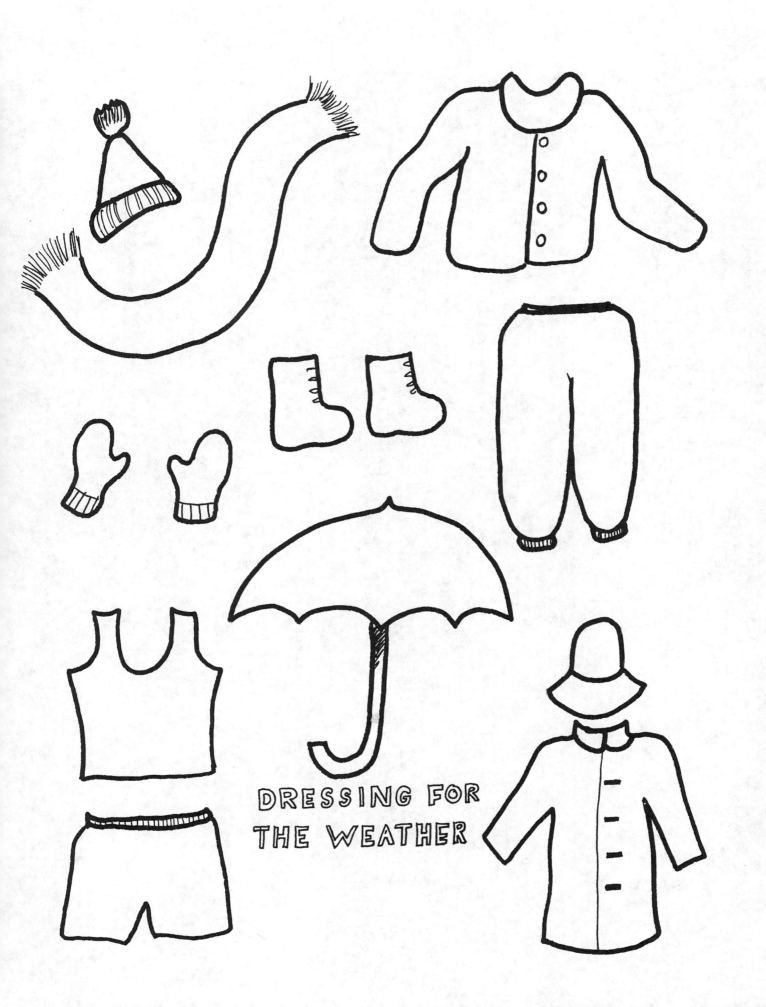

DRESSING FOR
THE WEATHER

MARCH

Dear Parents:

In March the winds blow and, as the weather warms up, the birds begin
to fly north.

SCIENCE
March brings birds,
spring and warmth

MUSIC
Green Bottle Band

SOCIAL STUDIES

BOOKS FROM THE LIBRARY

COOKING MATH
Green jello, Kool-Aid
and popsicles

LITERATURE
March Winds - poems
and finger plays
Jackie Robinson

HAPPY MARCH!

Parent page ART - Lion With A Curly Mane LITERATURE - POEM - "March Winds" SCIENCE - Grow a Grass Shamrock PHYS. ED. - Exercises 1-2 (five times) BOOK - Spring by Richard L. Allington, Ph.D.	ART - (Complete) Lion With a Curly Mane LITERATURE - FINGER PLAY - "Listen to the Wind" PHYS. ED. - Exercises 1-3 (five times) BOOK - Leprechauns Never Lie by Lorna Balian	ART - Curly Lamb LITERATURE - POEM - "Spring Will Soon Arrive" SCIENCE - Discuss B PHYS. ED. - Exercises 1-3 & C MATH COOKING - Green Finger Jello	ART - (Complete) Curly Lamb NURSERY RHYME - "Mary Had A Little Lamb" PHYS. ED. - Exercises 1-3 & C BOOK - Deep In The Forest by Brinton Turkle	ART - Dress Like A Leprechaun LITERATURE - POEM - "St. Patrick's Day" SOCIAL STUDIES - Discuss St. Patrick's Day PHYS. ED. - Exercises 1-4 & C
ART - (Complete) Dress Like A Leprechaun PHYS. ED. - Exercises 1-5 & E BOOK - St. Patrick's Day In The Morning by Eve Bunting	ART - (Complete) Dress Like A Leprechaun LITERATURE - POEM - "A Leprechaun" PHYS. ED. - Exercises 1-5 & B MATH COOKING - Green Kool Aid BOOK - The Hungry Leprechaun by Mary Calhoun	ART - Green Dot Shamrock LITERATURE - TRUE STORY - "Jackie Robinson" MUSIC - Green Bottle Band PHYS. ED. - Exercises 1-5 (very, very slowly) & C	ART - (Complete) Green Dot Shamrock LITERATURE - POEM - "Wearing Green" MUSIC - Green Bottle Band PHYS. ED. - Exercises 1-6 (very fast, very slow) BOOK - Corduroy by Don Freeman	ART - Hand Print LITERATURE - FINGER PLAY - "The Wind" MUSIC - Green Bottle Band PHYS. ED. - Exercises 1-7 & C MATH COOKING - Green Popsicles
ART - (Complete) Hand Print LITERATURE - FINGER PLAY - "The Strong Wind" MUSIC - Green Bottle Band PHYS. ED. - Exercises 1-7 (very quiet, much more quiet) BOOK - Teddy Bears Cure A Cold by Susan Gretz	ART - Shamrock MUSIC - Green Bottle Band PHYS. ED. - Exercises 1-8 (three times each) MATH COOKING - Cupcakes With Green Frosting BOOK - The Biggest Bear by Lynd Ward	ART - Make A Leprechaun LITERATURE - POEM - "Pot Of Gold" MUSIC - Green Bottle Band PHYS. ED. - Exercises 1-8 & B	ART - Shamrock Placemat NURSERY RHYME - "Jack and Jill Ran Up The Hill" PHYS. ED. - Exercises 1-8 & C BOOK - The Bear Who Saw The Spring by Karla Kuskin	ART - Colored Kites LITERATURE - POEM - "Flying A Kite Is Fun" PHYS. ED. - Exercises 1-8 (lay down and do them in your mind today) BOOK - Kite Flying by Dorothy C. Schmitz
ART - (Complete) Colored Kites LITERATURE - FINGER PLAY - "The Kite" PHYS. ED. - Exercises 1-8 (think about each exercise as you do it) BOOK - Let's Make A Kite by Jack Stokes	ART - Drop Painting PHYS. ED. - Exercises 1-8 MATH COOKING - Filled Celery Sticks BOOK - The Carp In The Bathtub by Barbara Cohen	ART - Kite With A Tail LITERATURE - POEM - PHYS. ED. - Exercises 1-8 (Do them backwards) BOOK - Word Birds, Spring Words by Jane Belk Moncure	ART - (Complete) Kite With A Tail LITERATURE - POEM - "A Long Tailed Kite" PIIYS. ED. - Exercises 1-8 & B BOOK - Spring Is Here! by Jane Belk Moncure	ART - Crayon Rubbing On Placemat PHYS. ED. - Exercises 1-8 & B MATH COOKING - Healthy Candy BOOK - Curious George Flies a Kite by Margaret Rey

I. ART

Children will develop skills in:

    Organization

    Sequence

    Use of small muscles (small motor)

A. **LION WITH CURLY MANE**

Round off corners of 9" x 12" paper for lion body. For head, cut 9" x 12" piece of paper in half, round corners. Use other half to cut four legs and a tail. Cut strips, 1" x 6" for lion's mane.

Roll strips around crayon or pencil to curl. Draw facial features with crayons. Paste head, body, legs, tail and mane

B. <u>CURLY LAMB</u>

Round off corners of 9" x 12" paper for body. Use hal[f]
9" x 12" sheet of paper for the head. Use the other ha[lf]
four legs and a tail.

Cut pieces of white construction paper into 1" x 3" strips, roll
on pencil or crayon to make shaggy coat.

Draw facial features with crayons. Paste head, legs and tail
on body. Then paste 1" x 3" pieces onto body to make the curly
lamb.

C. <u>COLORED KITES</u>

Cut a kite or diamond shape out of three colors. Three pieces
of yarn 4" long will be needed. Paste three kites on light blue
paper (12" x 18"). Paste yarn tails on each kite.

<u>PRETTY KITES</u>

See the pretty kites,
Flying in the sky.
Like a rainbow,
They catch your eye.

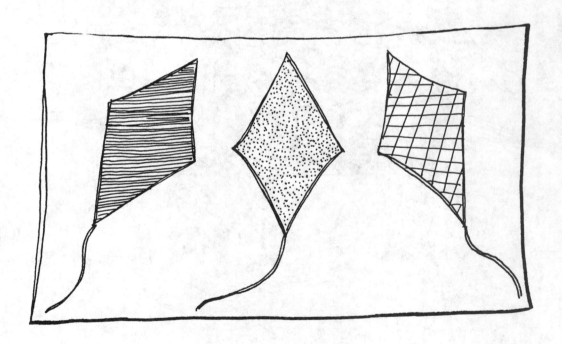

D. **KITE WITH A TAIL**

Cut kite out of 9" x 12" piece of construction paper. Cut eight bows out of white paper. You'll also need approximately 15" of yarn for each kite tail you make, plus 2' of yarn for the top of kite.

Staple yarn to bottom of kite. Glue two bows together with the yarn in the middle at four intervals along the yarn tail. Staple 2' of yarn to top of kite.

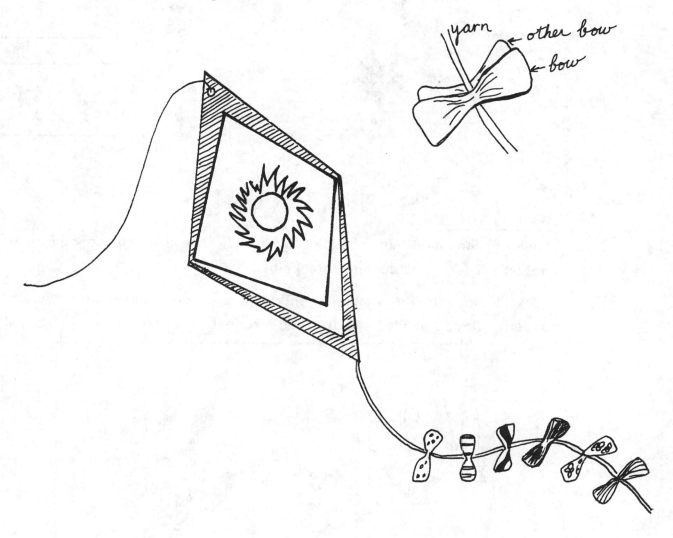

E. **DROP PAINTING**

Fill muffin tins with paint of all colors.

Use medicine dropper to drop different colors on the paper.

Fold paper in half to make design. Open paper and allow to dry.

F. **HAND PRINTS**

Place green paint in shallow tin. Slightly moisten sponge with water. Then, put sponge into paint.

Press hand onto the sponge evenly and then onto white construction paper. Dry. Shellac the finished product to preserve it.

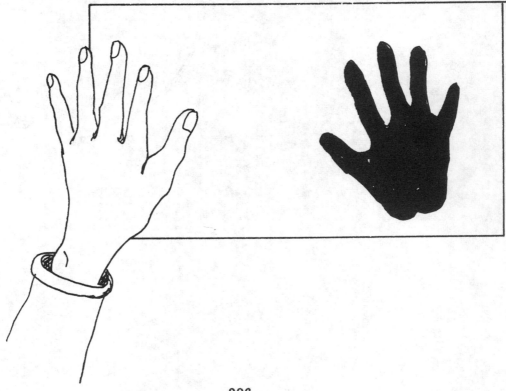

G. SHAMROCKS

To make an easy shamrock, trace the pattern on green paper.
Then cut it out. If desired, paste shamrock on white paper.

H. GREEN DOT SHAMROCK

Trace shamrock pattern on white paper.

Use hole punch to make dots from green paper. Collect dots
on small tray.

Spread glue on white shamrock then sprinkle dots until dots cover
shamrock. Dry.

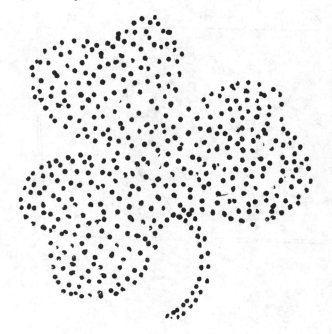

I. **SHAMROCK PLACEMAT**

Cut various sizes of shamrocks from green paper. Paste these on white (12" x 18") construction paper. Cut a fringe along the short sides to make a St. Patrick's Day placemat.

J. **CRAYON RUBBING ON A PLACEMAT**

Peel the paper off green crayons. Place shamrock or other patterns under the white paper. Use the side of the crayons to rub over the edges of the shamrock to make an impression on the top of the placemat. Fringe the edges if desired.

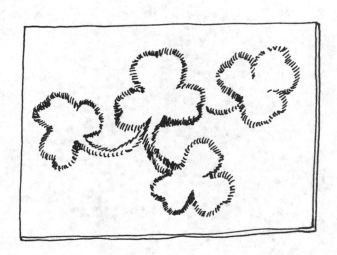

K. <u>DRESS LIKE A LEPRECHAUN</u>

Cut up the middle of a large brown paper bag (the kind in which you get groceries) and make a circle cut for the head.

Cut holes in sides for arms.

Decorate by pasting on various sized green shamrocks.

To make a leprechaun hat, trace leprechaun hat pattern onto green construction paper and cut it out. Put a black band around the base of the hat. Cut a strip of green paper to make crown fit on head. Staple to front of hat.

L. MAKE A LEPRECHAUN

Fold green 9" x 12" paper in half and cut on fold. Fold each half again. Cut hat from one piece and boots from the other.

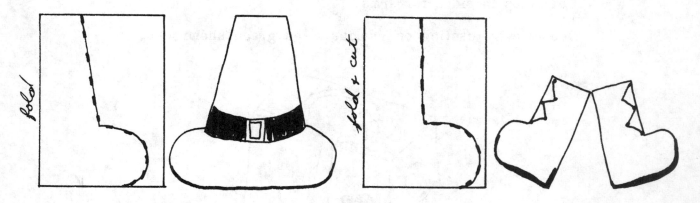

Paste hat at the top of the yellow 12" x 18" sheet of construction paper. Paste boots at the bottom. Draw the body of a leprechaun in between the hat and the boots.

MATERIALS CHART

MARCH

A. LION WITH CURLY MANE
9"x12" construction paper
Paste
Crayons

B. CURLY LAMB
9"x12" construction paper
White paper
Crayons
Paste

C. COLORED KITES
Colored construction paper
Yarn
Paste
12"x18" light blue construction paper

D. KITE WITH A TAIL
9"x12" construction paper
White paper
Yarn
Staple
Glue

E. DROP PAINTING
Muffin tin
Assorted paint
Medicine dropper
Assorted construction paper

F. HAND PRINTS
Green paint
Shallow tin
Sponge
Shellac

G. SHAMROCKS
Green paper
Paste
White paper

H. GREEN DOT SHAMROCK
White paper
Hole punch
Green paper
Paste/glue

I. SHAMROCK PLACEMAT
Green paper
Paste
12"x18" white construction paper

J. CRAYON RUBBING ON A PLACEMAT
Green crayons
White paper

K. DRESS LIKE A LEPRECHAUN
Large brown paper bag
Paste
Green construction paper
Black construction paper

L. MAKE A LEPRECHAUN
9"x12" green construction paper
Paste
12"x18" yellow construction paper
Crayons

II. LITERATURE

Children will develop the ability to identify and enjoy:

Characters

Main ideas

Details

Sequence of events

A. JACKIE ROBINSON

This is the story of how Jackie Robinson became the first black major league baseball player. Before Jackie Robinson played baseball, there were no black baseball players in the major leagues.

Young Jackie had four brothers, one sister and a hardworking mother who supported her family by cleaning and ironing for other people.

Jackie worked hard, too. At school he worked at his lessons. At sports, he worked to become the best he could in all sports. Jackie wanted to become a sports star like his brother, Mack, who had won a silver medal in track at the 1936 Olympics.

In college, people cheered as Jackie became a sports star and the first man to win letters in track, basketball, football and baseball.

After college and the Army, he decided to become a baseball player.

A baseball manager named Branch Rickey thought black men should be able to play major league baseball and he was told about Jackie Robinson. He met Jackie and saw he was a great baseball player. There were some people who didn't want black players to play major league baseball.

Jackie Robinson and Branch Rickey knew it would be very hard to ignore the people who would call him names and try to pick fights. They practiced having Jackie ignore those people. He kept his mind on winning each baseball game. That year his team, the Brooklyn Dodgers, beat all of the other teams and won the pennant. The next year, the Dodgers signed three more black players.

From that time on, baseball players have been judged on their sports ability and willingness to work hard, rather than on the color of their skin.

Jackie began to answer the few people who still called him names, but he also kept his mind on success.

He became a beloved and respected businessman after he stopped playing baseball. He traveled all around the country making speeches. He will always be remembered as the first black major league baseball player.

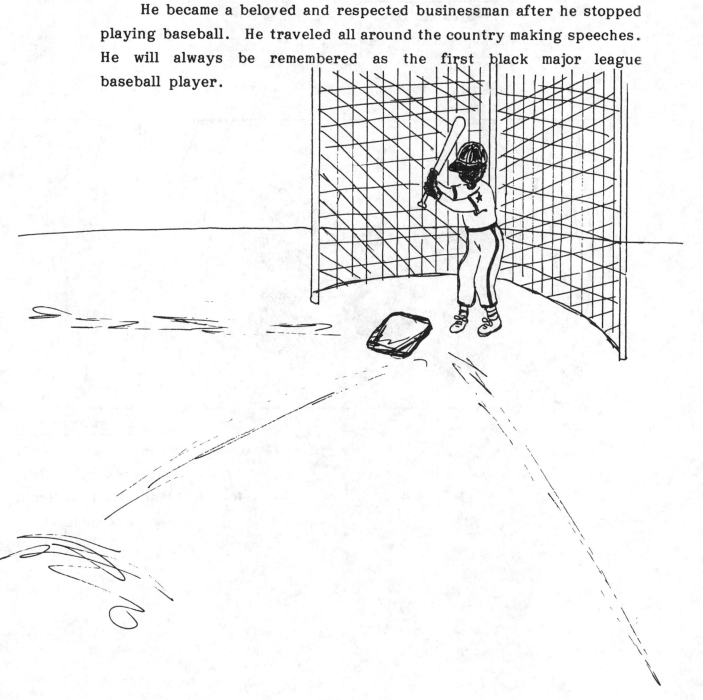

POEMS/FINGER PLAYS/NURSERY RHYMES

Children will develop the ability to participate in and enjoy:

Rhythm

Poetry

Sequence

Characters

B. POEMS FOR ST. PATRICK'S DAY

1. ST. PATRICK'S DAY

St. Patrick's Day, St. Patrick's Day.

Of Leprechauns beware.

Put a shamrock in your hat,

And find something green to wear.

2. A LEPRECHAUN

If you should meet a Leprechaun,

On St. Patrick's Day.

He will bring you Irish luck,

Today, and every day.

3. <u>POT OF GOLD</u>

Have you seen a Leprechaun
Hiding behind a tree?
I know he's really there,
Hiding from you and me.
If we can catch that Leprechaun,
So the story's told,
He just might lead us,
To his big pot of gold.

4. <u>WEARING GREEN</u>

We celebrate St. Patrick's day,
By wearing something green,
A shirt, a tie, a dress, a bow,
All around us, green can be seen.

C.   POEMS FOR A WINDY MARCH

1.   MARCH WINDS

March winds will blow
All the winter away.
And soon the springtime,
Will be on its way.

2.   SPRING WILL SOON ARRIVE

When the March winds blow,
We all know --
That spring will soon arrive.
We will cheer,
When buds appear --
For all nature is alive.

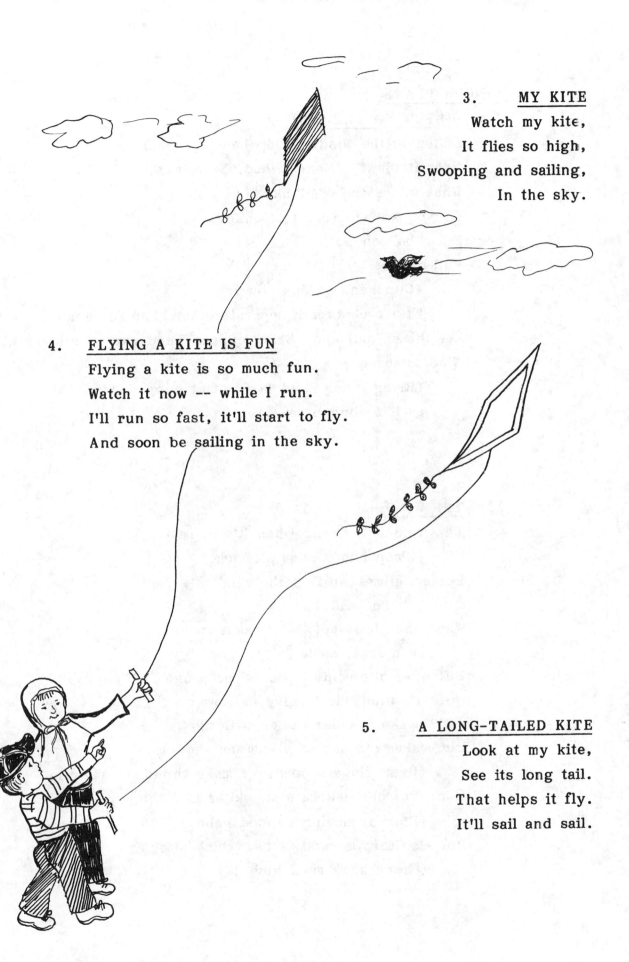

3. <u>MY KITE</u>

Watch my kite,
It flies so high,
Swooping and sailing,
In the sky.

4. <u>FLYING A KITE IS FUN</u>

Flying a kite is so much fun.
Watch it now -- while I run.
I'll run so fast, it'll start to fly.
And soon be sailing in the sky.

5. <u>A LONG-TAILED KITE</u>

Look at my kite,
See its long tail.
That helps it fly.
It'll sail and sail.

D. FINGER PLAYS

1. LISTEN TO THE WIND

Listen to the wind. (Cup hand to ear.)

Hear it blow? (Make "whoosh" noise.)

What makes the wind blow?

Do you know? (Point at child.)

Fill a balloon up

Full of air.

    (Cup hand to lips, blow;

    With each breath separate other hand further from mouth.)

Let the air out and (Bring cupped hand away from mouth.)

Wind is there.

    (Bring other hand in front of cupped hand

    as if feeling breeze.)

2. THE WIND

The wind is a friend when it's at rest,

    (Clasp hands over stomach.)

But sometimes we find the wind is a pest.

    (Shake head.)

When the air is hot, wind cools me off,

    (Fan face, smile.)

But when it's cold, it makes me cough. (Cough.)

It turns windmills to give us power,

    (Make circular motion with arm.)

But makes a storm of a summer shower.

    (Drum fingers on desk, make thunder noises.)

It pushes our sailboats and kites and things,

    (Blow at moving cupped hand.)

But also throws sand at us, which stings.

    (Grasp arms as if hurt.)

3. **THE KITE**

See the kite away up high.

    (Use one hand as kite sailing, twisting.)

Sailing, swooping in the sky.

Twisting and turning and dipping around,

'Til the wind goes away,

And it came fluttering down.

    (Hand comes slowly down.)

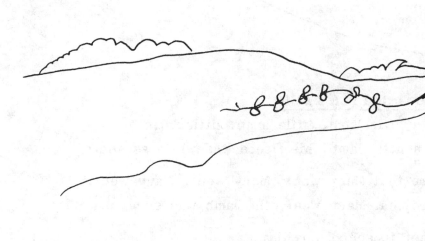

4. **THE STRONG WIND**

Feel the strong wind, it almost blows me down,

    (Bend body, almost falling.)

Hear it whistle through the trees and all around.

    (Cup hand to ear.)

Try to see the wind as it howls and blows.

    (Hand over eyebrows.)

But what does the wind look like? Nobody knows!

    (Shrug shoulders, palms up.)

E. **NURSERY RHYMES**

1. **JACK AND JILL**

    Jack and Jill ran up the hill,
    To fetch a pail of water.
    Jack fell down and broke his crown,
    And Jill came tumbling after.

2. **MARY HAD A LITTLE LAMB**

    Mary had a little lamb, little lamb, little lamb.
    Mary had a little lamb, his fleece was white as snow.

    Everywhere that Mary went, Mary went, Mary went,
    Everywhere that Mary went, the lamb was sure to go.

    Followed her to school one day,
        school one day, school one day.
    Followed her to school one day, which was against the rules.

    Made the children laugh and play,
        laugh and play, laugh and play,
    Made the children laugh and play, to see a lamb in school.

III. MUSIC

Children will develop the ability to participate in and enjoy music.

A. GREEN BOTTLE BAND

Collect a variety of jars and bottles. Fill the bottles with water that you have tinted green. (Use food coloring to tint the water.)

Fill these jars and bottles to various levels so that when tapped with a spoon they will sound various notes. When you have enough notes, you will be able to play a tune. For example: "Twinkle, Twinkle Little Star," Jingle Bells," or "The Farmer In The Dell."

IV. SCIENCE

Children will develop skills in:

Distinguishing differences

Similarities of attributes

A. GROW A GRASS SHAMROCK

Start this project the beginning of the month so that by St. Patrick's Day it will be ready to be observed.

Cut an old terry cloth towel or washcloth in the shape of a shamrock so it will fit in a foil pan. Place the cloth in the pan and wet it thoroughly. Sprinkle grass seed or bird seed on top of the cloth. Set the pan in a sunny place, but be sure to keep the cloth damp.

As the grass grows, the cloth will be transformed into a shaggy green shamrock. The children will enjoy watching the grass grow.

B. MARCH

March is the third month in the year and is named for Mars, the Roman God of War. A familiar saying is "March comes in like a lion and goes out like a lamb." This is to say the beginning of the month is blustery and cold. By the end of March, the days become more mild and sunny.

In March and April the cold, snowy days of winter come to an end and signs of spring become visible. Green buds begin to appear. The first pussy willows and wild flowers are found in the woods. Animals that have been hibernating -- bears, chipmunks, woodchucks, etc. -- awake from their long winter sleep. Birds that had flown south for the winter start to return. One of the earliest birds to return to the north is the robin. We are happy to see the first robin, as this is an indication that spring will soon be here.

We celebrate the first day of spring in the month of March. This usually occurs on March 21st, the "vernal equinox." On this day the sun rises directly in the east and sets directly in the west. The length of the day is equal to the length of the night.

V. SOCIAL STUDIES

Children will develop an awareness of:

Holidays

Traditions

Seasonal changes

A. ST. PATRICK'S DAY

One of the special days in March is March 17th. On this day we celebrate St. Patrick's Day. St. Patrick was the patron saint of Ireland who died on March 17th. It is said he founded 300 churches and baptized over 100,000 people. The story is told that he charmed all the snakes in Ireland to the sea where they drowned.

The shamrock is the national flower of Ireland. According to legend, St. Patrick planted this clover-like plant all over Ireland because its three small leaves represented the Holy Trinity. Thus, we observe this special day by wearing something green. In New York City, they hold a special St. Patrick's Day parade to honor the Irish.

Leprechauns are also associated with Ireland because the Irish just love to tell fairy stories. The Leprechauns were little old men who made shoes for the fairies of Ireland. People wanted to catch a Leprechaun to get them to tell where they kept their pot of gold. However, is was wise not to believe them as they always tried to get away without paying. They are usually pictured as being short, bearded and wearing a large green hat with a big buckle on the hatband.

VI. MARCH PHYSICAL EDUCATION FUN

Children will develop skills in:

Rhythm

Imaging

Use of large and small muscles

Good sports conduct

A. ## MOVE AS IF YOU ARE:
1.   Picking a shamrock.
2.   Batting a baseball.
3.   Catching a baseball.
4.   Throwing a baseball.
5.   Flying a kite.
6.   Counting gold.
7.   Pushing your car.
8.   Hammering.

B. ## BEAN CARRY

Each child (or team) gets a spoon and a dish with the same number of beans. They are "equal." They must use spoon to scoop beans and then walk along a taped line and place the beans in a bowl on the floor at the end of the line. There can be three winners in this game. The winning categories can be "fastest," "most beans in bowl," and the "least number of trips across line."

C. ## POT O' GOLD

Make a "Pot O' Gold" out of black construction paper. Make coins out of yellow paper. Paste coins on pot. Hide the pot someplace out of sight. Have children look for it and the one who finds it will hide it the next time. Play until everyone has a chance to hide the pot.

VII. MATH COOKING

Children will develop skills in:

Number awareness

Counting

Measuring

A. GREEN FINGER JELLO

3 small envelopes of green gelatin

4 envelopes of Knox® Unflavored gelatin

4 cups boiling water

Mix together until completely dissolved. Allow to cool in refrigerator. Cut into cubes.

Math: Count and discuss measurements of ingredients. Discuss "cube."

B. GREEN KOOL-AID

Make Kool-Aid®according to package directions.

Math: Count cups of water before mixing. Count cups of Kool-Aid® Are they the same?

C. GREEN POPSICLES

Make green Kool-Aid® Pour into ice cube trays. Put in freezer. When frozen, remove from trays for a St. Patrick's Day treat.

Math: Count cups of water. Discuss ice cube shapes.

D. <u>CUPCAKES WITH GREEN FROSTING</u>

Make cupcakes from package mix. Make a confectioners sugar frosting or purchase a prepared frosting. Add a few drops of green food coloring to the frosting. Allow children to frost their own cupcake. Sprinkle with green sugar crystals.

Math: Count ingredients. Count cupcakes. Are there enough cupcakes so that each child can have one . . . two?

E. **FILLED CELERY STICKS**

Clean and slice celery into sticks. Fill with cream cheese or peanut butter. Leave some sticks plain and sprinkle with a little salt.

Math: Compare celery sticks. Are some longer? Are some shorter? Are some equal?

F. **HEALTHY CANDY**

1 cup honey	1½ cups dried powder milk
1 cup peanut butter	1½ cups wheat germ
1 t. nutmeg	Crushed corn flakes

Combine above ingredients. Shape into small balls. Roll in crushed corn flakes or crushed nuts. Ready to enjoy.

Math: Count and discuss measurement of ingredients. Count spheres of "Healthy Candy." How many spheres are there?

READ ALOUD BOOKS FROM THE LIBRARY
MARCH

Children will develop the ability to enjoy and gain knowledge from books.

1. ## SPRING
   Allington, Richard L., Ph.D. and Krull, Kathleen
   Illustrated by Lynn Uhde
   Raintree Children's Books, Milwaukee, 1981
   32 pages, color illustrations

   Pictures and words help young chilren recognize the changes that happen to plants, animals and humans and their activities in the spring.

2. ## LEPRECHAUNS NEVER LIE
   Balian, Lorna
   Illustrated by author
   Abington, Nashville, 1980
   Unpaged, illustrations

   A wise little leprechaun tricks a lazy girl and her equally non-industrious grandmother into working hard to find his pot of gold. He never exactly lies to them, but he gives them just enough information so they end up cleaning and re-roofing their house and digging up their potato patch. In the end, the girl and her grandmother are clean, dry and well-fed, and the leprechaun still has his gold. May need to be paraphrased or read in sections because of its length, but a good story for young children.

3. **ST. PATRICK'S DAY IN THE MORNING**
   Bunting, Eve
   Illustrated by Jan Brett
   Houghton Mifflin, New York, 1980
   Unpaged, color illustrations

   > Little Jamie is told he is too young to be in the St. Patrick's Day Parade. He gets up very early and, with pieces of his family's uniforms, a flute and his dog, he travels the parade route across the Irish countryside. He visits the local townspeople, gets an Irish flag from the woman at the bakery and marches to the top of Acorn Hill. This book may be a little long for very young children, but it can be easily paraphrased or read in sections and it shows a young boy's triumph and also Irish life.

4. **THE HUNGRY LEPRECHAUN**
   Calhoun, Mary
   Illustrated by Roger DuVoisin
   Morrow, 1962
   Unpaged, illustrations

   > Young Patrick O'Michael O'Sullivan O'Callahan and a hungry leprechaun tried to turn dandelion soup into gold, but the leprechaun didn't have enough magic to do it. His magic didn't turn rocks to gold either, but it did seem to help produce a new vegetable which the hungry boy and the hungry leprechaun named potatoes. They cooked and ate some while saving some for sprouting and some for neighbors.

5. THE CARP IN THE BATHTUB

Cohen, Barbara

Illustrated by Joan Halpern

Lothrop, 1972

48 pages

> Leah and Harry adopt a carp, which mother has given a temporary home in their bathtub, until she cooks it for Passover.

6. CORDUROY

Freeman, Don

Puggin, 1976

32 pages

> A little girl makes herself and a friendless Teddy Bear happy when she purchases him from the store.

7. TEDDY BEARS CURE A COLD

Gretz, Susan and Sage, Allison

Four Winds Press, New York, 1984

Unpaged, color illustrations

> Andrew the bear has a sore throat and fever. He convinces the other bears he is sick when he can't eat. The bears mobilize their forces to help him get better until his fever goes down and they begin to feel he is taking advantage of the situation. He feels better and goes sledding but when they get home, Louise bear isn't feeling well enough to eat and **she** goes to bed. Bright colors and pictures show bears doing very human things.

8. THE BEAR WHO SAW THE SPRING

Kuskin, Karla

Harper, New York, 1961

Unpaged, illustrations

> This rhyming story tells about a small dog and a big bear who become friends and enjoy the wonders of each season as it comes along, beginning with spring.

9. SPRING IS HERE!

Moncure, Jane Belk

Child's World, 1975

Unpaged, color illustrations

> Simple words and multi-colored drawings describe a young boy's delight in the sounds, smells, tastes and creatures which are especially enchanting during spring. He also wonders what will happen in the summer to the flowers, the wind, his turtle, frogs, ducks, rabbits and gardens. A song and music are on the last page -- "Take A Walk In The Spring."

10. WORD BIRDS, SPRING WORDS

Moncure, Jane Belk

Illustrated by Vern Gohman

Child's World, Elgin, IL 1985

Unpaged, color illustrations

> Very large print (two lines measure one inch) and large bright pictures help introduce children to spring words. Most pages contain one word such as "mud puddles" or "suds" and a picture which explains and gives deeper meaning to the word. Pictures show how to make a word house and how to put spring words in it.

11. CURIOUS GEORGE FLIES A KITE

Rey, Margaret

Illustrated by H.A. Rey

Houghton Mifflin, Riverside Press, Cambridge, 1958

> Curious George, the monkey, who is interested in everything, jumps over a wall to play with some bunnies. George follows a fisherman and goes fishing and swimming before flying a kite. The kite takes George up in the air. He is saved by the same man in the yellow hat who appears in many Curious George books.

12. KITE FLYING

Schmitz, Dorothy Childers

Editied by Howard Schroeder

Crestwood House, Mankatu, MN, 1978

30 pages, color illustrations

(Fun Seeker Series)

> This is a history of kites including a page of directions on how to build your own kite. This book is too difficult for most young children, but it will provide the adult with interesting information to discuss with young children.

13. LET'S MAKE A KITE

Stokes, Jack Tilden (1923)

H.Z. Walck, New York, 1976

Unpaged, color illustrations

> A beginners everying-you-ever-need-to-know-about-making-and-flying-a-kite book. It even tells how to get kites up into the air and what the best location and weather is for kite flying. Detailed instructions are included for making and decorating kites. The pictures are bright and the vocabulary simple.

14. <u>DEEP IN THE FOREST</u>
Turkle, Brinton
Dutton, 1976
30 pages

> No words, but children familiar with Goldilocks will recognize that the cub bear has paid her a visit. The baby bear has his adventures (much as Goldilocks did) as he finds his way around the cabin in the woods. After Goldilocks' mother and father come home, they surprise the terrified bear and he runs back into the woods. We are certain that he will never visit the cabin again. Well, **almost** certain!

15. <u>THE BIGGEST BEAR</u>
Ward, Lynd
Houghton Mifflin, 1952, 1973

> Johnny finds out that it's not an easy process trying to tame a wild bear cub.

SHAMROCKS

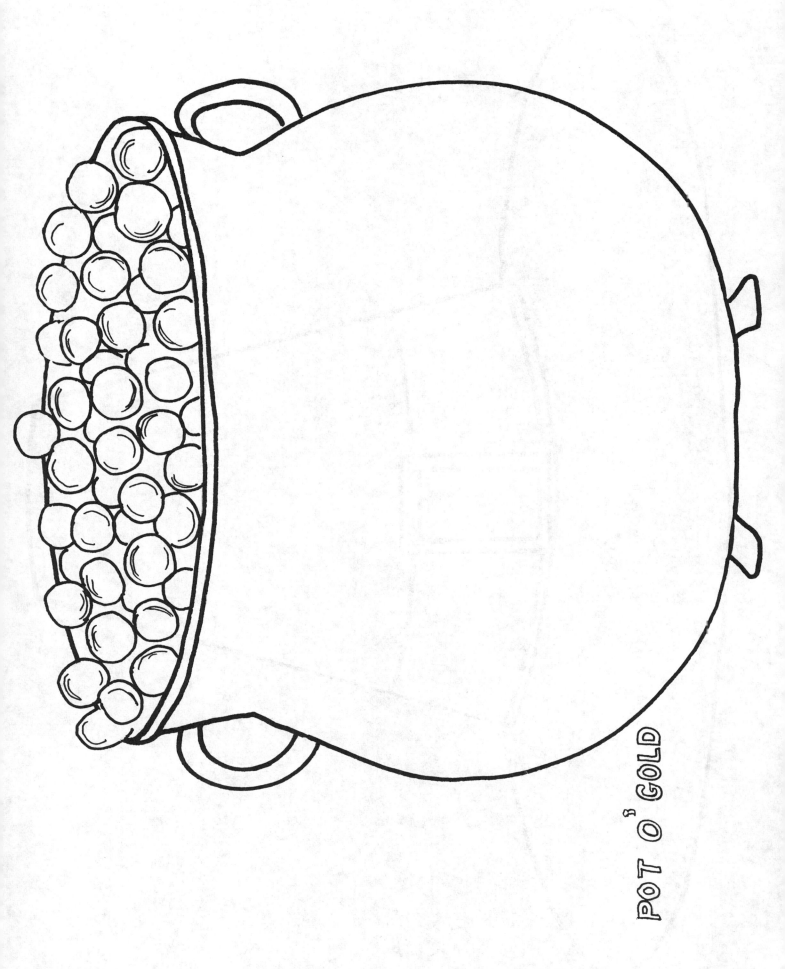

POT O' GOLD

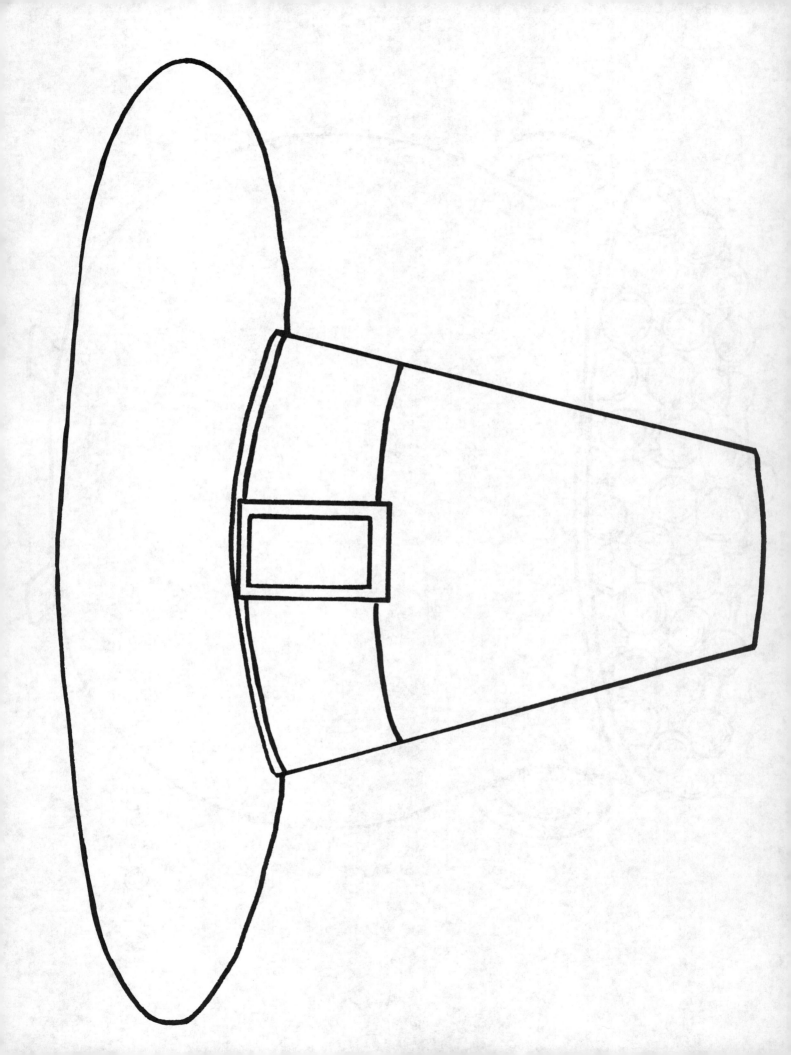

APRIL

Dear Parents:

April brings rain, plants, Spring and Easter!

ART
Raindrop Puppets
Paper Plate Bunnies

LITERATURE
Rainy Day Worms
The Egg Who Couldn't Make Up His Mind

SCIENCE
Earth, plants, animals
and people change

SOCIAL STUDIES
Easter

BOOKS FROM THE LIBRARY

MATH COOKING
Bunnies Lunch

PHYSICAL EDUCATION
Pretend you are a very little seed
growing into a huge green plant

HAPPY APRIL!

Parent Page ART - Paper Bag Bunnies PHYS. ED. - Exercise 1 (five times) MATH COOKING - Bunny's Lunch BOOK - Sky Dragon by Ronald Wegen	ART - Circle Bunny MUSIC - "See The Easter Bunny" PHYS. ED. - Exercise 1 (five times) MATH COOKING - Every Thing About Easter Rabbit by Wiltrud Roser BOOK -	ART - Easy Easter Baskets LITERATURE - FINGER PLAY - "A Tisket, A Tasket, I'm Looking For My Basket" PHYS. ED. - Exercises 1-2 (five times each)	ART - Paper Easter Eggs LITERATURE - POEM - "Easter Eggs" - NURSERY RHYME - "April Showers" PHYS. ED. - Exercises 1-2 & B	ART - Easter Bonnet MUSIC - "Bunny" SOCIAL STUDIES - Discuss Easter BOOK - The Country Bunny and The Little Gold Shoes by Dubois Heyward
ART - (Complete) Easter Bonnet LITERATURE - POEM - "Easter Hat" - NURSERY RHYME - "Rain Before Seven" SOCIAL STUDIES - Recall discussion about Easter PHYS. ED. - Exercises 1-3 BOOK - Follow The Wind by Alvin Tresselt	ART - Hard Boiled Easter Eggs LITERATURE - STORY - "The Egg Who Couldn't Make Up His Mind" - NURSERY RHYME - "It's Raining, It's Pouring" PHYS. ED. - Exercises 1-3 & C MATH COOKING - Individual Egg Salad	ART - Paper Plate Bunny LITERATURE - POEM - "Finding A Treat - STORY - Recall "The Egg Who Couldn't Make Up His Mind" PHYS. ED. - Exercises 1-3 & C MATH COOKING - Bunny Cake BOOK - Thunderstorm by Mary Szilagyi	ART - Chicken In A Shell LITERATURE - FINGER PLAY - "The Butterfly" SOCIAL STUDIES - Discuss "Easter B" PHYS. ED. - Exercises 1-4 & C (do slow, do fast)	ART - Mr. Rabbit In A Sprinkling Can LITERATURE - ACTION POEM - "Little Bunnies" PHYS. ED. - Exercises 1-4 MATH COOKING - Bunny Salad BOOK - The Rain Puddle by Adelaide Holl
ART - Baby Chick In A Shell SCIENCE - Discuss "Earth Changes" PHYS. ED. - Exercises 1-5 BOOK - Rain Drop Splash by Alvin Tresselt	ART - Pussy Willow Pictures or Puffed Rice Pussy Willow LITERATURE - POEM - "Hello Spring" PHYS. ED. - Exercises 1-6 (do very quietly, do very, very quietly)	ART - Spring Collection Picture LITERATURE - POEM - "April Rains" PHYS. ED. - Exercises 1-7 & B BOOK - Cloudy With A Chance of Meatballs by Mudi Barrett	ART - (Complete) Spring Collection Picture LITERATURE - FINGER PLAY - NURSERY RHYME - "Pitter Patter" - "Rain, Rain Go Away" SCIENCE - Discuss "Plants Change" BOOK - The Carrot Seed by Ruth Krauss	ART - Smiling Dandelion NURSERY RHYME - "Rain, Rain Go Away" MUSIC - ACTION POEM - "We're Walking In The Rain" PHYS. ED. - Exercises 1-8 (do big, do small) BOOK - Splish Splash by Ethel Kessler
ART - Umbrella LITERATURE - POEM - "Splash, Splash The Raindrops Fall" - NURSERY RHYME - "Rain Before Seven" PHYS. ED. - Exercises 1-8 BOOK - Rain! Rain! by Carol Greene	ART - Raindrop Puppet LITERATURE - FINGER PLAY - "Rainy Day Worms" - NURSERY RHYME - "It's Raining, It's Pouring" PHYS. ED. - Exercises 1-8 BOOK - Spring Things by Maxine Winokur	ART - Cupcake Paper Flowers SCIENCE - Discuss "Animal Changes" PHYS. ED. - Exercises 1-8 & B MATH COOKING - Individual Potato Salad BOOK - Peeper, First Voice of Spring by Robert McClung	ART - Duck Puppet SCIENCE - Discuss "People Changes" PHYS. ED. - Exercises 1-8 (add one of your own) BOOK - The Bear Who Saw Spring by Karla Kuskin	ART - Paper Cup Flower LITERATURE - FINGER PLAY - "The Rain" PHYS. ED. - Exercises 1-8 (do very, very slowly twice) BOOK - Caught In the Rain by Beatriz Ferro

I. ART

Children will develop skills in:

Organization

Sequence

Use of small muscles (small motor)

A. <u>PUSSY WILLOW PICTURES WITH FINGERPRINTS</u>

Use the paint brush and brown paint to paint branches on a 9" x 12" sheet of construction paper. Dip your finger into the gray paint and press on the brown branches at various places. Keep dipping the finger in the paint and pressing until enough "pussy willows" have been pressed onto the branches. This is good for fine motor control.

B. <u>PUFFED RICE PUSSY WILLOW</u>

Cut out a vase from the dark paper and paste on pastel construction paper (9" x 12"). Draw stems with a magic marker coming from the vase. Glue puffed rice on the stems to make a pussy willow picture.

Fold on dotted lines to form a frame for your picture.

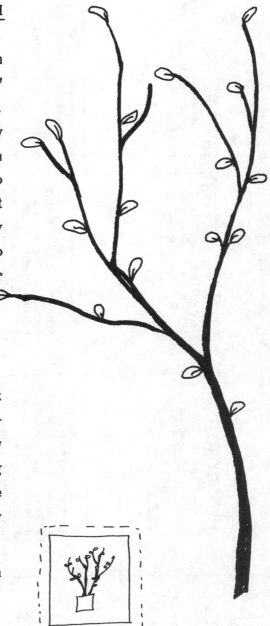

C.   SPRING COLLECTION PICTURE

Using seed and flower catalogues or magazines, children will cut out pictures about spring. Pictures of flowers, planting and preparing the soil, people working in gardens, children playing, blue sky and sunshine are all suitable pictures.   The pictures could be of new animal babies, farm or woodland animals or birds chirping for food.

Paste the pictures on a sheet of 12" x 18" manilla paper. When finished, have children explain their pictures.

D.   SMILING DANDELIONS

From yellow construction paper cut one circle 4½" and one circle 3½" in diameter.   From brown construction paper cut a brown circle 2" in diameter.   Fringe the two yellow circles.

Staple all three circles onto the tongue depressor.   Use green magic marker to color the stick.   Bend up the fringe all around the two yellow circles.   Make a face on the brown circle with magic markers.

E.   UMBRELLA

Using umbrella pattern, copy the umbrella on 9" x 12" construction paper.

Cut out bows from construction of contrasting colors.

Paste the bows on the umbrella.   Using magic marker, draw a handle for the umbrella.

For variety, you may use varied colored curling ribbon and staple them on the umbrella.

F. RAINDROP PUPPET

Using raindrop pattern, cut out puppet. Draw in facial features.

Fasten arms and legs onto raindrop body with paper fasteners.

Punch a hole in the top of the raindrop and put yarn through and make a loop.

Children can make the raindrop puppet jump up and down.

G. __CUPCAKE PAPER FLOWERS__

Cut vase out of colored paper
and paste on 12" x 18" sheet
of construction paper. Cut three
strips of green for stems. Cut
green leaves. Paste stems and
leaves in place. Paste a cupcake
paper at the top of each stem.
Paste small dots in the middle
of the "flower."

Variation: Use coffee filters for
big, floppy flowers. Paint the
filter all different colors. When
dry, paste on large paper. Add
the stem and leaves -- these can
be drawn or painted on the
picture.

H. PAPER CUP FLOWER

Cut strips all around a 5 oz. dixie cup from the top to the base. Spread the strips out flat around the base and place it on a 12" x 18" piece of bright blue construction paper. Staple the base of the cup to the paper. The base is the center of the flower and the strips are the petals.

Cut a vase out of the colored paper and paste on the blue paper. Now, draw stems connecting the flower to the vase. Also, draw leaves on the stems.

I. **BABY CHICK IN A SHELL**

Clue half of a real egg shell on cardboard. Glue two cotton balls in the egg shell, one on top of the other. Glue two small orange eyes and a beak made of construction paper.

J. **PAPER BAG BUNNIES**

Cut bunny ears from pink paper and staple on bag. Cut pink nose from construction paper. Using the same pink construction paper, cut whiskers.

Paste nose and whiskers on face. Draw in face with crayons. Finish by pasting on the cotton tail.

K.   CIRCLE BUNNY

Trace circles on pink or white paper.   Cut out circles.   Mark one circle as shown:

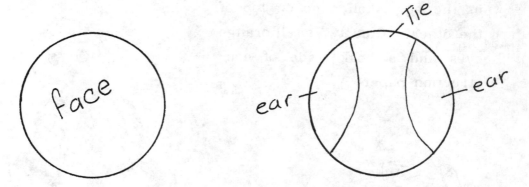

Cut circle to make ears and tie.   Draw face on other circle. Paste ears and bow on rabbit face.   Color a fancy bow tie. Plaste rabbit on 12" x 18" sheet of construction paper.

L.   EASY EASTER BASKETS
Use decorative plastic margarine containers.   Punch a hole on
each side.   Use the pipe cleaners for a handle.   Fill with Easter
grass.   Put in dyed eggs and jelly beans.

M. <u>DUCK PUPPET</u>

Fold a 12" x 18" sheet of white construction paper and draw a "hill." Cut out. Make beak and eyes of orange. Paste on the white paper. Cut pupils and eyelashes out of black paper. Paste tongue depressor between the white paper to use as a handle.

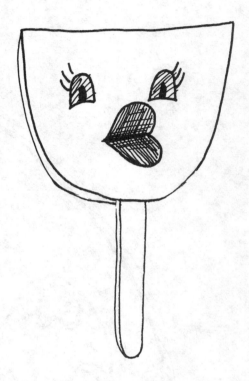

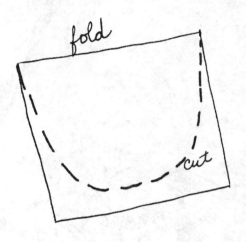

N. <u>PAPER PLATE BUNNY</u>

Cut rabbit ears out of white construction paper. Color the center of the ears red or pink. Paste ears to paper plate. Draw rabbit's face on the paper plate. Staple the tongue depressor on for a handle.

O. PAPER EASTER EGGS

Trace around egg patterns. Draw as many as the paper will allow. Cut out the eggs. Decorate the eggs by coloring or painting designs on back and front. Use for the "Egg Hurt" activity.

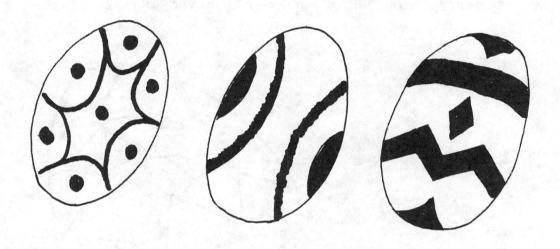

P. HARD BOILED EASTER EGGS

Allow hard boiled eggs to cool thoroughly. Dye by using regular egg dye. Eggs can also be colored with crayons. Child's name can be put on egg with crayon and then dipped in coloring solution.

Q. CHICKEN IN A SHELL

Cut large oval egg from wall paper or white paper. Draw jagged line across half of egg and cut. If white paper is used, it should be decorated. Make a chick's head out of yellow or white construction paper. Color beak and eyes black. Paste chick to bottom half of egg shell. Fasten top and bottom shell together with paper fastener so top half of shell can be moved to reveal chick.

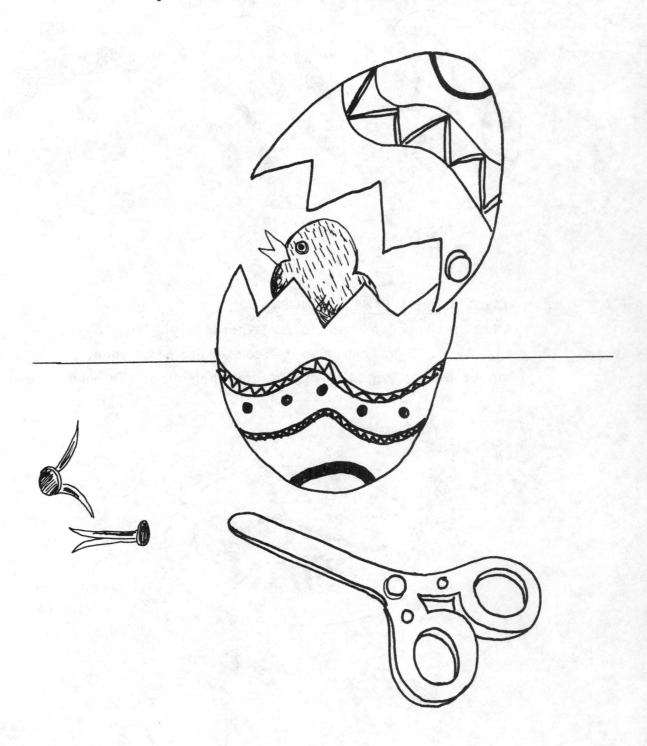

R. <u>EASTER BONNET</u>

Decorate your paper plate with tissue paper flowers and leaves. Use crepe paper, if preferred. Staple or glue decorations on bonnet. Poke a hold on each side. Put a ribbon through from the top and tie under chin.

Have an Easter Parade and each child will wear the Easter Bonnet they created.

S.   **MR. RABBIT IN A SPRINKLING CAN**

Using rabbit pattern and 9" x 12" white construction paper, trace rabbit face and paws. Cut out.

Using sprinkling can pattern and 9" x 12" sheet of yellow construction paper, trace sprinkling can and cut out.

Paste sprinkling can and rabbit face and paws on 9" x 12" green construction paper.

Draw rabbit's face and whiskers.

A. PUSSY WILLOW PICTURES WITH FINGERPRINTS	B. PUFFED RICE PUSSY WILLOW	C. SPRING PICTURE COLLECTION	D. SMILING DANDELION
Paint brush Brown paint 9"x12" construction paper Gray paint	Dark 9"x12" construction paper Paste Pastel 9"x12" construction paper Magic marker Glue Puffed rice	Pictures about spring Paste 12"x18" manilla paper	Yellow construction paper Brown construction paper Staple Tongue depressor Green magic marker
E. UMBRELLA	F. RAINDROP PUPPET	G. CUPCAKE PAPER FLOWERS	H. PAPER CUP FLOWER
9"x12" construction paper Paste Magic marker Curling ribbon Staple	Construction paper Crayons Paper fasteners Hole punch Yarn	Colored paper 12"x18" construction paper Green paper Paste Cupcake paper Coffee filters Crayons	Dixie cup 12"x18" bright blue construction paper Staple Colored paper Crayons
I. BABY CHICK IN A SHELL	J. PAPER BAG BUNNIES	K. CIRCLE BUNNY	L. EASY EASTER BASKETS
Glue Egg shell Cardboard Cotton balls Orange construction paper	Pink paper Staple Lunch bag Paste Crayons Cotton balls	Pink paper White paper Crayons Paste 12"x18" construction paper	Plastic margarine tubs Hole punch Pipe cleaners Easter grass Dyed eggs Jelly beans
M. DUCK PUPPET	N. PAPER PLATE BUNNY	O. PAPER EASTER EGGS	P. HARD BOILED EASTER EGGS
12"x18" white construction paper Orange construction paper Paste Black construction paper Tongue depressor	White construction paper Crayons Paste Paper plate Staple Tongue depressor	Construction paper Paint/crayons	Hard boiled eggs Egg dye Crayons
Q. CHICKEN IN A SHELL	R. EASTER BONNET	S. MR. RABBIT IN A SPRINKLING CAN	
Wallpaper/white paper Crayons Yellow construction paper Paste Paper fasteners	Paper plate Tissue paper/crepe paper Leaves Staple/glue Ribbon	9"x12" white construction paper 9"x12" yellow construction paper Paste 9"x12" green construction paper Crayons	

II. LITERATURE
Children will develop the ability to
identify and enjoy:

Characters

Main ideas

Detail

Sequence of events

A. THE EGG WHO COULDN"T MAKE
    UP HIS MIND

Eggmond Egg was very
worried. It was getting closer
and closer to Easter. Many special
things were being prepared.
Delicious chocolate bunnies, jelly
beans and eggs were ready to
be put into Easter baskets.

Dozens of eggs were boiled and ready
to be colored. Most of the eggs had already
selected the colors they wanted to be. The
eggs knew how pretty they would look in
an Easter Basket. All except Eggmond
Egg. He just couldn't seem to decide on
a color.

The coloring day finally arrived and Eggmond
still hadn't made up his mind. What pretty colors
there were! There were beautiful shades of red,
yellow, purple, blue, green and orange to pick from.
But he was so undecided.

"Let's see, this is a really pretty shade of blue." It reminded
him of the color of the sky. So, he picked up the blue brush
and gave himself a couple of dabs of blue. Then, he spied the
red. It was as bright and shiny as an apple sitting on a teacher's

desk. He put a little blop of it here and there.

Then he saw the yellow. It was as bright and golden as sunshine on a summer day. He put the brush in the yellow and made some wide yellow lines. They looked nice. He looked over and saw a deep rich green. A green that reminded him of the green needles in a pine forest. He liked it so much he made some nice green lines.

"What color should I try next?" he sang to himself. He looked at the orange. That was a bright cheerful color. It was the color of a pumpkin you would pick to make a jolly jack-o-lantern on Halloween. This was fun!

"Well," he said. "Just a touch of it here and there will be nice."

To finish it off he took the purple brush in his hand. It was such a nice deep purple. It was lush and colorful as a cluster of purple grapes. With the brush he made a little mark here and a little mark there.

"Well," he said. "I think I'm ready for Easter."

He found an egg size hat. He put it on his head and then took a look at himself in the mirror. This is what he saw.

Don't you think Eggmond is the best looking Easter egg of all?

POEMS/FINGER PLAYS/NURSERY RHYMES

Children will develop the ability to participate in and enjoy:

    Rhythm

    Poetry

    Sequence

    Characters

B.   POEMS FOR SPRING

1.   "HELLO" TO SPRING

      We say goodby to winter,
      And say "hello" to spring.
      The sunshine warms the earth,
      We hear the robins sing.
      We see the new buds sprouting
      On every bush and tree.
      And soon the earth is all aglow
      In its springtime finery.

2.   APRIL RAINS

      April rains come falling down,
      Splishing, splashing, all around.
      We hate a rainy day, although -
      The rain helps make the gardens grow.

3.   SPLISH, SPLASH, THE RAINDROPS FALL

      Splish, splash, the raindrops fall.
      Splish, splash, over all.
      My red umbrella will keep me dry.
      While the raindrops keep falling from the sky.

C. EASTER POEMS

1. EASTER EGGS

At Easter time we color eggs,
Shades of yellow, red and blue.
We make them pretty as can be,
We'll make some for me and some for you.

2. FINDING A TREAT

Hippity hop, hippity hop.
Will the Easter Bunny stop?
Will he leave a treat behind,
An Easter basket for me to find?

I'll look over here, I'll look over there,
I'll look behind things, I'll look everywhere.
I'll look until I find my treat,
And then I'll sit right down and eat.

3. EASTER HAT

I'll make a pretty Easter hat,
To wear at Easter time.
I'll put some flowers on it,
And a bow will make it fine.
We'll fasten on some ribbons,
All pretty pink and blue,
Then we'll take a picture,
And I'll give it to you.

D. FINGER PLAYS

1. THE RAIN

I sit before the window now (Seat yourself, if possible.)

And I look out at the rain. (Shade eyes; look around.)

It means no play outside today (Shake head; shrug.)

So inside I remain. (Rest chin on fist; look sorrowful.)

I watch the water dribble down

    (Follow up-to-down movements with eyes.)

And turn the brown grass green. (Sit up; take notice.)

And after a while I start to smile

At Nature's washing machine. (Smile; lean back; relax.)

2. BUTTERFLY

Bright colored butterfly,

    (Place hands back to back; wiggle fingers.)

Looking for honey,

Spread your wings and fly away,

While it's sunny.

3. PITTER, PATTER

Oh! Where do you come from,

You little drops of rain,

Pitter, patter, pitter, patter (Tap fingers on table or floor.)

Down the windowpane.

Tell me little raindrops,

Is that the way you play,

Pitter, patter, pitter, patter (Tap fingers as before.)

All the rainy day?

4. <u>A TISKET, A TASKET, I'M LOOKING FOR MY BASKET</u>

A tisket, a tasket, I'm looking for my basket.

I'll look up, (Looking at high places.)

And I'll look down. (Looking at low places.)

I'll look carefully all around. (Turning and looking.)

I'll be happy when I find, (Point to self; nod head "yes.")

The treat Mr. Bunny left behind. (Rub tummy and smile.)

5. <u>RAINY DAY WORMS</u>

The rain is falling all around, (Hands make rain falling.)

Splish, splash, splish, splash. (Wiggle fingers.)

Making puddles on the ground,

Splish, splash, splish, splash.

The squishy worms crawl about,

   (Hands and arms slither around.)

Wiggle, waggle, wiggle, waggle.

They disappear when the sun comes out,

Zip. Zip. Zip. Zip.

   (Point thumbs down; right, left, right, left.)

6. <u>LITTLE BUNNIES</u>

(Children crouch down; hop around.)

Furry little bunnies, like to go hippity hop.

They wiggle their nose, (Wiggle nose.)

And twitch their whiskers,

   (Place hands under nose, wiggle fingers.)

While their ears go flippity flop.

   (Place hands on each side of head, move them back
   and forth.)

E. NURSERY RHYMES

1. RAIN BEFORE SEVEN

Rain before seven,
Fine before eleven.

2. APRIL SHOWERS

March winds and April showers,
Help bring us May flowers.

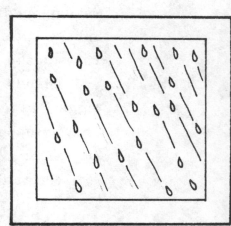

3. IT'S RAINING, IT'S POURING

It's raining, it's pouring,
The old man is snoring;
He got into bed
And bumped his head,
And he couldn't get up
Until morning.

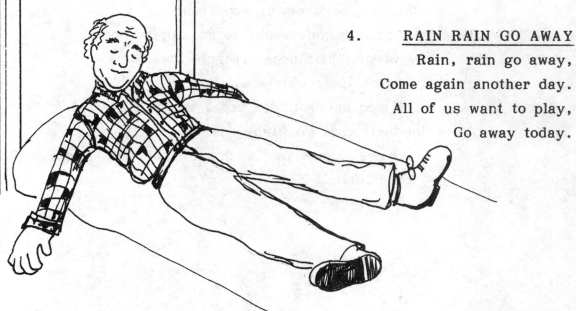

4. RAIN RAIN GO AWAY

Rain, rain go away,
Come again another day.
All of us want to play,
Go away today.

III. MUSIC

Children will develop the ability to participate in and enjoy music.

A. <u>WE'RE WALKING IN THE RAIN</u>

(Tune: Farmer In The Dell)

We're walking in the rain, (Walking, holding umbrella.)

Oh, we're walking in the rain,

We'll carry our umbrellas,

As we go walking in the rain.

And when the rain is done,

Put umbrellas down, (Put umbrella down.)

And run around,

Oh, we'll have so much fun. (Jump and clap hands.)

B. <u>SEE THE EASTER BUNNY</u>

(Tune: Here We Go Round The Mulberry Bush)

See how the bunny hops along, hops along, hops along.

See how the bunny hops along, (Children crouch and hop.)

On an Easter morning.

This is the way he wiggles his nose, wiggles his nose,

Wiggles his nose. (Children wiggle nose.)

This is the way he wiggles his nose,

On an Easter morning.

This is the way he flops his ears, flops his ears,

Flops his ears. (Use hands flopping for ears.)

This is the way he flops his ears,

On an Easter morning.

See how he jiggles his cotton tail, cotton tail.

Cotton tail. (Put one hand behind and wiggle it.)

See how he jiggles his cotton tail,

On an Easter morning.

C. <u>BUNNY</u>

(Tune: This Is The Way We Wash Our Clothes)

(To be used when passing out a treat.)

Here comes the bunny, hop, hop, hop.

Hop, hop, hop. Hop, hop, hop.

Here comes the bunny, hop, hop, hop.

With his Easter Basket.

I wonder if he'll stop, stop, stop.

Stop, stop, stop. Stop, stop, stop.

And bring a treat for me.

Thanks, Mr. Bunny. Thanks a lot.

Thanks a lot, thanks a lot.

Thanks, Mr. Bunny. Thanks a lot.

I'm happy as can be.

Chilren can be seated at desks, tables or in a circle on the floor.
If on the floor, have a paper plate for each child's treat. Pick
a "Bunny" to start. Sing the verses as the child passes around
the group. By the third verse the next child should have been
selected. First "Bunny" returns to their own spot and gives
basket with treat to the next "Bunny." Sing verses again as
the "Bunny" picks the next child. Do this until each child has
received their treat and has had a chance to be Mr. Bunny.

IV. SCIENCE

Children will develop skills in:

Distinguising differences

Similarities of attributes

A. EARTH CHANGES

In the springtime days are getting longer. It is lighter when we wake up in the morning and it stays lighter in the evening. We have more hours of daylight than we had in the winter.

The ice and snow are melting as the days gradually become warmer. Instead of snow, we often have rain. The ground thaws as the rain falls and softens it. The warm sunshine and the springtime showers help the plants start to grow.

Sometimes we have tornadoes and hurricanes in the springtime which are the result of sudden changes in the temperature.

B. PLANTS CHANGE

As the spring rains fall and the sun warms the earth, new shoots push through the soil. Some of the earliest plants to show their faces are the tulips and crocuses. They are quite hardy and even though the temperatures may still be cool, they will blossom and help us to know that spring has arrived.

Leaf buds begin to appear on the trees and bushes. Fruit trees burst into bloom with beautiful colored blossoms. We admire the beauty of the various fruit trees when they are in bloom: apple, cherry, peach and pear. Our nation's capitol, Washington, D.C., has cherry trees that are known for their beauty when they blossom each spring.

As the spring rains nourish the earth, the grass starts to change from brown to green. All around us the land takes on a fresh new look for spring.

C.   ANIMALS CHANGE

The animals that hibernate wake up from their long winter sleep and start to look for food. The birds which had migrated to the south start to return. They look for a good place to build a nest so they can lay their eggs. In a short while the eggs will hatch and baby birds will be chirping to be fed.

Most animals in the woods and forests and farms will have new babies in the spring. Spring is the time of birth and new life.

Furry animals will start to lose their winter coats. For now that the weather will be warmer, they will no longer need their thick winter coats of fur. Birds also lose some of their fuzzy down that protected them from the bitter cold of winter.

D.   PEOPLE CHANGE

Farmers start to prepare their ground for planting. Crops need to be planted as soon as the farmer knows the danger of freezing temperatures are over. For freezing temperatures can destroy new crops. So the farmer must be very careful not to plant too soon in the spring.

The warmer temperatures of spring mean we no longer have to wear our heavy winter things. Children start to play outdoors more and more. They are able to wear lighter clothing, without heavy boots and mufflers and snowsuits.

Spring is a time of new beginnings. People like to clean up their yards, put fresh paint on their houses and start planting shrubs and flowers in their gardens.

We welcome spring!

V. SOCIAL STUDIES

Children will develop an awareness of:

Holidays

Traditions

Seasonal changes

A. EASTER

Easter is a special religious holiday that is celebrated by Christians all over the world. This joyous holy day celebrates the resurrection of Jesus Christ. The Bible says that on the third day after the crucifixion, the body of Christ disappeared from His tomb. The stone had been rolled aside and the tomb was empty. An Angel appeared to His followers and said, "He is risen."

Although Easter is always celebrated on a Sunday, it's actual date varies from year to year. It falls on the first Sunday after the first full moon after March 21st (the vernal equinox). This falls sometime between March 22nd and April 25th.

Christian families often attend church in honor of Jesus. Churches at Easter often are decorated with white lilies, the symbol of purity and light.

B. EASTER CUSTOMS AND TRADITIONS

Many of the customs and traditions of Easter have come to us down through the years. It is believed that the name "Easter" comes down from Eostre, a Teutonic goddess of spring. The tradition of "dressing up" for Easter probably comes to us from Emperor Constantine, who had his leaders dress up in their most elegant robes on Easter. Also, Easter is celebrated in the springtime when the earth is shedding the snow and ice of winter and putting on a new coat of "green."

The use of eggs at Easter represent new life. The custom

of exchanging eggs began in ancient times. The Egyptians and Persians dyed eggs in pretty colors and gave them to their friends.

The tradition of the Easter Bunny probably came from ancient Egypt. The rabbit symbolized birth and new life and some ancient people associated it with the moon. It is believed that the rabbit became a symbol because the date of Easter is determined by the moon.

Today, children believe that the Easter Bunny brings eggs and candy on Easter morning. Many places have Easter egg hunts. In the United States, on the Monday of Easter, thousands of children are welcomed by the President to participate in an egg rolling contest. This is held on the lawn of the White House in Washington, D.C.

VI. APRIL PHYSICAL EDUCATION FUN

Children will develop skills in:

Rhythm

Imaging

Use of large and small muscles

Good sports conduct

A. MOVE AS IF YOU ARE:

1. A very little seed growing slowly into a huge green plant.
2. A soft rain falling.
3. A bear waking up after being asleep all winter.
4. Washing windows
5. Painting your garage.
6. Planting a tree.
7. Sweeping rain puddles off your sidewalk.
8. Playing baseball.

B. EGG HUNT

Hide paper "colored eggs." Children hop around to find as many eggs as they can. Each child will have a turn to count their eggs for the group. Variations: Give each child one colored paper egg. He/she should tell what color it is, then hunt for eggs that match that color.

C. PIN THE EAR ON THE BUNNY

Make a large picture of a bunny with one ear missing. Put the picture on a wall or a door. Cut one bunny ear. Roll a piece of tape and put on the back of the bunny's ear. Put a blindfold over the child's eyes. Aim them toward the picture and let them try to put the ear on the bunny. (Play the same way you would play "Pin The Tail On The Donkey."

VII. MATH COOKING

Children will develop skills in:

  Number awareness

  Counting

  Measuring

A. BUNNIES LUNCH

Discuss various foods that bunnies like to eat. Make sure the following foods are mentioned: lettuce, carrots, cabbage, radishes, celery, spinach and turnips.

Assign children to bring in a sample of each kind of vegetable. When all the vegetables have been brough in, have a discussion time to identify each one. Then, cut into small pieces and put on paper plates with the name on it. Pass each plate around for children to sample. Encourage children to sample each kind of vegetable.

Math: Count the different kinds of vegetables. Count the first fractions as you cut up the vegetables -- ½, ¼, etc.

B. BUNNY SALAD

Lettuce	Maraschino cherries
Pear	Marshmallows
Raisins	Cottage cheese

Place lettuce leaf on a plate. Place on chilled pear half upside down on the lettuce leaf. Use the raisins for eyes, cherry for the nose and put a ball of cottage cheese for the tail. Shape the marshmallows for ears.

Math: How many raisins will we need for eyes? How many cherries will we need for a nose?

C. BUNNY CAKE

       1 cake mix   Jelly beans

       Prepared frosting   Licorice

       1 pkg. coconut

Prepare cake mix according to the directions on the package. Bake in two 8" or 9" cake pans. When cake has cooled, cut according to the following directions.

 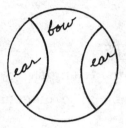

Assemble cake on a cookie sheet. Frost and decorate with coconut. Use jelly beans to make the face. Use licorice for whiskers. Color some coconut green and use for grass around the bunny.

Math: Count jelly beans. Discuss cutting cake in $\frac{1}{2}$, $\frac{1}{4}$.

D. **INDIVIDUAL EGG SALAD**

    1 hard cooked egg (chopped)

    1 T. mayonnaise or salad dressing

    ½ t. mustard

    ¼ t. finely chopped onion

Mix in bowl. You may put this on bread or crackers.

Another idea:

EGG TRIANGLES

Cut bread into triangles by removing crusts. Spread with egg salad. Cut each slice diagonally into quarters.

Math: Cut egg into fractions (½, ¼) before chopping. Discuss measurements of ingredients. Discuss bread triangle shape, if used.

E. **INDIVIDUAL POTATO SALAD**

Each child has:

    1 medium boiled potato (cooled)

    2 T. mayonnaise or salad dressing

    ¼ t. finely chopped onion

    1 T. chopped celery or green pepper

Peel potato. Chop the potato in a dish and add mayonnaise and other ingredients. Mix.

Math: Count number of ingredients. Count potatoes available. Are there enough so each person can have one? More?

READ ALOUD BOOKS FROM THE LIBRARY

APRIL

BOOKS

Children will develop the ability to enjoy and gain knowledge from books.

1. <u>Cloudy With A Chance of Meatballs</u>
   Barrett, Judi
   Illustrated by Ron Barrett
   Antheneum, 1982
   28 pages

   The citizens who live in Chewand Swallow are supplied with all of the food they need. Three times a day food rains from above, satisfying all of their needs. Something goes wrong, however, and the weather changes to meatballs the size of basketballs and other disconcerting menu items.

2. <u>Caught In The Rain</u>
   Beatriz, Ferro
   Illustrated by Michele Sambin
   Doubleday, New York, 1980
   25 pages, color illustrations

   What can you do when you are caught in the rain? This book answers that question by providing a suggestion on each page. It also tells about a "portable roof" called an umbrella. The pictures have many beautiful wet-blue-green colors in them.

3. **Rain! Rain!**
    Greene, Carol
    Illustrated by Larry Frederick
    Prepared under the direction of Robert Hillerich, Ph.D.
    Children's Press, Chicago, 1982
    Color illustrations
    (A Rookie Reader book)

    > Not more than five or six words every other page tell the rhyming
    > story of rain.   There are twenty-nine words in the word list
    > at the end of the book. This is a good "choral reader." Children
    > will be able to learn to recite the words after going through
    > the books several times.

4. **The Country Bunny and the Little Gold Shoes**
    Heyward, DuBosi
    Illustrated by Marjorie Hock
    Houghton Mifflin, 1974
    48 pages

    > No one gave her much encouragement, but pluck and persistence
    > are rewarded when a little country bunny finally becomes an Easter
    > Bunny.

5. <u>The Rain Puddle</u>
Holl, Adelaide (1910)
Illustrated by Roger Duvoisin
Lothrop, New York, 1965
Unpaged, illustrations

> Each animal looks into a rain puddle and thinks its reflection is another animal which has fallen in the puddle. When the sun "shone warm and bright" the rain dried and the animals decide that the others safely escaped from the puddle. The pictures are in bright primary colors and the mystery of the animals in the puddle is left for the readers and listeners to solve.

6. <u>Splish, Splash</u>
Kessler, Ethel and Leonard
Parent's Magazine Press, New York, 1973
32 pages, illustrations

> The signs of spring include ice melting, plants growing and rain splish splashing. Turtles and bears wake up and birds return. Pussy willows begin to grow and insects return. The weather continues to warm up and summer brings ice cream and swimming.

7. <u>The Carrot Seed</u>
Krauss, Ruth
Illustrated by Crockett Johnson
Harper and Row, New York, 1945
22 pages

> Easy (primer) vocabulary and charming simple drawings tell the story of a small boy's perserverance. Though everyone else doubts he will be able to grow anything, the boy cares for the seed he has planted. A wonderful giant carrot grows just as he had faith it would.

8. Spring Things

Kumin, Maxine Winokur

Illustrated by Arthur Marokvia

G.P. Putnam Sons, New York, 1961

48 pages

> A verse story in which a young boy learns and appreciates all of the wonderful new things that spring brings. He especially enjoys a new calf his parents entrust to him. There is a vocabulary list.

9. The Bear Who Saw The Spring

Kuskin, Karla

Harper and Row, Evanston, New York, 1961

Unpaged

> Story written with some rhyming phrases. A small dog and a bear explore spring, summer, fall and winter changes.

10. Peeper, First Voice of Spring

McClung, Robert

Illustrated by Carol Lerner

William Morrow and Company, New York, 1977

> Spring, summer and fall and what happens to insects, turtles, butterflies, birds and especially peepers -- a type of tree frog. Large nature drawings are included.

11. Everything About Easter Rabbits

Roser, Wiltrud

Translated by Eva L. Mayer

Thomas Y. Crowell Company, New York, 1972

> Everything you ever wanted to know about the habits of the G.O. Easter Rabbit. (G.O. stands for genuine original.)

12. Thunderstorm
     Szilargyl, Mary
     Illustrated by author
     Bradbury Press, New York, 1985
     Unpaged, color illustrations

   Soft, lovely illustrations show the arrival and departure of a summer
   rain -- thunder and lightning storm. It frightens a young girl
   and her dog but mother comforts them and after the storm is
   over they go back outside to play.

13. Follow The Wind
     Tresselt, Alvin
     Illustrated by Roger Duvoisin
     Lothrop, Lee and Shepard Inc., New York, 1950, 1959, 1961
     Unpaged, color illustrations

   Multicolored drawings show the wind blowing the things that are
   told about in the story. The kite, boy's hat, windmill, bird,
   cloud, storm, sailboat, mountain and the wind goes on and on
   until finally it grows gentle and sleeps.

14. Rain Drop Splash
     Tresselt, Alvin
     Illustrated by Leonard Weisgard
     Lothrop, Lee and Shepard Inc., New York

   Drip, drip the rain went on and on. It rained on the flowers,
   animals and frogs in the woods. It rained on the pond which
   ran down the mountain. It rained on the lake which flooded
   a meadow and road near a farm and church. It rained in the
   city and finally ran down the river and into the sea. Large
   black, white, yellow and brown drawings.

15. _Sky Dragon_
    Wegen, Ronald
    Illustrated by author
    Greenwillow Books, New York, 1982
    24 pages, color illustrations

    Don't let this title fool you!   This book is not about dragons.
    It's a lovely book about three children who use their imaginations
    and see animal shapes in the cloudy sky.   In the morning after
    a snow, they begin to build a snow fort that turns into a wonderful
    snow dragon.   There are very few words in this book and the
    ones that are included are in huge type!

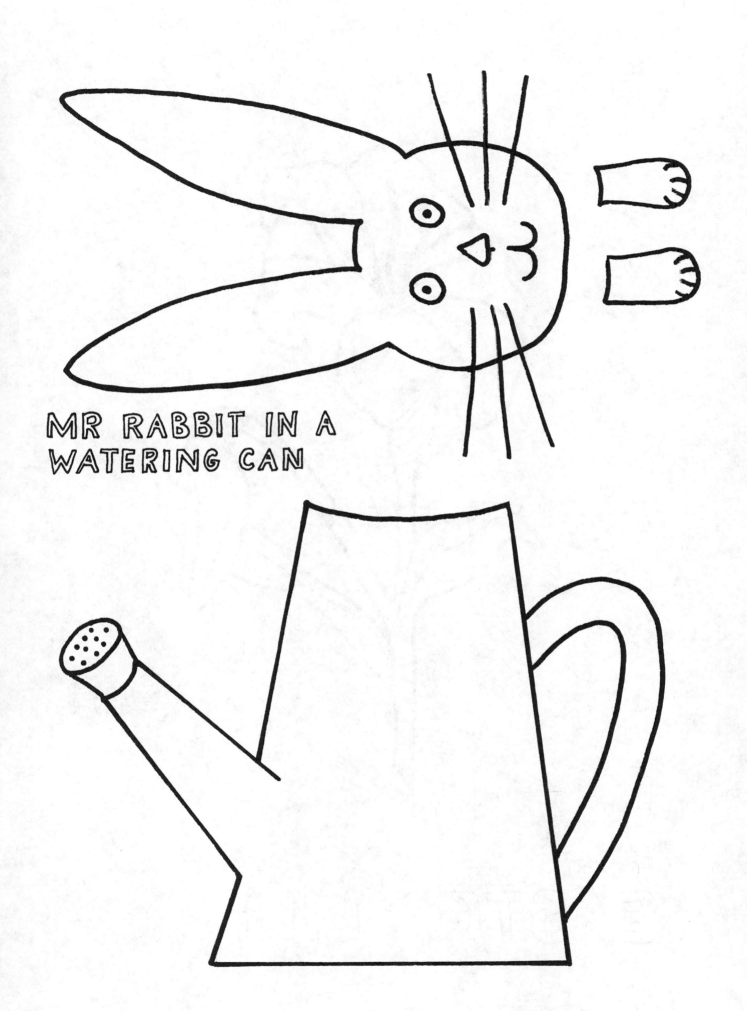

MR RABBIT IN A
WATERING CAN

EASTER LILY

UMBRELLA

RAINDROP
PUPPET

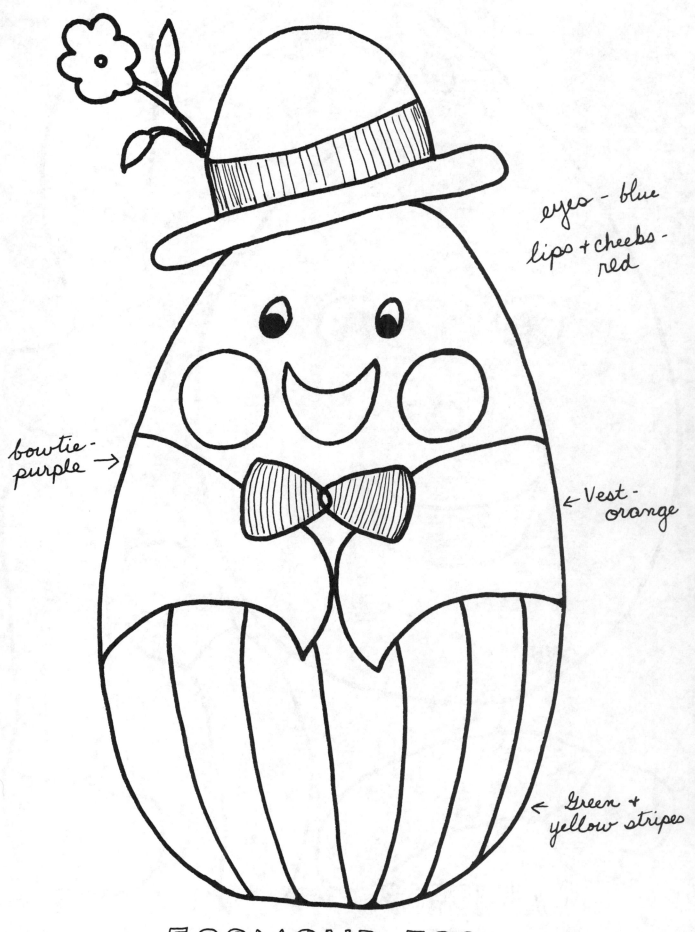

eyes - blue
lips + cheeks - red

bowtie - purple →

← Vest - orange

← Green + yellow stripes

EGGMOND EGG

Dear Parents:

May is beautiful! We celebrate Mother's Day and welcome the lovely flowers.

ART
May Basket
Surprise for Mother!

SOCIAL STUDIES
Memorial Day
Armed Forces Day
Mother's Day
Victoria Day

MATH COOKING
Hand cookies
Homemade butter

BOOKS FROM THE LIBRARY

MUSIC
Happy Mother's Day

LITERATURE
Mother's Day poems and stories

HAPPY MAY!

SUGGESTED DAILY LEARNING PLANS

MAY

Parent Page ART - Mother's Day Plant MUSIC - ACTION - "Happy Mother's Day" SOCIAL STUDIES - Discuss "May" and "May Holidays" PHYS. ED. - Exercises 1-2 BOOK - Anno's Counting Book by Mitsumasa Anno	ART - Flower Garden LITERATURE - STORY - "A Mother's Day Story" - NURSERY RHYME - "Old Woman" PHYS. ED. - Exercises 1-2 (five time) & B BOOK - Blue Bug's Surprise by Virginia Poulet	ART - (Complete) Flower Garden LITERATURE - Recall "A Mother's Day Story" SCIENCE - Discuss "See, Hear and Smell Spring PHYS. ED. - Exercises 1-3 BOOK - My Mother and I by Aileen Fisher	ART - Bookmarks For Mother LITERATURE - ACTION POEM - "For Mother's Day" PHYS. ED. - Exercises 1-4 & B MATH COOKING - Hand Cookies BOOK - My Hands by Aliki	ART - May Basket LITERATURE - FINGER PLAY - "The Garden" SCIENCE - Recall discussion "See, Hear and Smell Spring" PHYS. ED. - Exercises 1-4
ART - (Complete) May Basket LITERATURE - POEMS - "Flowers For Mother" and "Mom, You Are So Nice" PHYS. ED. - Exercises 1-4 BOOK - Blue Bug To The Rescue by Virginia Poulet	ART - Mother's Day Cards LITERATURE - POEM - "I Love You Mom" SOCIAL STUDIES - Discuss "Victoria Day" PHYS. ED. - Exercises 1-4 MATH COOKING - Suckers BOOK - Who Likes The Sun? by Beatrice S. DeRegniers	ART - (Complete) Mother's Day Cards LITERATURE - POEM - "A Bouquet for Mother" & "To Mother" PHYS. ED. - Exercises 1-5 & B	ART - Pin Cushion LITERATURE - POEM - "Rainy Days" and "After The Rain" PHYS. ED. - Exercises 1-5 (do as if you are a baby) BOOK - Really Spring by Gene Zion	ART - (Complete) Pin Cushion LITERATURE - FINGER PLAY - "Our Umbrella Will Keep Us Dry" SOCIAL STUDIES - Discuss "Decoration and Armed Forces Day" PHYS. ED. - Exercises 1-5 BOOK - Grandpa And Me by Patricia L. Gauch
ART - Note & Pencil Holder MUSIC - ACTION - "This Is The Way PHYS. ED. - Exercises 1-6 MATH COOKING - Homemade Butter BOOK - Grandpa And Me by Patricia Lee Gauch	ART - Bird House LITERATURE - FINGER PLAY - "Little Birds" & "Mr. Carrot" SCIENCE - Activity - Let's Watch Seeds Grow PHYS. ED. - Exercises 1-7 (do quietly, do noisily)	ART - Tulip Time LITERATURE - POEM - "May Flowers" - FINGER PLAY - "Rain Helps The Flowers Grow" PHYS. ED. - Exercises 1-7 (do big; do small) MATH COOKING - Wheaties Treat BOOK - Spring Time For Jeanne-Marie by Francoise	ART - Fabric & Pipe Cleaner Flowers LITERATURE - POEM - "My Little Garden" PHYS. ED. - Exercises 1-8 & B (do as if you are a giant) BOOK - Sun Up by Alvin R. Tresselt	ART - Silhouettes LITERATURE - FINGER PLAY - "Eensy, Weensy Spider" PHYS. ED. - Exercises 1-8 BOOK - Who Took The Farmer's Hat by Joan L. Nodset
ART - (Complete) Silhouettes LITERATURE - Recall "Eensy, Weensy Spider" SCIENCE - Activity - (Continue) "Let's Watch Seeds Grow" PHYS. ED. - Exercises 1-8 & B	ART - Nature Walk Collage LITERATURE - FINGER PLAY - "My Garden" PHYS. ED. - Exercises 1-8 BOOK - Beneath Your Feet by Seymour Simon	ART - Make A Farm Book LITERATURE - NURSERY RHYME "Old Woman Under The Hill" PHYS. ED. - Exercises 1-8 MATH COOKING - Haystacks BOOK - My Day On The Farm by Chiyoko Makatani	ART - Farmer and Tractor PHYS. ED. - Exercises 1-8 & B BOOK - Blueberries For Sal by Robert McCloskey	ART - (Complete) Farmer and Tractor PHYS. ED. - Exercises 1-8 (do slow, do fast) BOOK - Blue Bug's Vegetable Garden by Virginia Poulet

I. ART

Children will develop skills in:

    Organization

    Sequence

    Use of small muscles (small motor)

A. A BIRDHOUSE

Cut birdhouse from 4" piece of red construction paper. Paste on white 9" x 12" construction paper. Draw brown or black pole. Draw and color grass. Draw and color flowers and birds.

B. **A FLOWER GARDEN**

Cut green construction paper 3" wide and 18" long. Fringe the green paper for the grass. Cut five stems for flowers, ½" x 6". Cut ten leaves, two for each flower.

Using yellow and pink construction paper, cut flowers. Using a 3" square of paper, fold in half, and fold in half again. Round off corners, fringe. Cut five flowers.

Paste grass on 12" x 18" sheet of blue construction paper. Paste stems on paper, approximately 3" apart. Paste leaves on stems and paste flowers on top.

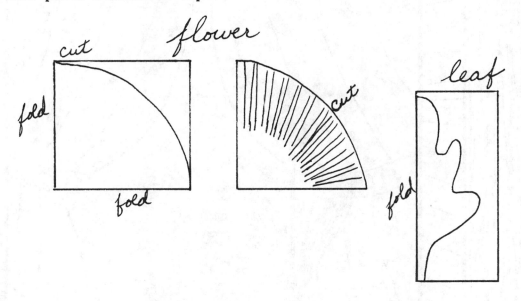

C. TULIP TIME

Using flower pot pattern, trace on brown paper. Trace tulip from colored paper. Cut stem and leaves out of green construction paper.

Paste leaves and stem on flower pot. Paste tulip on stem.

D. <u>MAY BASKET</u>

Copy basket pattern on brown construction paper. Cut out basket.

For flowers: Cut out circles or squares of various colors of crepe or tissue paper. Put two or three pieces together to give a layered look. Pinch all layers together in the middle. Tightly Wrap one end of a pipe cleaner around the pinched paper. Paste one or two leaves on the pipe cleaner to finish the stem.

Make four or five flowers to put in the basket.

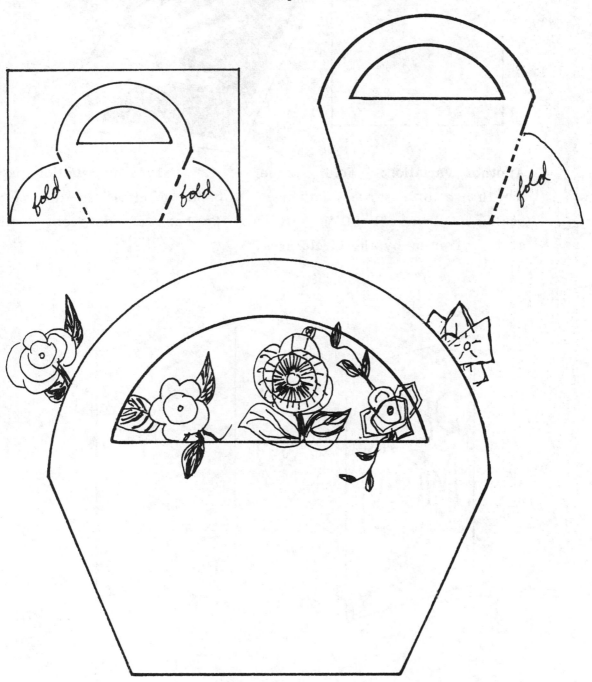

E.   MOTHER'S DAY CARDS

Fold white construction paper in half. Dip hand in pan of paint and press on paper. When the hand print is dry, open the card. Write "Happy Mother's Day" inside and sign.

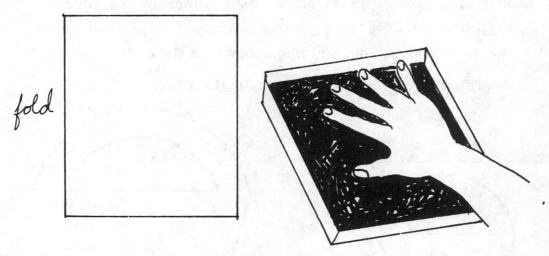

Another variation: Fold a sheet of 12" x 18" construction paper lengthwise into three sections. Cut out a circle in the middle section. Print "I LOVE YOU" on the back of the front section so it is framed by the circle area.

F. **A PIN CUSHION FOR MOTHER**

Fill a washed peanut butter jar lid with cotton. Cut out a circle of material large enough to fit over the cotton and cover the sides of the lid.

Put glue on the sides of the lid and hold material in place until the glue starts to hold.

Tie ribbon or colorful yarn around the lid.

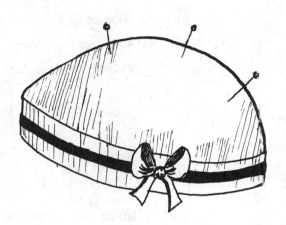

G. **PAPER PLATE NOTE AND PENCIL HOLDER**

Cut a paper plate in half. Decorate the underside of the half paper plate. Decorate one half of a whole paper plate. Then staple the half plate to the whole plate with the decorated areas showing. Tie a piece of ribbon or yarn on the pencil and staple the other end to the half plate. Staple a short piece of ribbon or yarn to the top of the plate so it can be hung on a hook or nail. Place a small pad of paper on the plate half so it is easily available.

H. BOOKMARKS FOR MOTHER

Cut felt into 1½" x 10" strip.
With yarn in needle, overcast all
around bookmark. Finish off the
top with a yarn tassel.

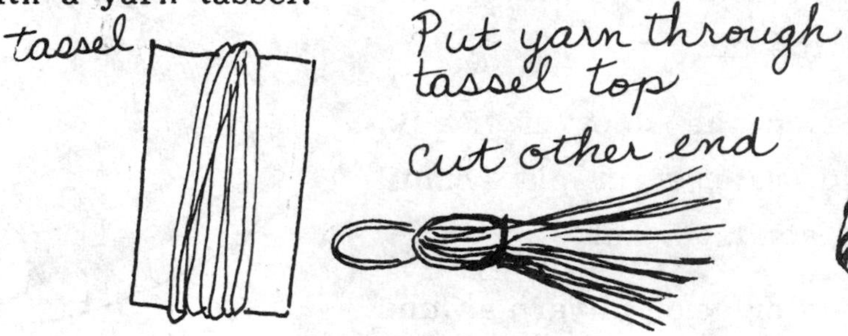

tassel

*Put yarn through
tassel top
Cut other end*

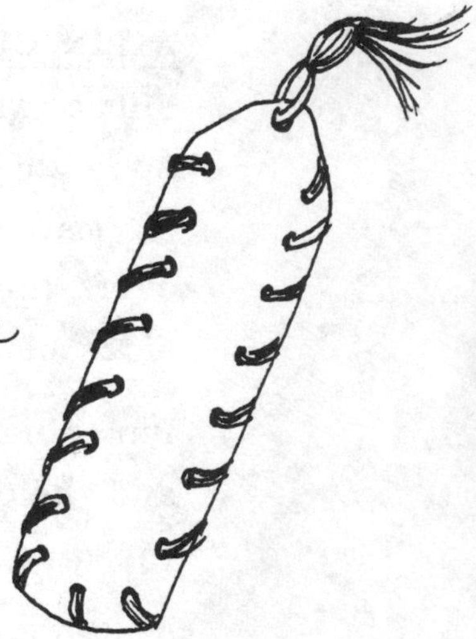

Cut ribbon to measure 1" x 10"
strip. Cut letters to spell
MOTHER from gold or silver
paper. Paste letters on ribbon.

MOTHER

Cut ribbon to measure 1" x 10"
strip. Cut heart out of pink
or white paper. Write "I LOVE
YOU" on the heart and paste it
on the ribbon.

I LOVE YOU

I.   MOTHER'S DAY PLANT

A couple of weeks before Mother's Day, have children plant several
seeds of marigolds, petunias, geraniums, etc. in a foam cup filled
with potting soil.   Water according to instructions.   Seeds should
start to sprout so that plant could be taken home as a gift for
mother.

Optional: Tie a ribbon around the foam cup or wrap tissue paper
around the cup.

J. FABRIC AND PIPE CLEANER FLOWERS

If there isn't time to grow a flower for mother, collect colorful fabrics to make some fabric flowers.

Bend the pipe cleaners in a petal shape. Glue fabric under the pipe cleaner. When dry, trim excess fabric away. Use a pipe cleaner for the stem. Make a circle at one end and glue to the petal. Glue foam block to bottom of cup. Poke flower stem into block. Make several flowers.

Bend pipe cleaner

glue fabric underneath

trim when dry

stem

glue to fabric petal.

K. SILHOUETTES

Tape a sheet of 12" x 18" black construction paper on the wall in a dark room. Have the child sit in front of the strong light so that his or her profile is clearly outlined on the black paper. Then carefully trace along the outline. When finished, remove from the wall and carefully cut out the silhouette. Mount this on white paper. Great for Mother's Day gift!

L. NATURE WALK COLLAGE

Plan a nature walk to a field and wooded area. Give each child a plastic bag. Discuss some things they should be watching for: seeds, twigs, pods, stems, buds, etc. Have them put the things they collect in the bag.

When they return from the nature walk, place items collected on construction paper. Glue onto paper. You may want to label items.

M. MAKE A FARM BOOK

This will take a week or two to complete. One day at a time, discuss a farm animal. Show a picture of the selected animal. Perhaps read a story about this animal. Discuss what it looks like, its habits, etc. Have children draw a picture using information that has been discussed. Have children write a comment on each page. (Give help with this if necessary.)

N. FARMER AND TRACTOR

Paste an orange rectangle and small orange square on a sheet of 12" x 18" construction paper.

Paste circles on to make tractor tires.   Draw a farmer driving the tractor.

MATERIALS CHART

MAY

A. A BIRD HOUSE
Red construction paper
9"x12" white construction paper
Crayons

B. A FLOWER GARDEN
Green construction paper
Yellow construction paper
Pink construction paper
12"x18" blue construction paper
Paste

C. TULIP TIME
Brown paper
Colored paper
Green paper
Paste

D. MAY BASKET
Brown construction paper
Assorted crepe/tissue paper
Pipe cleaners
Paste
Green paper

E. MOTHER'S DAY CARDS
White construction paper
Shallow pan
Paint
12"x18" construction paper

F. A PIN CUSHION FOR MOTHER
Peanut butter jar lid
Cotton
Cloth material
Glue
Ribbon/yarn

G. PAPER PLATE NOTE AND
PENCIL HOLDER
Paper plates
Crayons
Staple
Ribbon/yarn
Pencil
Small pad of paper

H. BOOKMARKS FOR MOTHER
Felt
Yarn
Needle
Ribbon
Paste
Pink/white paper
Gold/silver paper

I. MOTHER'S DAY PLANT
Flower seeds
Foam cup
Potting soil
Ribbon/tissue paper

J. FABRIC AND PIPE CLEANER
FLOWERS
Colorful fabric
Pipe cleaner
Glue

K. SILHOUETTES
12"x18" black construction paper
Strong light
White paper

L. NATURE WALK COLLAGE
Plastic bag
Construction paper
Nature walk collection
Glue

M. MAKE A FARM BOOK
Crayons
Construction paper

N. FARMER AND TRACTOR
Paste
Orange paper
12"x18" construction paper
Crayons

II. LITERATURE

Children will develop the ability to identify and enjoy:

Characters

Main ideas

Details

Sequence of events

A. A MOTHER'S DAY STORY

Betsy and her little brother, Tim, had a big problem. They knew Mother's Day was coming. They wanted to do something special for their mother because they wanted to show how much they loved her.

Betsy had planted some seeds in a plastic carton in school, and now she had a nice little plant to give to her mother. The teacher had all the children plant some flower seeds at the beginning of the month. They had watered them and then placed the containers in the sun. Before they knew it, the plants were growing tall and strong.

Betsy also had a nice card that she had made in school. She had drawn some pretty pictures on it and she had printed "Dear Mom, We love you." She had signed her name and Tim's. Tim didn't go to school yet.

The children would love to buy their mother a nice bottle of perfume, or maybe the bracelet she had admired in the store. Their big problem was they didn't have enough money.

Betsy and Tim thought and thought. They had to come up with an idea for something special.

Betsy jumped up and shouted, "I've got it!"

She said it so loud she startled Tim and he almost fell off his chair.

"Tell me, tell me," he said. "What'll we do?"

"We'll make her a coupon book," Betsy said.

"A coupon book?" said Tim. "What's that?"

Betsy explained, "We'll get some pieces of paper that are about the size of tickets. We'll staple them together at one end like a book. Do you understand?"

Tim shook his head to say "no", so Betsy continued to explain.

"On each ticket we'll print something we can do to help mom."

"I can't print," said Tim sadly.

"I know," said Betsy. "**You** can draw some pretty flowers on the cover."

"Then on each ticket I'll print something that we can do to help mom around the house. For example, on one ticket I can print "COUPON -- GOOD FOR WASHING DINNER DISHES.""

"Or a coupon could be good for dusting the house, or running the vacuum," said Tim excitedly, as he caught on.

Betsy and Tim worked on the coupon book. In a little while they had it filled with all kinds of errands and jobs they could do to help their mother. They could hardly wait for Mother's Day to come. They'd give their mother the plant and the card and the coupon book. Most important they wanted to give their mom a big hug and kiss and tell her that they loved her today and every day.

POEMS/FINGER PLAYS/NURSERY RHYMES

Children will develop the ability to participate in and enjoy:

Rhythm

Poetry

Sequence

Characters

B.   POEMS

1.   FLOWERS FOR MOTHER

These flowers are so pretty.

They're red, and white, and blue.

I love you with all my heart.

So, I give them all to you.

2.   MOM, YOU ARE SO NICE

You are so nice,

I want you to know

You're my special Mom,

And I love you so.

3.   I LOVE YOU, MOM

Mother, when you smile at me,

I'm just as happy as I can be.

For all the nice things that we share.

For all your love and tender care.

Here's something important I want to say.

I love you more every day.

4. <u>A BOUQUET FOR MOTHER</u>

Dear Mom,

I picked these flowers just for you

To make a nice bouquet.

To let you know you are the best.

Today and every day.

5. <u>TO MOTHER, ON HER SPECIAL DAY</u>

Dear Mother on your special day,

I want to say, "Thank you."

For all your love and guidance

And the fun we have had, too.

And I want you to know,

That today and every day.

I love you so.

C. POEMS FOR SPRING

1. RAINY DAYS

Rainy days aren't fun at all,
For little girls and boys.
For they must stay inside and play,
With puzzles and other toys.
But when, at last, the clouds are gone,
And the sun begins to shine,
The children run outside and play,
And everything is fine.

2. AFTER THE RAIN

When it rains and there's puddles on the ground,
Mother says, "Be careful, there's water all around."
So I'll be very careful, when I play and run,
I'll step right in the middle of every one!

3. MAY FLOWERS

April brought us showers,
But it is plain to see,
That May will bring us flowers
That are pretty as can be.

D. FINGER PLAYS

1. EENSY, WEENSY SPIDER

An eensy, weensy spider (Opposite thumb and pointer fingers)
Climbed up the waterspout, (Climb up each other.)
Down came the rain
And washed the spider out. (Hands sweep down.)
Out came the sunshine (Arms form circle overhead.)
And dried up all the rain (Arms sweep upward.)
And the eensy, weensy spider
Climbed up the spout again. (As above.)

2. THE GARDEN

(Teacher picks "farmer." The other children are grouped
together. The "farmer" takes children one at a time and
places them in a row. Each child crouches down when placed
in the row.) Teacher and children chant together.

See the farmer plant the seeds,
    plant the seeds, plant the seeds.
See the farmer plant the seeds, He plants them in a row.
Now he has to water them, water them, water them.
Now he has to water them so the seeds will start to grow.
Then the seeds will start to grow,
    start to grow, start to grow.
Then the seeds will start to grow. Grow up big and tall.
See how big and tall they are, tall they are, tall they are.
See how big and tall they are, standing in a row.
The farmer is so very proud, very proud, very proud.
The farmer is so very proud to see his garden grow.

3. <u>MY LITTLE GARDEN</u>

In my little garden bed (Extend one hand, palm up.)
Raked so nicely over (Use three fingers for rake.)
First the tiny seeds I plant.
Then with soft earth cover, (Use planting, covering motion.)
Shining down, the great round sun (Circle with arms.)
Smiles upon it often.
Little raindrops, pattering down, (Flutter fingers.)
Help the seeds to soften.
Then the little plant awakes,
Down the roots go creeping, (Fingers downward.)
Up it lifts its little head
  (Fingers held close together point upward.)
Through the brown earth peeping.
High and higher still it grows,
  (Raise arms, fingers still cupped.)
Through the summer hours.
Till some happy day the buds
Open into flowers. (Spread fingers.)

4. <u>MISTER CARROT</u>

Nice Mister Carrot
Makes curly hair, (Hand on head.)
His head grows underneath the ground (Bob head.)
His feet up in the air. (Raise feet.)
And early in the morning
I find him in his bed (Close eyes, lay head on hands.)
And give his feet a great big pull (Stretch legs out.)
And out comes his head!

5.　MY GARDEN

This is my garden, (Extend one hand forward, palm up.)
I'll rake it with care.

　　(Make raking motion on palm with three fingers of other
　　hand.)

And them some flower seeds (Plant motion.)
I'll plant in there.
The sun will shine (Make circle with hands.)
And the rain will fall.　(Let fingers flutter down to lap.)
And my garden will blossom

　　(Cup hands together, extend upward slowly.)

And grow straight and tall.

6.　RAIN HELPS THE FLOWERS GROW

First, the rains come down, (Hands make rain; wiggle fingers.)
Then the sun comes out.　(One hand held up for sun.)
And soon the flowers begin to sprout.

　　(Whole body crouched down; start to stand slowly.)

They grow and they grow
And the bud opens wide.

　　(Hands and arms together in front; move slowly apart.)

Then we see the pretty flower inside.

　　(Hands and arms spread apart for flower.)

7. <u>OUR UMBRELLA WILL KEEP US DRY</u>

Here comes a cloud, 'way up high in the sky.

    (Raise one hand for cloud.)

See the rain fall as it goes sailing by.

    (Lower hand, wiggle fingers.)

We're going to get wet. Oh, me, oh, my!

    (Hands over head to cover it.)

So we'll put up our umbrella,

    (Action of putting up umbrella; holding it while walking

    around.)

To keep us nice and dry.

8. <u>LITTLE BIRDS</u>

Fly, little birds, fly. (Children move arms like wings.)

Fly 'way up high in the sky. (Move around room.)

Look for a place to rest. (Looking around as they move.)

Find a tree to make a nest.

Pick a partner, one, two, three, (Find a partner.)

Sit together in a tree. (Partners sit together on floor.)

E.   NURSERY RHYMES

1.   OLD WOMAN

There was an old woman who lived in a shoe.

She had so many children, she didn't know what to do.

She gave them some soup without any bread.

She told them three stories and sent them to bed.

2.   OLD WOMAN UNDER THE HILL

There was an old woman
Who lived under a hill.
And if she's not gone,
She lives there still.

III. MUSIC

Children will develop the ability to participate in and enjoy music.

A. **THIS IS THE WAY**

(Tune: This Is The Way We Wash The Clothes)

This is the way I make my bed, make my bed, make my bed.

This is the way I make my bed. (Making bed.)

I am my mother's helper.

This is the way I dust the house, dust the house, dust the house.

This is the way I dust the house. (Dusting motion.)

I am my mother's helper.

This is the way I set the table, set the table, set the table.

This is the way I set the table. (Setting table.)

I am my mother's helper.

This is the way she hugs me tight, hugs me tight, hugs me tight.

This is the way she hugs me tight. (Hug yourself.)

Because I am her helper.

B. **HAPPY MOTHER'S DAY**

(Tune: Yankee Doodle)

I'll pick some flowers for my mom,

To make a nice bouquet. (Pick flowers.)

I'll give her a smile, (Smile.)

And a hug, (Hug self.)

And say, "Happy Mother's Day."

  (Raise voices on "Happy Mother's Day.")

IV. SCIENCE

Children will develop skills in:

Distinguishing differences

Similarities of attributes

A. SEE AND LISTEN AND SMELL SPRING

What happens in the spring? Birds return from the south. Watch for the first robin in the spring. Also, watch for the new green shoots that are starting to push up through the soil. Tulips and crocuses are early flowers and can be seen when spring starts. Trees and bushes are starting to show buds and the grass is changing from brown to a bright, fresh green color. In the fields and lawns, we start to see many, many bright, yellow dandelions.

Listen to the sounds of spring. Enjoy singing of many different kinds of birds and croaking of frogs in the ponds and streams. As the weather grows warmer, listen to the buzzing of bees and insects as they fly through the air. Listen to the sound of raindrops as they hit the window, or fall splashing on the street. Listen to the wind as it whistles through the trees and the loud rolling sound of thunder during a spring storm.

There are special smells to spring. The fresh smell in the air of early morning. The smell when the spring rain is falling. Freshly cut grass has a distinct smell, too, and we must remember the sweet fragrances of lovely flowers that are starting to bloom.

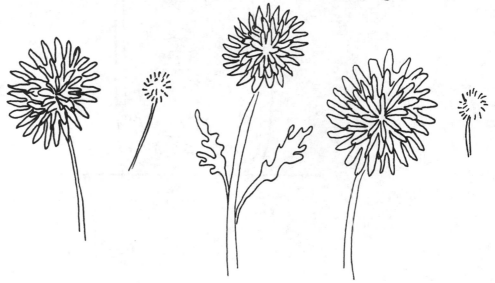

B. SCIENCE ACTIVITY

Place a different kind of seed in each straight-sided jar. Hold the seeds against the side of the jar with blotting paper or paper toweling that has been dampened. Label the jar with the kind of seed: carrot, lettuce, radish, corn or lima beans.

Make sure the paper in the jar stays damp or the seeds will die.

Children will enjoy checking the daily progress of all the seeds.

V. SOCIAL STUDIES

Children will develop an awareness of:

Holidays

Traditions

Seasonal changes

A. MAY

May is one of the most welcome and most beautiful months of the year. The ice and snow of winter is gone. The sun has warmed the earth and the birds are nesting in the trees. The first green shoots are poking through and some of the wild flowers are in bloom.

Many, many years ago, in ancient times in Rome, May 1st was a day for outdoor festivals. It was celebrated with flower-decked parades. In another part of the world, the English celebrated May by erecting Maypoles which they trimmed with Hawthorne blossoms or Mayflowers. They danced around the Maypoles to welcome spring.

We have several days in May which are special to the people in the United States. May 30th is observed as Memorial Day, or Decoration Day. This day was first designated as a legal holiday in 1869. On this day, we honor the memory of those who died in the Korean War, World War I, World War II, the Spanish-American War, the Civil War and the Vietnam Conflict.

The third Saturday of the month is Armed Forces Day. The people of the United States honor the men and women of the military services.

B. <u>VICTORIA DAY</u>

Victoria Day is a special day celebrated in Canada and in England to honor Queen Victoria, who was born on May 24, 1819. The people of the British Commonwealth have always celebrated the birthday of the ruling monarch. Queen Victoria was such a popular ruler that her birthday came to have a special meaning. After her death in 1901, people continued to celebrate her birthday.

In the early 1900's, the people of Canada combined Queen Victoria's Birthday and Empire Day, which was May 25th. In this way they could honor Queen Victoria and the British Empire at the same time.

Canadians now celebrate Victoria Day and the official birthday of the reigning monarch as a legal holiday on May 24th, or the Monday before that date. This is often the weekend when summer activities begin and recreational locations open for the summer season. Usually this event is celebrated with fireworks in the evening.

VI. MAY PHYSICAL EDUCATION FUN

Children will develop skills in:

Rhythm

Imaging

Use of large and small muscles

Good sports conduct

A. **MOVE AS IF YOU ARE:**

1. Dusting furniture.

2. Washing dishes, pots and pans.

3. A baby grasshopper.

4. Vacuuming.

5. Emptying the garbage.

6. Washing walls.

7. A little tiny dog.

8. Swimming.

B. **BIG BALL ROLL**

Tape a "start" line and a "finish" line on the floor (or carpet). Children stand or sit on start line and roll a large ball to the finish line. If it does not go over the finish line, they must do it again. If you are using this as a relay, they go to the other end and pick up the ball and give it to the next child.

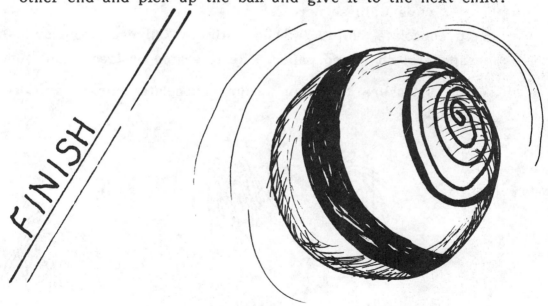

VI. MATH COOKING

Children will develop skills in:

     Number awareness

     Counting

     Measuring

A.   HOMEMADE BUTTER

     Small sterilized baby food jars

     Heavy whipping cream

     Salt

Pour about 2 oz. of whipping cream into each baby food jar. Let each child shake the jar. Children will continue to shake jars until: the cream looks whipped, flecks of butter begin to appear, and they feel a lump forming in the jar.

Drain off the milk. Add a little salt. Use on crackers or biscuits.

Math: Group count shakes of jar; teacher puts marks on board each time children get to 10 or 20 or 100. How many shakes did it take?

B.   HAYSTACKS

     12 oz. pkg. semi-sweet or milk chocolate chips

     2 cups Chinese noodles

Melt chocolate chips. Then, stir in Chinese noodles. Drop by teaspoonful on waxed paper. Refrigerator or freeze and serve.

Math: Measure two cups; count chocolate chips; count completed haystacks.

C. <u>WHEATIES TREAT</u>

       12 oz. pkg. chocolate chips
       4 cups Wheaties®

Melt chocolate chips (over hot water). Gently mix in four cups of Wheaties® Drop by tablespoonful on waxed paper. Place in refrigerator to set.

Math: Count chocolate chips; measure four cups; count Wheaties® treats. Are there enough for each child to have one?

D. <u>HAND COOKIES</u>

       ½ cup shortening (half butter or margarine, softened)

1 cup sugar	1 t. baking powder
1 egg	½ t. soda
1 t. vanilla	½ t. salt
2 ⅔ cup flour	¼ t. nutmeg
	½ cup sour cream

Heat oven to 425°. Mix shortening, sugar, egg and vanilla. Blend in remaining ingredients. Divide dough into three parts. Roll each part ¼" thick on a floured board. Trace around child's hand. Cut remaining dough into hands. Bake 6-8 minutes. Cool. Decorate as desired.

Yield: approximately six hand cookies and one dozen 2" cookies.

Optional: For chocolate cookies mix one part dough with one ounce unsweetened chocolate. For peanut butter, mix one part dough with one tablespoon peanut butter.

Math: Discuss measurements; decide how to divide dough into three "equal" parts. Show children what "equal" means.

E.   SUCKERS

        1 cup water

        1 cup sugar

        $\frac{2}{3}$ cup plus 2 T. light corn syrup

        2 T. butter

        3 t. flavoring; root beer, cherry, butterscotch, etc.

        Food coloring (to match flavor)

        Popsicle or sucker sticks

Brush a baking sheet, parchment paper or sucker molds with butter.   Place sucker sticks on surface.   Leave enough room to allow space between suckers.

Combine first five ingredients and cook to hard crack stage.   Add food coloring.   Pour or spoon mixture so suckers do not touch.

Math: Count ingredients; count sticks.

READ ALOUD BOOKS FROM THE LIBRARY

MAY

Children will develop the ability to enjoy and gain knowledge from books.

1. My Hands

    Aliki

    Thomas Y. Crowell Company, New York, 1962

    > This is a Let's-Read-And-Find-Out Science Book. Children find out wonderful uses of hands and fingers.

2. Anno's Counting Book

    Anno, Mitsumasa

    Thomas Y. Crowell Company, New York, 1976

    28 pages

    > Beautifully illustrated (no words) counting book. Mr. Anno, one of Japan's leading illustrators and book designers, shows the growth in a village and countryside by adding buildings and groups of plants, animals, pictures and cubes to illustrate number.

3. Who Likes The Sun?

    DeRegniers, Beatrice Schenk

    Woodcuts by Leona Pierce

    Harcourt Brace and World, New York, 1961

    Unpaged

    > A child thanks the sun for shadows and warmth. She appreciates the flowers, light and animals. She writes and encourages other children to write a "Sun Song."

4. __My Mother and I__
   Fisher, Aileen
   Illustrated by Kazue Muzumura
   New York, 1967

   > A story written in rhyme. A young girl returns from school to find her mother has gone to help the girl's sick grandmother. The girl visits insects, flowers and animals and thinks about their mothers. She is happy when her mother returns.

5. __Spring Time For Jeanne-Marie__
   Francoise (pseud.)
   Scribner, New York, 1955
   Unpaged
   (Author's full name: Francoise Seignobose)

   > Jeanne-Marie and her sheep search for Jeanne-Marie's duck. They ask the postman, school children and fisherman. Finally, Jean-Pierre, a boy on a boat, takes Jeanne-Marie and her sheep down the river to ask everyone they meet about the duck. They all say "No", they haven't seen the duck. Finally, they find the duck and make a new friend of the boat boy.

6. __Grandpa and Me__
   Gauch, Patricia Lee
   Drawings by Symeon Shimin
   Coward, McCann, Geoghegan Inc., New York, 1972

   > A story in unrhymed verse tells of a small boy and his grandfather at the lake during the summer and how they share their thoughts and experiences.

7. Blueberries For Sal
McCloskey, Robert
Illustrated by the author
Viking Press, 1948
55 pages

> Sally mistakes the mother bear for her mother, and mother mistakes the cub bear for Sally when they are all hunting for blueberries. It comes out all right by the end of this delightful story.

8. My Day On The Farm
Nakatani, Chiyoko
Illustrated by the author
Thomas Y. Crowell Company, New York, 1976
29 pages, color illustrations

> A young boy and his mother visit a farm. He sees the cows, sheep and goats. He also visits the pig and her piglets. He stays long enough to see how each type of animal goes to sleep.

9. Who Took The Farmer's Hat
Nodset, Joan L.
Illustrated by Fritz Siebel
Harper and Row, New York, 1963
31 pages, illustrations

> A sentence or two on each page tells the story of a farmer who looks all over the farm to find his old brown hat. He talks to all of the birds and animals on the farm. Finally, he sees that a bird has been using it for a nest and has layed a beautiful little egg in it. He buys a new brown hat!

10. <u>Blue Bug To The Rescue</u>
    Poulet, Virginia
    Illustrated by Mary Maloney and Stan Fleming
    Children's Press, Chicago, 1976
    31 pages, illustrations

    Blue Bug warns the other bugs about poisonous plants in the garden. He stops them one by one from eating the toxic plants. The pictures of the plants and bugs are very large and will help children recognize the bugs and the toxic plants. The last two pages have the pictures and names of eleven toxic plants. Each page of the book has only one or two words on it.

11. <u>Blue Bug's Surprise</u>
    Poulet, Virginia
    Illustrated by Mary Maloney and Stan Fleming
    Children's Press, Chicago, 1977
    31 pages, color illustrations

    Blue Bug picked one each of twelve different types of flowers to give his friend, Freebee the Bee. Freebee gave Blue Bug a big kiss in return. Very few words and a gentle story with many learning opportunities make this typical of all of the Blue Bug Books. Each flower is drawn so that it's name can be learned by little children.

12. <u>Blue Bug's Vegetable Garden</u>
    Poulet, Virginia
    Illustrated by Donald Charles
    Children's Press, Chicago, 1973
    31 pages, color illustrations

    Very few words and the pictures tell the story of Blue Bug, who looked all over the vegetable garden for a certain vegetable. As he looked, he passed by corn, a beet, beans, carrots, tomatoes, cucumbers, a pumpkin, peas and turnips until he finally found his favorite -- the onion. Strong illustrations and words indicating directions make this an excellent book for very young children.

13. Beneath Your Feet
Simon, Seymour
Illustrated by Daniel Nevins
Walker and Company

A book about soil that is as interesting to the young listener as it is to the adult reader. It includes many simple observations, exercises and experiments, as well as easy to read background information on different types of soil, its components and from where it comes.

14. Sun Up
Tresselt, Alvin R.
Illustrated by Roger Duvoisin
Lothrop, New York, 1949
Unpaged, illustrations

The farm wakes up to a bright summer day which becomes hotter and hotter. In the afternoon, it gets even hotter until a summer shower brings welcome rain and relief. All is clear by the end of the day when the farm residents go back to sleep.

15. Really Spring
Zion, Gene
Pictures by Margaret Bly Graham
Harper and Row, New York, 1956

Large print and pictures. A little boy is the catalyst for a huge city-wide spring clean-up, paint-up, fix-up effort. Soon, nature imitated the flowers and leaves that had been painted all over town.

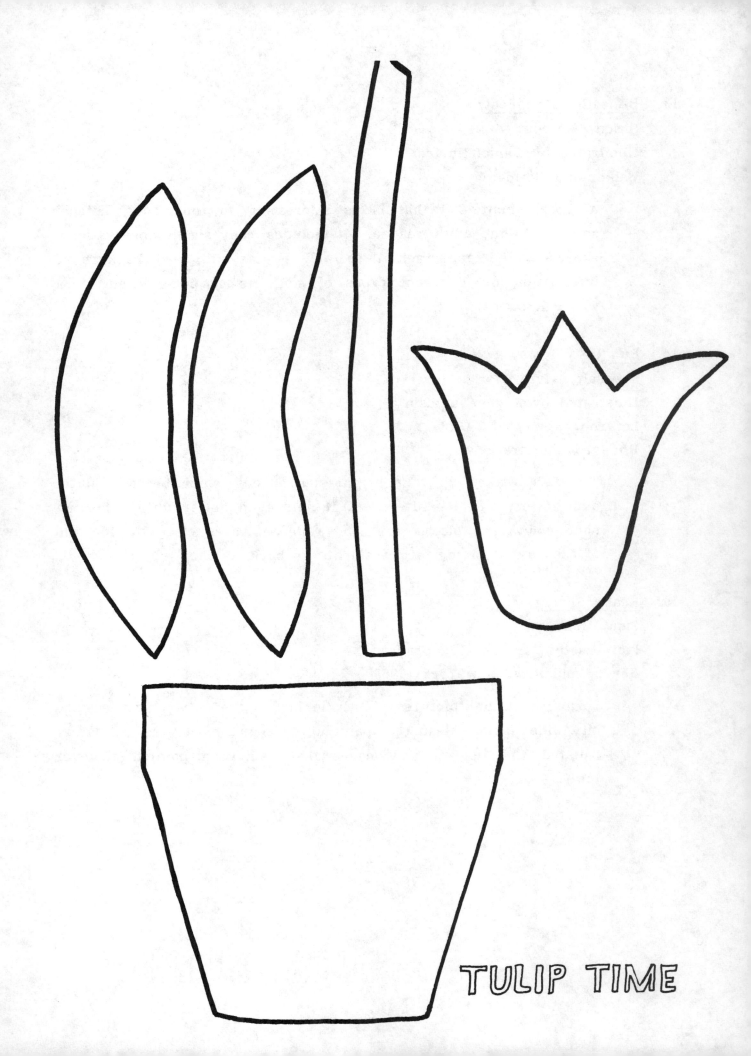

TULIP TIME

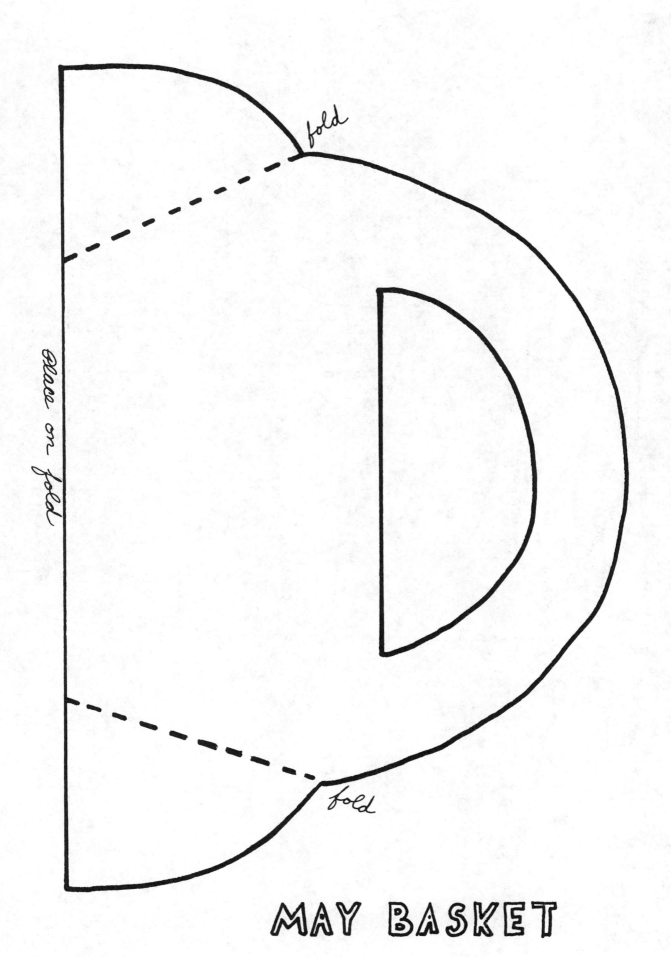

fold

Place on fold

fold

MAY BASKET

JUNE

Dear Parents:

June is the beginning of summer. We celebrate Father's day and Flag Day!

SCIENCE
Fireflies and warm weather
Why do we need the sun?

SOCIAL STUDIES
Flag Day and
Father's Day

BOOKS FROM THE LIBRARY

ART
Horrible Harry
Birds and more birds

MATH COOKING
Number and Alphabet Pretzels

PHYSICAL EDUCATION
Pushing and pulling

LITERATURE
Father's Day Poems

HAPPY JUNE!

SUGGESTED DAILY LEARNING PLANS

JUNE

Week	Day 1	Day 2	Day 3	Day 4	Day 5
1	Parent Page ART – Spool Flowers LITERATURE – POEM – "Happy Father's Day" SCIENCE – Discuss "June" PHYS. ED. – Exercises 1-2 (five times) MATH COOKING – Candle Salad	ART – Horrible Harry LITERATURE – POEM – "Sounds of Summer" MUSIC – Picnic Time PHYS. ED. – Exercises 1-3 (five times) BOOK – Why Frogs Are Wet by Judy Hawes	ART – Busy Bees & Beehive LITERATURE – POEM – "Honey Bees" PHYS. ED. – Exercises 1-4 (two times fast, one time slow)	ART – Desk Set for Father LITERATURE – POEM – "I Love You Dad" NURSERY RHYME – "Rock-A-Bye Baby" PHYS. ED. – Exercises 1-4 (very quietly) MATH COOKING – Ice Cream Treat BOOK – Frog and Toad Are Friends by Arnold Lobel	ART – (Complete) Desk Set for Father LITERATURE – POEM – "To Dear Dad" PHYS. ED. – Exercises 1-5 (very big) BOOK – Frog On His Own by Mercer Mayer
2	ART – Mr. Turtle LITERATURE – POEM – "Tommy Turtle" PHYS. ED. – Exercises 1-5 (very small) MATH COOKING – Rice Crispy Candy BOOK – The Story of a Toad by Robert M. McClung	ART – Father's Day Card LITERATURE – POEM – "You're My Dad" NURSERY RHYME – "Hey Diddle Diddle" PHYS. ED. – Exercises 1-6 BOOK – My Goldfish by Herbert H. Wong and Matthew F. Vessel	ART – Birds, Birds LITERATURE – FINGER PLAY – "The Sand Dragon" SCIENCE – Discuss "The Sun" PHYS. ED. – Exercises 1-6 MATH COOKING – Alphabet or Number Pretzels	ART – June Balloon LITERATURE – POEM – "The Balloon Ride" SCIENCE – Recall "The Sun" PHYS. ED. – Exercises 1-6 BOOK – The Frog In The Well by Alvin Tresselt	ART – (Complete) June Balloon SOCIAL STUDIES – Discuss "Flag Day" PHYS. ED. – Exercises 1-8 BOOK – Some Frogs Have Their Own Rocks by Robert and Claire Wiest
3	ART – Lady Bugs LITERATURE – POEM – "Lady Bug, Lady Bug" SCIENCE – Discuss "Sun" PHYS. ED. – Exercises 1-8 BOOK – The Grouch Ladybug by Eric Carle	ART – Make A Sailboat LITERATURE – POEM – "The Sailboat" MUSIC – Going Fishing PHYS. ED. – Exercises 1-8 MATH COOKING – Chocolate Chip Pizza	ART – (Complete) Make A Sailboat LITERATURE – POEM – "The Pollywogs" SOCIAL STUDIES – Discuss "Father's Day" PHYS. ED. – Exercises 1-8 & B BOOK – Goldie Is A Fish by Carroll Lane Fenton	ART – Ducks On A Pond LITERATURE – POEM – "Catch A Fish" SOCIAL STUDIES – Recall "Father's Day" PHYS. ED. – Exercises 1-8 & B BOOK – What I Like About Toads by Judy Hawes	ART – Activity Wheel LITERATURE – POEM – "Animal Symphony" PHYS. ED. – Exercises 1-8 & B MATH COOKING – Lemon Sherbet
4	ART – (Continue) Activity Wheel LITERATURE – POEM – "The Owl" PHYS. ED. – Exercises 1-8 & B BOOK – All About Fish by Carl Burger	ART – (Complete) Activity Wheel LITERATURE – STORY – "Little Justin and the Dragon" PHYS. ED. – Exercises 1-8 & B MATH COOKING – Bambino Pizzas BOOK – The Care of Water Pets by Gertrude Pels	ART – Butterflies LITERATURE – POEM – "Lightning Bugs" SCIENCE – Discuss "The Sun" PHYS. ED. – Exercises 1-8 & B BOOK – Caterpillars by Dorothy Sterling	ART – (Complete) Butterflies LITERATURE – Recall "Little Justin and the Dragon" FINGER PLAY – "Little Huey Dragon" PHYS. ED. – Exercises 1-8 & B BOOK – Moths by Dorothy Childs Hogner	ART – Creepy Caterpillar LITERATURE – POEM – "Fuzzy Caterpillar" PHYS. ED. – Exercises 1-8 & B BOOK – The Very Hungry Caterpillar by Eric Carle

I. ART
Children will develop skills in:
   Organization
   Sequence
   Use of small muscles (small motor)

A. SPOOL FLOWERS
Cut 5" stem with leaves attached and circle at the top from green paper. Spread out a paper baking cup and glue it to the stem. Glue another paper baking cup inside, leaving this one closed. Roll the bottom of the stem slightly and put it into an empty thread spool.

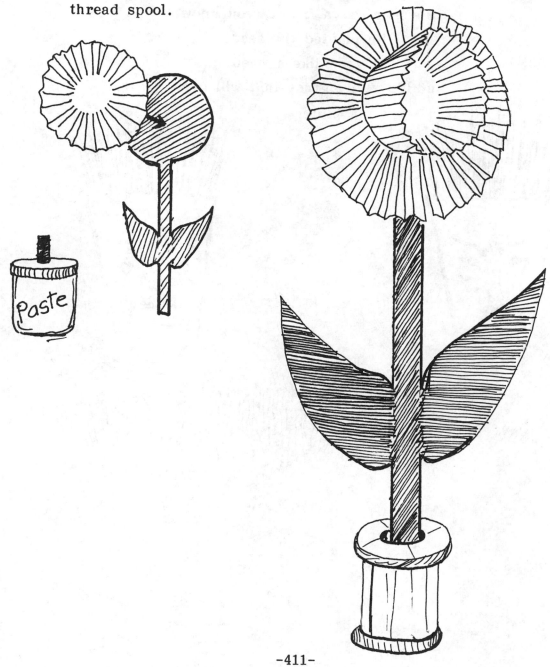

B. HORRIBLE HARRY

Have children draw a face on a styrofoam cup. Fill with potting soil. Plant grass seed in the soil. Water soil and place cup in the sun. Water the soil as needed and soon the grass will start to grow. When the grass is long enough, it will look like Harry has a head of hair.

Horrible Harry

Horrible Harry,

His face was so scary,

His hair was a fright, you know.

We planted the seed,

It grew like a weed,

But it's really grass that will grow.

C. BUSY BEES AND A BEEHIVE

Trace beehive and bees on manilla paper. Use crayons to fill in features of bees. Cut out bees and beehive. Paste on 9" x 12" light blue construction paper. Draw in grass and trees and flowers

D. __BUTTERFLIES__

Put several colors of paint in small bowls. Trace butterfly pattern on pastel paper. Cut out pattern. With spoon, place several different colors on the wings. Use straws to blow paint on wings. What a pretty butterfly!

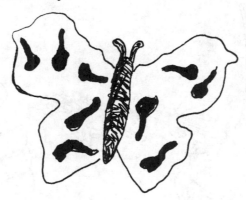

Another butterfly: Trace butterfly pattern on 12" x 18" black construction paper. Cut out inside of wings leaving black outline. Paste colored tissue or cellophane paper to fill areas cut away. Paste colored paper to black outline.

Optional: Cut out two black butterflies. Cut away inside of wings. Paste colored paper between the two layers. Attach a string and hang from the ceiling.

E. CREEPY CATERPILLAR

Fold 12" x 18" manilla paper in half the long way. Fold lengthwise
paper in half. Fold in half again. Cut rounded piece cff
each corner. Open up caterpillar, but keep folded lengthwise.
Put eyes and mouth at one end for the head. Make a design
in each section of the body. Cut feet out of the brown construction
paper. Paste feet on inside of caterpillar's body.

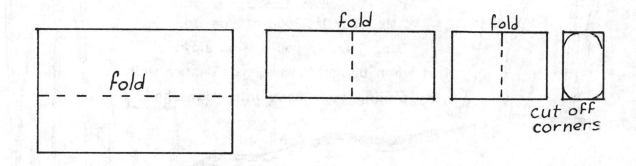

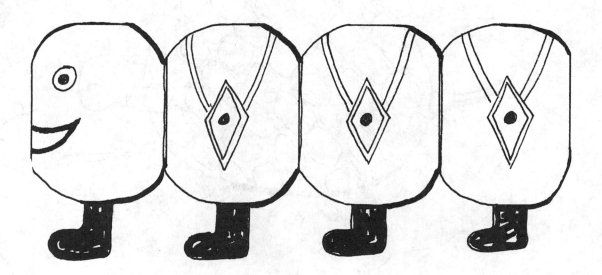

F.   MR. TURTLE

Cut out one large brown circle from brown construction paper. Cut two small green circles from green construction paper. Cut one green tail. Cut one green head.

With crayons, make pattern on turtle's body. Cut small green circles in half to make the turtle's four feet. Use crayons to draw facial features. Paste feet, tail and head under brown circle.

Mr. Turtle

Mr. Turtle, look at you go.
Mr. Turtle, you are so slow.
But when danger comes, you'll stay well,
By pulling your body into your shell.

G. LADY BUGS

Trace lady bug pattern. Cut out lady bug from 9" x 12" sheet of manilla paper. Color head black, body part black. Color wings red with black dots. Color antennae black. Paste together.

Lady Bug

Lady bug, lady bug,
How are you today?
Lady bug, lady bug,
Are you going to stay?
Lady bug, lady bug,
Or, will you fly away?

H. BIRDS, BIRDS AND MORE BIRDS

Trace birds on manilla paper. Color and cut out. Hang by string, yarn or fish line.

I.   JUNE BALLOON

Trace balloon pattern on manilla paper.   Trace basket pattern on brown paper.   With crayons, make a design on the balloon. Glue yarn to rounded top of balloon.   Punch a hole in each side of the basket.   Tie each end of the yarn through a hole in the basket.   (If desired, hang balloons from ceiling.   Tie yarn or string through to top of the balloon to hang.)

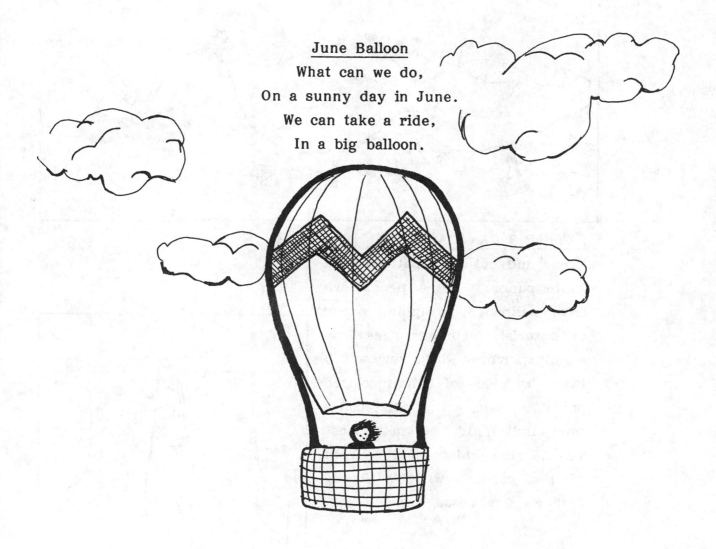

June Balloon
What can we do,
On a sunny day in June.
We can take a ride,
In a big balloon.

J. DUCKS ON A POND

Trace and cut two ducks and flower out of white paper. Trace and cut lily pad out of green paper. Trace and cut duck's bill and feet out of orange paper. Paste on 12" x 18" sheet of light blue construction paper. Draw eye for duck and draw duck's wing. Use blue crayon to make water.

K. FATHER'S DAY CARD

Trace and cut shirt pattern from white paper. Trace tie pattern from wallpaper, wrapping paper or material. (Using pages from a wallpaper book works very well.) Fold the piece of bright colored paper in half. Cut shirt collar where indicated. Glue tie in place. Then, glue shirt on the front of the card. Write a Happy Father's Day message inside.

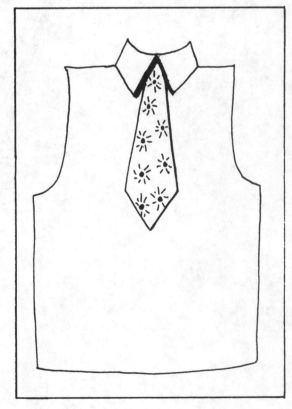

L.   MAKE A SAILBOAT

Trace sails on white paper. Trace boat, flag and mast on bright paper. Cut water from medium blue paper. Cut brown paper 1" shorter than the light blue background paper. (Both should be 9" x 12" at the beginning of the project.) Cut inside of brown paper to make a frame. Paste boat and mast flat on paper. Paste three corners of each sail to paper, making sails bulge out. Paste part of flag, bend to make it look like it is waving in the breeze. Color in birds and water. Cut medium blue to look like water and paste to the frame. Staple frame to sides of picture. Because the background sheet is longer than the frame, this will give a dimensional look to the boat.

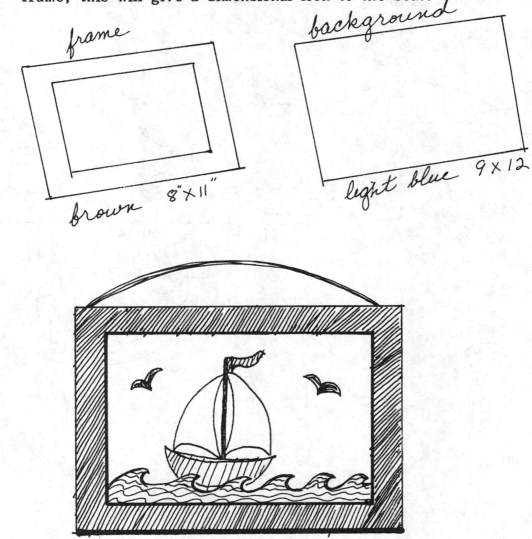

-421-

M. ACTIVITY WHEEL

Start with two pieces of 9" x 12" white construction paper. Using circle pattern, cut two circles. Trace section to be cut out of top circle. Divide bottom circle into four equal sections. In each section draw a summer, fun time activity. For example: swimming, fishing, playing ball, riding a bike, etc. Color pictures. Fasten top circle with section cut out to the bottom circle with the metal fastener.

Optional: This activity wheel could be used for different things -- science, health, animals, etc. For instance, foods that are good for you could be drawn in each section. Or, farm animals or animals found in the woods can be used in the wheel.

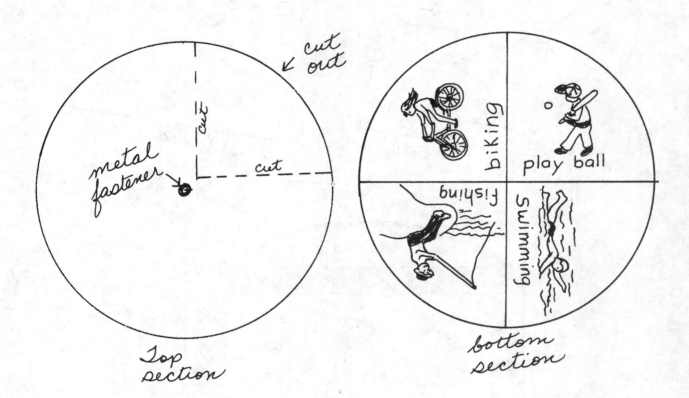

N. A DESK SET FOR FATHER

Use different size cans or cardboard containers. Cover sides with glue. Next, wind string or yarn around the containers. Make sure containers are entirely covered.

Another idea: If desired, instead of string or yarn, use contact paper or wallpaper to cover all items. Fill large containers with pencils, pens and markers. Fill small containers with paper clips. Put note paper in the box. This makes a nice desk set for Dad!

MATERIALS CHART

JUNE

A. SPOOL FLOWER Green paper Paper baking cups Glue Empty thread spool	**B. HORRIBLE HARRY** Styrofoam cup Crayons Potting soil Grass seed	**C. BUSY BEES AND BEEHIVE** Manilla paper Crayons 9"x12" light blue construction paper	**D. BUTTERFLIES** Paint String Spoon Straws Small bowls Paste Pastel paper Colored paper 12"x18" black constr. paper Colored tissue/cellophane
E. CREEPY CATERPILLAR 12"x18" manilla paper Crayons Brown construction paper Paste	**F. MR. TURTLE** Brown construction paper Green construction paper Crayons Paste	**G. LADY BUGS** 9"x12" manilla paper Crayons Paste	**H. BIRDS, BIRDS AND MORE BIRDS** Manilla paper Crayons String/yarn/fish line
I. JUNE BALLOONS Manilla paper Brown paper Crayons Glue Yarn/string Hole punch	**J. DUCKS ON A POND** White paper Green paper Orange paper 12"x18" light blue construction paper Crayons	**K. FATHER'S DAY CARD** White paper Wall paper/wrapping paper/material (cloth) Bright colored paper Glue	**L. MAKE A SAILBOAT** White paper Staple Bright paper Medium blue paper 9"x12" light blue construction paper Paste 9"x12" brown constr. paper
M. ACTIVITY WHEEL 9"x12" white construction paper Crayons Paper fasteners	**N. A DESK SET FOR FATHER** Vegetable/soup can Tuna fish can Glue String/yarn Box Contact paper/wall paper Pens-pencils-markers-paper clips		

II. LITERATURE

Children will develop an ability to identify and enjoy:

Characters

Main ideas

Details

Sequence of events

A. LITTLE JUSTIN AND THE DRAGON AND THE VEGETABLES

Once upon a time Little Justin woke up in the morning and ran downstairs to eat breakfast. Things seemed just like every other day so Little Justin wasn't sure that his magic friend, the fire breathing dragon, had been able to do anything about the vegetable problem.

Yesterday, Little Justin had visited the dragon's cave and had told the dragon how much he and his friends hated vegetables. The fire breathing dragon had blinked his shiny red eyes, carefully breathed a little fire near Little Justin's ear and said, "I am a magic dragon. It's a hard job, but I can make them all disappear if you and your friends are very, very sure that you would like a world without vegetables."

"Yes! Yes!" shouted Little Justin and he had run home happily singing "No more broccoli . . . no more peas . . . no more lima beans . . . no more spinach!" Little Justin was very happy.

Breakfast was so normal that Justin wasn't expecting big changes at lunch. However, when Justin returned from his morning play time, his mother was very upset. "Justin, I'm not sure what happened," she said. "I seem to have run out of all of your favorite foods for lunch. There is no vegetable soup, spaghetti sauce or chili. I can't even find a lettuce leaf, celery stalk or an onion to put into a tuna salad sandwich." And, his mother scurried around the kitchen making a list of all the things she was suddenly "out of."

A trip to the store did not help much. Justin and Mother looked up and down the aisles trying to find the things on their list. There was no pizza, no sloppy joe sauce, and almost no canned soup! Dinner and snacks were terrible! There was no french fries or corn on the cob to go with Mother's fried chicken. There was no popcorn and no potato chips!

Little Justin had told all of his friends that he would make all of the vegetables disappear. He had taken all of the credit and now he began to take all of the blame. His friends began to call up and shout at him. Were they mad! They were beginning to realize all of the good things that had vegetables in them!

Some of Little Justin's friends told him they would never play with him again . . . ever! Shawn, his best friend, said that he would not even invite Little Justin to his birthday party. Other friends came over to get games, books and balls they had left at Little Justin's house because they did not want to ever play with him again.

Little Justin went to bed feeling terrible. He was very sad and lonely.

Early the next morning while the stars still twinkled faintly in the sky, Little Justin slipped from his warm bed. He found his way down the road to the dragon's cave. He carefully poked the dragon awake with a big stick.

"Good morning, Mr. Dragon." This time Little Justin was **very** polite. "Please, please help me! I am in **terrible** trouble. All of my friends are mad at me. I have no one to play with anymore. My mother is busy shopping all day trying to find vegetables. Our meals and snack times are awful. I didn't know all of the great things we would have to do without after all the vegetables disappeared. Could you bring the vegetables back, but leave out spinach and broccoli and . . ."

"No," said the dragon sleepily, but firmly. "Since I have

made them all disappear, I must bring them all back. Making them reappear is even harder work than making them disappear. I will only do this because you are my good friend. Walk ever so slowly back home and by the time you get home, all of the vegetables will be back."

Little Justin hugged the dragon's slippery, shiny, scaly green neck and then ever so slowly walked home down the still dark road.

He walked so slowly that before he got home, the sun had reappeared and so had all the vegetables.

Little Justin started feeling better right away. His friends started coming over to tell him that since the vegetables were back, they weren't angry any more. Mother made great meals and snacks and had time to play with him. The refrigerator was full of beautiful vegetables and the kitchen shelves were full of cans of chili, spaghetti and vegetable soup. Everything was almost the same as it had been before the vegetables disappeared. The only thing that had changed was that now, each day, Little Justin eats every vegetable Mother gives him . . . broccoli, peas, spinach and lima beans.

Little Justin and the Dragon lived happily ever after.

POEMS/FINGER PLAYS/NURSERY RHYMES

Children will develop the ability to participate in and enjoy:

  Rhythm

  Poetry

  Sequence

  Characters

B. POEMS FOR FATHER'S DAY

  1. HAPPY FATHER'S DAY

      Hurrah, hurrah,
      It's Father's Day.
      It gives us all
      A chance to say,
      We love you more
      Everyday.
      Happy, Happy Father's Day.

  2. TO DEAR DAD

      I'm so lucky to have a Dad like you,
      We share so much fun in everything we do.
      You are so special in every way,
      I wish you the very best Father's Day.

  2. I LOVE YOU DAD

      For helping me and teaching me,
      All the things that you do,
      On this Father's Day, I say,
      "I love you."

  4. YOU'RE MY DAD

      Father's Day comes once a year,
      But I want you to know,
      That you're my dad, every day,
      That's why I love you so.

C. POEMS

1. THE BALLOON RIDE

What can we do on a bright day in June?
We can take a ride in a big balloon.
We can sail right over the trees and the flowers,
We can float through the air for hours and hours.
We'll look down on the ground below,
And wave to everyone we know.
Look at us away up high,
Why, we can almost touch the sky.
And when, at last, our ride is done,
We'll say, "That was a lot of fun."

2. THE SAILBOAT

Sailboat, sailboat, where will you go?
Why sailing over the waves, you know.
Sailboat, sailboat, take me along?
Will you sing me a sailing song?
Sailing, sailing as free as we please.
Sailing along on a summer breeze.
We'll sail and sail, together we'll roam,
And when we're tired, we'll head for home.

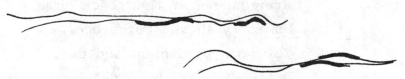

3. CATCH A FISH

I sure wish, I could catch a fish,
On this lovely summer day.
If not, I'll buy it,
My mom can fry it,
And I'll eat it right away.

4. LIGHTNING BUGS

In summer when it's evening
We look right at the dark.
Here and there we spot·a glow,
A shining little spark.
A flash of light, a twinkle,
Just like a little star.
Just keep on looking,
See how many there are.
Little sparks of light,
Flashing here and there.
It's the lightning bugs we see,
They're flying everywhere.

5. HONEY BEES

Buzzy bees, you are so busy
Working in your honey comb.
Gathering honey from the flowers,
Bringing nectar right back home.
I'm sorry all you buzzy bees,
You work hard night and day,
But your honey is so delicious,
I'm going to steal it away!

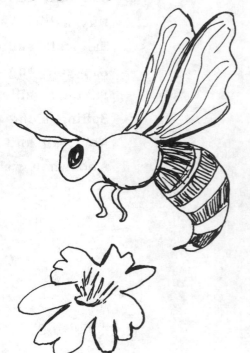

6. TOMMY TURTLE

Tommy Turtle, look at you go.
Tommy Turtle, you are so slow.
But when danger comes, you'll stay well,
By pulling your body into your shell.

7. LADYBUG, LADYBUG

Ladybug, Ladybug,
How are you today?
Ladybug, Ladybug,
Are you going to stay?
Ladybug, Ladybug,
Or will you fly away?

8. **SOUNDS OF SUMMER**

Listen to the sounds of summer
On a warm June day.
The chatter of the squirrels
As they run and play.
The soft buzz of the bees
As they move from flower to flower.
The croaking of the frogs
After a warm rain shower.
The birds in the trees
As they sing a lovely song.
These are the sounds we hear
All summer long.
The sound of children's voices
As they laugh and play.
These are the sounds we hear
On a warm summer day.

9.   **THE OWL**

Whoo, whoo, says the owl in the tree,
I'm just as wise as I can be.
Whoo, whoo, he said as he blinked his eyes,
Asking questions makes me sound very wise!

10. FUZZY LITTLE CATERPILLAR

Fuzzy little caterpillar,
Eating day and night.
Growing fatter all the time,
What an unusual sight.
You spin a cocoon around yourself,
Until you're snug inside.
To stay through the cold winter,
You have a safe place to hide.
Then in the spring, one sunny day,
A strange sight we will spy.
For instead of a fuzzy caterpillar,
You'll be a butterfly.
And when your wings are ready,
Maybe, in a day,
What once was a fuzzy caterpillar,
Will spread wings and fly away.

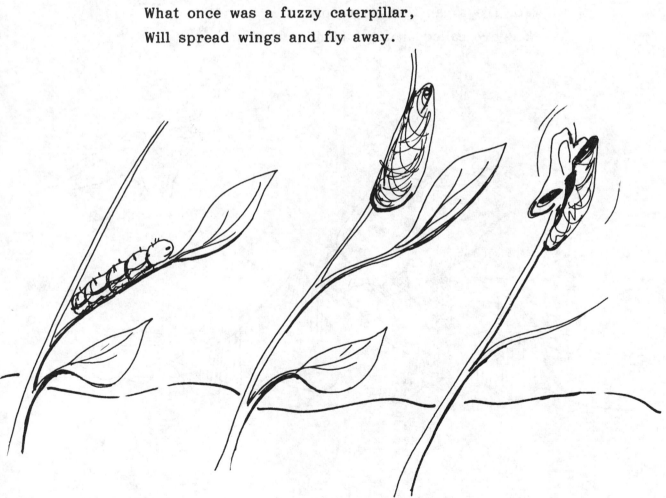

11.   THE POLLYWOGS

Look at all the pollywogs,
Swimming in the stream.
There are so many gathered there,
Hundreds, it would seem.
Watch them as the days go by,
Notice something strange?
Their tails will soon grow short,
We'll see their bodies change.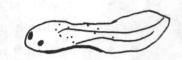
For soon we'll see some tiny legs,
Look how fast they grow.
Bigger and stronger every day,
And then, what do you know?
They'll turn into tiny frogs,
And hop onto the land.
For frogs can live either place,
They're called an amphibian.

12. ANIMAL SYMPHONY

The song of a bird is clear and sweet,
He sits in a tree and sings, "Tweet, tweet."
Mr. Owl, so calm and wise,
Says, "Whoo, whoo," as he blinks his eyes.
The duck in the pond says, "Quack, quack, quack."
I'll fly away, but I'll be right back."
The big dog barks and says, "Bow-wow."
The furry little kitten says, "Meow."
The rooster crows, "Cock-a-doodle-doo."
The big brown cow says, "Moo, moo, moo."
The horse in the pasture says, "Neigh, neigh."
"Baa, baa," said the little lamb, "I like to play."
"Oink, oink," said the pig, "When is it time to eat?"
"Buzz, buzz," said the bee, "My honey is so sweet."
"Croak, croak," said the frog, "It's time for my rest."
Now which animal sound did you like the best.

D. FINGER PLAYS

1. THE SAND DRAGON

   Today I was in my sandbox,
   And I made myself a dragon. ("Play" with sand.)
   I wanted to show it to my mom,
   So I put it in my wagon.
       ("Lift" dragon and put in wagon.)
   I pulled it over bumpy grass,
       ("Pull" wagon a few steps.)
   And yelled and waved my hand. (Wave hand.)
   Mom smiled and said, "What dragon, child?" (Turn around.)
   There was nothing there but sand.

2. LITTLE HUEY DRAGON

   (Make appropriate hand motions.)
   Little Huey Dragon counts to three,
   Little Huey Dragon bends one knee.
   Little Huey Dragon stretches his wings,
   Little Huey Dragon whistles and sings. (La, la.)
   Little Huey Dragon touches his toes,
   Little Huey Dragon touches his nose.
   Little Huey Dragon makes a funny face,
   Little Huey Dragon runs in place.
   Little Huey Dragon lays on the floor,
   Little Huey Dragon starts to snore.

E. NURSERY RHYMES

1. ### ROCK-A-BYE, BABY
   Rock-a-bye, Baby on the tree top!
   When the wind blows the cradle will rock.
   When the bough breaks the cradle will fall,
   And down will come baby, cradle and all.

2. ### HEY DIDDLE DIDDLE THE CAT AND THE FIDDLE
   Hey diddle diddle, the cat and the fiddle,
   The cow jumped over the moon.
   The little dog laughed to see such a sight,
   And the dish ran away with the spoon.

III. MUSIC

Children will develop the ability to participate in and enjoy music.

A. PICNIC TIME

(Tune: London Bridge Is Falling Down)

Summer time is picnic time, picnic time, picnic time.

We'll pack a lunch, here's yours, here's mine,

In our picnic basket.

Go to the park to spend our day,

    spend our day, spend our day.

We'll have fun, we'll run and play,

On our picnic.

We will have a lot of fun, lot of fun, lot of fun.

Then our picnic day is done.

Pack up the basket,

The picnic's over, time to go, time to go, time to go.

We'll walk home so very slow,

What a great picnic!

B. GOING FISHING

(Tune: This Is The Way We Wash Our Clothes)

This is the way we hunt for worms,

    hunt for worms, hunt for worms.

This is the way we hunt for worms, when we're going fishing.

See a worm and grab it fast, grab it fast, grab it fast.

See a worm and grab it fast, before it gets away.

Look at it wiggle in my hands,

    in my hands, in my hands,

Look at it wiggle in my hands, he's a nice fat worm.

Put it in the jar and cap the top, cap the top, cap the top.

Put it in the jar and cap the top, look how many we've caught.

We'll take our poles and go to the lake, go to the lake,

    go to the lake.

We'll take our poles and go to the lake,

    to see how many we'll catch.

We might catch 1, 2 or 3, 1, 2 or 3, 1, 2 or 3.

How many we catch, we'll have to see,

When we go fishing.

IV. SCIENCE

Children will develop skills in:

Distinguishing differences

Similarities of attributes

A. **JUNE SCIENCE**

June is the sixth month of the year. It is believed that the Romans named the month "Juno" after the patron goddess of marriage. June is one of the most popular months of the year for marriages.

We welcome the month of June because it is the beginning of summer. Many beautiful flowers are in bloom, especially roses. Often June is called the rose month because these lovely, fragrant flowers are in full bloom. Trees and shrubs are arrayed in fresh new green leaves.

It is the month of new beginnings for many of nature's creatures. Young birds are learning to fly. Calves and foals are happy in the pastures. Baby fawns test their wobbly legs in the deep woods.

The insect world is also full of activity. Bees and butterflies move from flower to flower. Also, in some areas on warm June evenings, the twinkling of fireflies can be seen.

B. **THE SUN**

Why do we need the sun? We live on the planet earth. Earth is one of nine planets which go around the sun.

We must have the sun in order to live. The sun gives our heat, light and energy to us. The energy from the sun goes into green plants. The plants change sun energy, water and carbon dioxide into food. Animals eat the plants and other animals. People eat plants as vegetables and animals as meat. Thus, we get energy from the sun when we eat meat and plants.

The sun provides the heat that warms our oceans, lakes and streams. We know how cold it can get in winter when the sun is not as close to us as it is in the summer.

C. <u>The sun is very big and very hot.</u> It looks small because it is so far away. We know that it is very strong because in the summer it can give us a terrible sunburn if we are not careful.

The sun also causes weather. It warms air and warm air goes up. Cooler air fills in the space left by the warm air. When air moves in this way we call it wind.

D. <u>The sun also helps dry up</u> some of the water in puddles, streams, lakes and oceans. The dried up water in the air is called vapor. It helps make clouds and falls back to the earth as rain and snow.

The sun provides heat, energy, weather changes and food.

You can see that the sun is very important to us here on earth.

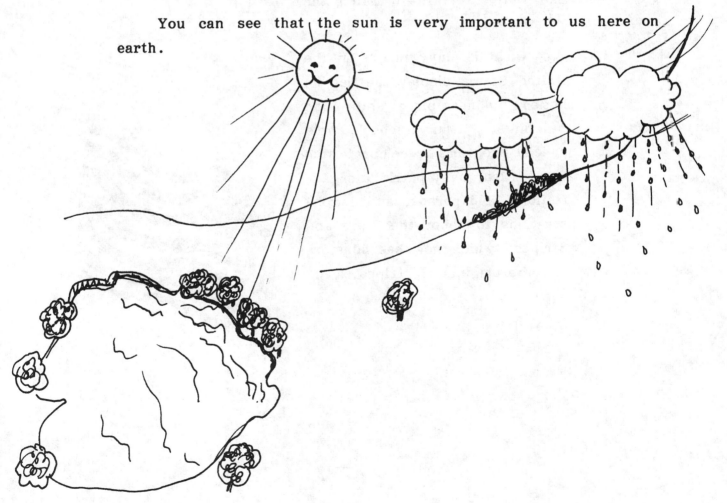

IV. SOCIAL STUDIES

Children will develop an awareness of:

    Holidays

    Traditions

    Seasonal changes

In the United States we celebrate two special holidays during the month of June: Flag Day and Father's Day.

A. FLAG DAY

Flag Day is celebrated on June 14th, commemorating the day in 1777 when the Continental Congress adopted the Stars and Stripes as the official flag of the United States of America. At the time it was adopted, our flag had only 13 stars to match the 13 stripes.

On this day, people in the United States display the flag on homes, business places and public buildings. Many schools hold special programs to celebrate this day. Also, many patriotic organizations hold parades and demonstrations to honor the Stars and Stripes, which now has 50 stars and the original 13 stripes.

B. FATHER'S DAY

Father's Day is celebrated both in Canada and the United States. This special day for fathers is always held on the third Sunday in June.

The first Father's Day was celebrated many years ago in 1910, in the city of Spokane, Washington. Eventually the custom spread throughout the United States and Canada.

On this day, in a show of love and appreciation, fathers receive cards and gifts from their families.

VI. JUNE PHYSICAL EDUCATION FUN
Children will develop skills in:

   Rhythm

   Imaging

   Use of large and small muscles

   Good sports conduct

A. <u>MOVE AS IF YOU ARE:</u>
   1.   Pushing a swing.
   2.   Pushing a baby stroller.
   3.   Pulling weeds out of your garden.
   4.   Pulling a heavy wagon.
   5.   Pushing a two wheeler while someone learns to ride it.
   6.   Pushing a big, friendly dog out the door.
   7.   Pulling a monkey into its cage.
   8.   A fish.

B. <u>BIG BALL PUSH</u>
   Children sit in a circle with legs crossed. Child who is "it"
   has the ball and describes another child in the circle. For example:
   "I am pushing this ball to someone with a blue and red dress
   and a blue ribbon." "It" then rolls it to the person he/she describes.
   That person catches the ball and is "it."

   If the person misses the ball, the turn passes to the left.

VII. MATH COOKING

Children will develop skills in:

Number awareness

Counting

Measuring

A. ## RICE KRISPIE CANDY

Peanut butter   Rice Krispies®

Marshmallow fluff   Chocolate chips (optional)

Combine equal amouts of peanut butter and marshmallow fluff. Add Rice Krispies® until the mixture is very hard to mix. Roll into balls or spread in a pan. Chill and cut into squares. Optional: Add chocolate chips to the mixture.

Math: Concept of half (peanut butter and marshmallow fluff), shape (square and cube), count chocolate chips.

B. ## ALPHABET OR NUMBER PRETZELS

½ cup water   1 pkg. dry yeast

2 cups flour   1 T. sugar

Dissolve yeast in water. Combine flour and sugar. In a large bowl, work flour mixture and yeast mixtures with a large spoon. When about 1½ cups of flour mix have been worked in, start to knead the mixture on the table while working in the remaining mix. Divide the dough into 12-15 parts. Shape the dough into letters and place on greased pans. Beat 1 egg slightly with 1 tablespoon of water. Paint the unbaked letters with the egg-water mixture and sprinkle with salt. Bake at 425° for 20-25 minutes or until golden brown.

Math: measurement awareness, count dough parts, read numbers and letters, and counting practice.

C. ICE CREAM TREAT

      1 cup cream (half and half) 1 cup milk

      1 t. vanilla   ½ cup sugar

      Pinch of salt

You will need one empty ½ gallon milk carton and one empty small **metal** can per child

Pour above ingredients into a large bowl and mix.

Pour the ice cream mix into the small can. Cover with a small plastic bag and secure it with a rubberband. Place in milk carton. Around the can pack ice. Salt the ice, pack again and salt again. Repeat this until the container is completely packed. Let this stand about 10 or 15 minutes, until a ring of ice crystals form around the edge. Remove the cover and let the children stir until ice cream is frozen hard. It will taste like ice milk.

Math: measurement awareness.

D. CHOCOLATE CHIP PIZZA

      ½ cup sugar   ½ cup brown sugar, packed

      1 stick butter   ½ cup peanut butter

      ½ t. vanilla   1 egg

      1½ cups flour

Mix above ingredients together. Spread on ungreased pizza pan. Bake at 375° for 10 minutes. Remove from oven and sprinkle ½ cup chocolate chips on top. Optional: ½ cup marshmallows. Return to oven for 5-8 minutes.

Math: Measurement awareness, count chocolate chips or marshmallows.

E. **BAMBINO PIZZAS**

   Ritz®crackers   Pizza sauce

   Mozzarella cheese   Pepperoni

Spread crackers with pizza sauce. Sprinkle on grated mozzarella cheese and place one slice of pepperoni on top. Place on cookie sheet. Bake at 350° until cheese melts.

Math: Counting crackers, pepperoni, one to one. Are there enough pizzas for each child to have one?

F. **CANDLE SALAD**

   Lettuce leaf   Slice of pineapple

   Half of banana   Marachino cherry

Place lettuce leaf on salad plate. Place pineapple slice on lettuce. Put half of banana in center of slice. Top with a marachino cherry (use toothpick to hold).

Math: Count number of ingredients, fractions (½ banana).

G. **LEMON SHERBET**

   3 oz. concentrated frozen lemonade

   2 cups crushed ice

   1 egg

Put above ingredients in blender. Blend until mixture is thick and slushy. Serve at once, or store covered in freezer. Other flavors of frozen juice may be substituted.

Math: Measurement awareness, count ingredients.

READ ALOUD BOOKS FROM THE LIBRARY

JUNE

Children will develop the ability to enjoy and gain knowledge from books.

1. <u>All About Fish</u>
    Burger, Carl
    Illustrated by author
    Random House, New York, 1960

    > Includes chapters titled "What Is A Fish Anyway," Salt Water Fish," "Fresh Water Fish," "Fish As Pets," and "Some True Fish Tails." This book is good background information or to read as paraphrased sections for very young readers.

2. <u>The Grouchy Lady Bug</u>
    Carle, Eric
    Thomas Y. Crowell Company, New York, 1977
    41 pages

    > In a book dedicated to lady bugs, Mr. Carle tells the story of a lady bug who challenges increasingly large opponents - from another lady bug to a whale - to fight. She backs down on each fight by deciding that each is "not big enough" to fight. Hungry and tired, she finally accepts another lady bug's offer to share an aphid dinner.

3. The Very Hungry Caterpillar
    Carle, Eric
    Philomel Books (Division of Putham), New York, 1983

      Colorfully illustrated life story of a caterpillar who eats a large
      variety of food including fruit, ice cream and watermelon. He
      cures his sick stomach by eating a nice green leaf after which
      he makes a cocoon falls asleep and emerges a beautiful butterfly.

4. Goldie Is A Fish
    Fenton, Carroll Lane
    Illustrated by author
    The John Day Company, New York, 1961

      Black, white and blue drawings help simple words describe Goldie's
      life in the aquarium. There are 21 brief chapters in the 48 page
      book. Some of the chapters are "What Are Fish?" "How Fish
      Swim" and "Fish That Sting."

5. What I like About Toads
    Hawes, Judy
    Illustrated by James and Ruth McCrea
    Thomas Y. Crowell, New York, 1969

      The life cycle of toads is described. Interesting facts about
      toads are treated in an almost story-like way with multi-colored
      drawings and few sentences on each page.

6   Why Frogs Are Wet
    Hawes, Judy
    Illustrated by Don Madden
    Thomas Y. Crowell, New York, 1968
    (This is a Let's-Read-And-Find-Out book)

      Large drawings and easy words which explain why frogs are wet.
    It also describes how toads jump, see and eat.

7. Moths

Hogner, Dorothy Childs

Illustrated by Nils Hogner

Thomas Y. Crowell Company, New York, 1964

Dorothy Childs Hogner has written at least eight other books on nature subjects. This book describes the life cycle of the moth and diagrams of the moth's "inside" and "outside" are included.

8. Frog and Toad Are Friends

Lobel, Arnold

Harper, 1979

64 pages

Five stories with easy vocabulary help students understand the joys of close friendships.

9. Frog On His Own

Mayer, Mercer (1943)

Dial Press, New York, 1973 (2)

30 pages, illustrations

This is a wordless book. The delightful story is told entirely by "reading" the pictures. A spirited little frog escapes from a small boy's pail and gets himself into one scrape after another until finally he is pinned down by a cat who means business. The small boy and his dog scare the cat away just in time to save the happy frog's life. The tired frog rides contentedly home in the small boy's arms.

10. Buffo - The Story of a Toad
   McClug, Robert M.
   Illustrated by author
   William Morrow and Company, New York, 1954

   Buffo grows from an egg to a mature toad. His story includes escapes from his enemies and descriptions of the insects he eats. Large print and green, tan, black and white drawings.

11. The Care of Water Pets
   Pels, Gertrude
   Illustrated by Ava Morgon
   Thomas Y. Crowell Company, New York, 1955

   Chapters include "How To Choose Your Fish," "How To Set Up Your Aquarium," "How To Feed Your Fish" and more of the same.

12. Caterpillars
   Sterling, Dorothy
   Illustrated by Winifred Lubell
   Doubleday and Company Inc., Garden City, NY, 1961

   Tells the complete story of the miracle of the process by which caterpillar eggs are laid, hatched, the pupae spin cocoons and finally emerge as beautiful butterflies.

13. The Frog In The Well
Tresselt, Alvin
Lothrop, Lee and Shepard Company, New York, 1958

Brightly colored pictures illustrate the story of a frog who left his well to discover a wonderful world that he had not suspected existed. After exploring a meadows, farm marsh and woods, he settled down on a lily pad with a "million singing frogs."

14. Some Frogs Have Their Own Rocks
Wiest, Robert and Claire
Children's Press, Chicago, 1970

Strong black and white drawings and a **very** few words (on opposite page) tell the story of the frogs perspective on the life of a frog. Including the title, there are less than eighty words in this book.

15. My Goldfish
Wong, Herbert and Vessel, Matthew F.
Illustrated by Arvis L. Stewart
Addison-Wesley, Reading, MA, 1969

A little boy wins a goldfish and observes it in a bowl, an aquarium and his uncle's goldfish pond. Large, multi-colored drawings. After looking at other fish, the little boy likes his own best.

DUCKS ON A POND

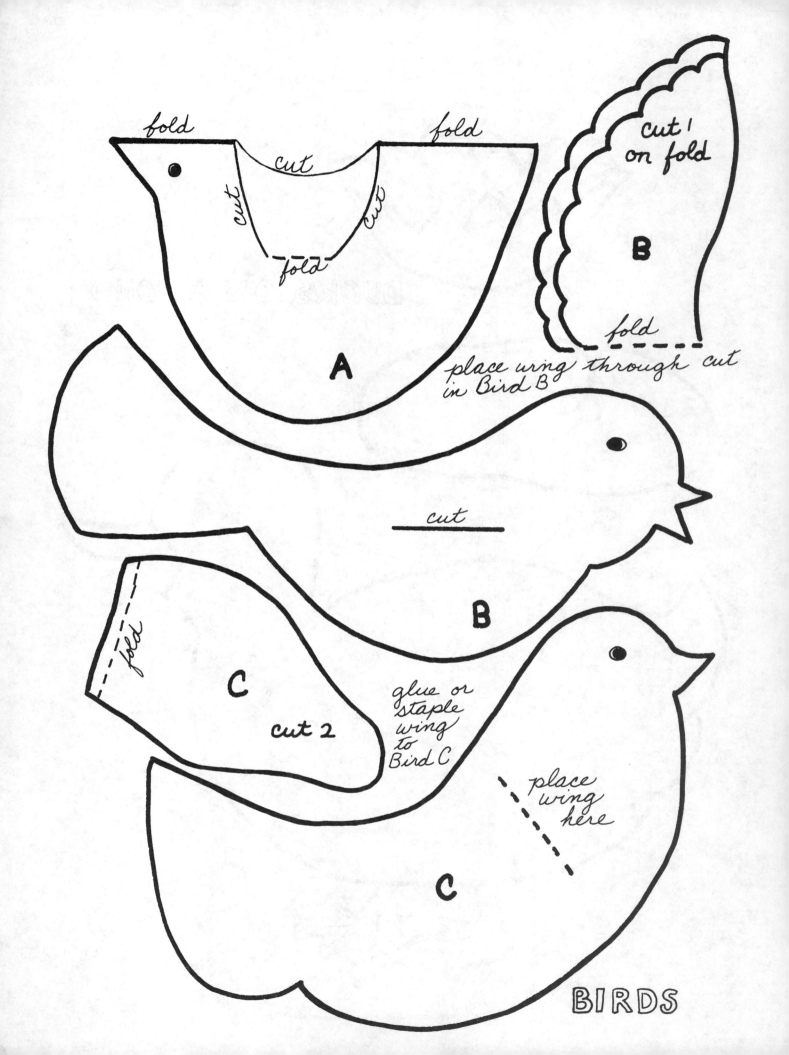

fold

cut

cut

cut

cut

fold

fold

fold

A

cut 1 on fold

B

fold

place wing through cut in Bird B

cut

B

C

cut 2

glue or staple wing to Bird C

place wing here

C

BIRDS

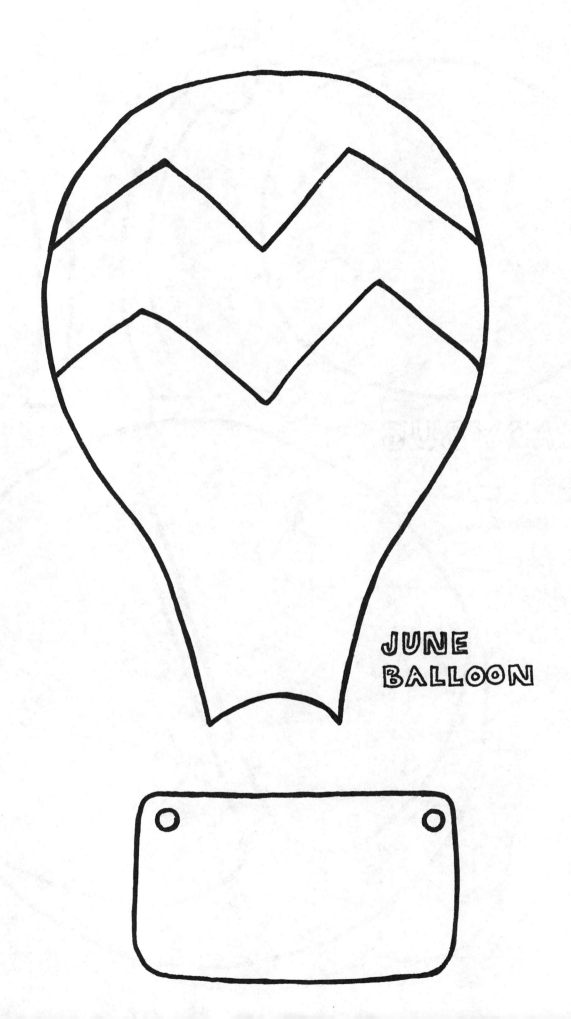

JUNE
BALLOON

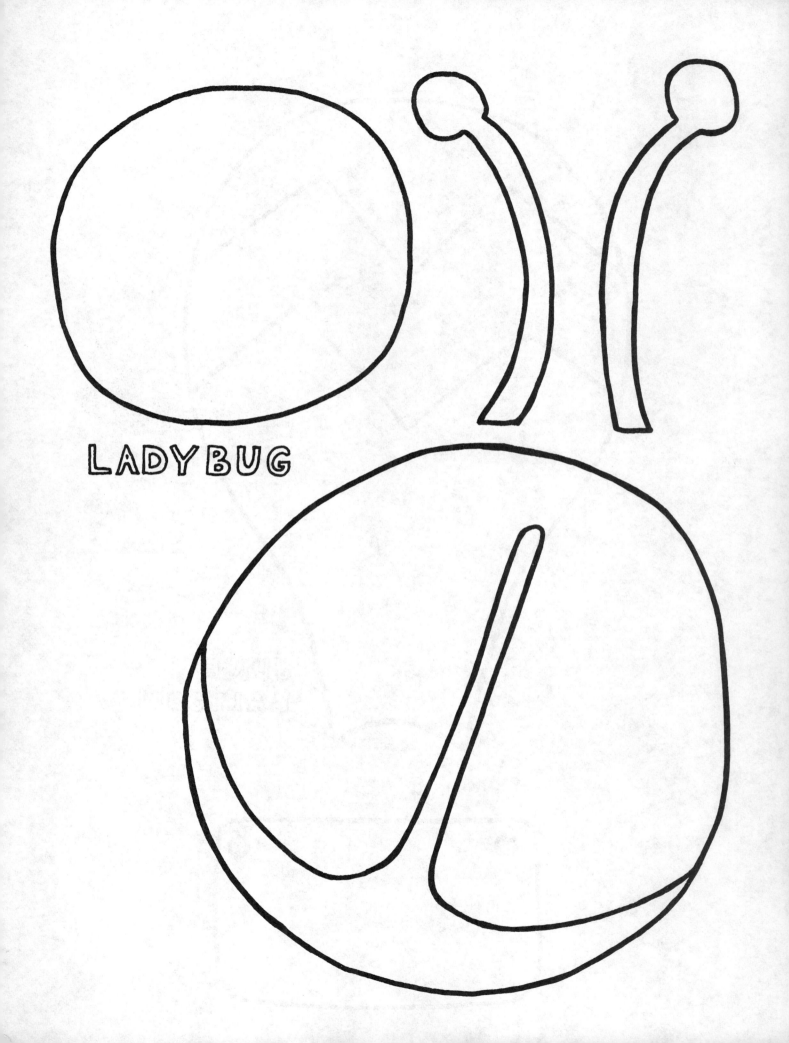

LADYBUG

BUSY BEES

AND

BEEHIVE

MAKE A SAILBOAT

FATHERS DAY CARD

cut to peak
of collar

draw line

cut line

cut line

draw line

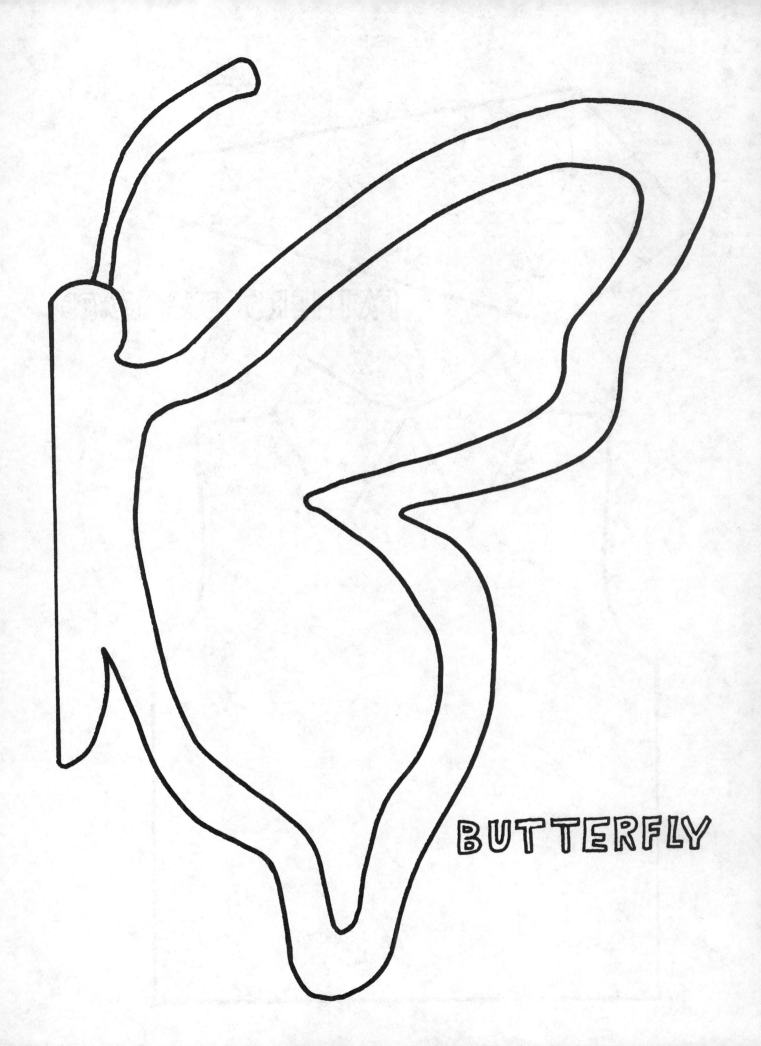

BUTTERFLY

JULY
AUGUST

Dear Parents:

July and August are vacation time, so don't look for learning plans these months.   Instead, here are activities to simulate both sides of the young brain.

The left, more logical side, will be helped to develop by the summer math activities.   The right, more creative side, will grow through listening to and discussing the dragon and fantasy Read Aloud Books From The Library.

SUMMER MATH
Counting
Inventory
More Or Less   Shapes
Ordering   Sizes   Bingo
Sequence

BOOKS FROM THE LIBRARY
A dozen dragon and other
fantasy books.

Have a super happy summer!

SUMMER MATH ACTIVITIES

1. ## COUNTING
    Start establishing 1-5 by counting beans, buttons, pennies, rocks, etc. When children have mastered 1-5, go on to 6-10. Do finger counting; count how many fingers on each hand, both hands.

    Count with children. Count how many children are present, count tables, count chairs, count days on the calendar. Combine listening with counting. Have children close their eyes while the teacher bounces a ball. Have them count aloud and together, at first. Then, have them count silently and give each one a chance to tell how many bounces they counted.

2. ## TAKE INVENTORY
    Make a chart and count together to fill the amounts. Things that could be put on the chart to be counted: children, hands, feet, eyes, ears, noses, fingers, watches, rings, hats, coats, scarfs, chairs, tables, etc.

    An example of the chart to be made:

feet	12	rings	2	chairs	10
noses	6	watches	4	Tables	1
ears	12	hats	0	balls	0
eyes	12	scarves	1	glasses	1

3.   MORE OR LESS

Introduce ten objects (use paper clips, pencils, pens, erasers, keys, bottons, etc.).   Arrange these items into two unequal groups.   Which group has "more" and which group has "less"?   Have children count the objects in each group together.   Establish what "more" and "less" means and then have children indicate which group has "more" and which group has "less."

Using the same objects, change the amounts several times.   Each time a change is made have the children count both groups to find which has "more" and which has "less."

Use pictures to help establish concept of "more" and "less."   For example: dining table and chairs, basket of fruit (oranges and apples), cats and dogs, money (pennies and nickels), jackets and hats.

Count number of people.   How many boys?   How many girls?   Which has more?   Which has less?

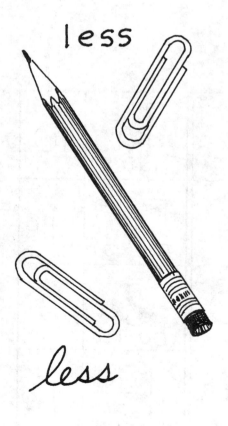

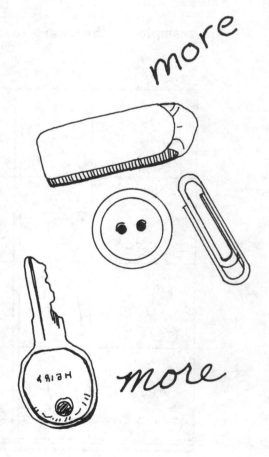

4. <u>CIRCLE</u>

Make eight circles out of different colors of tagboard. Make each circle a different size. Explain that a circle is round like a ball. Discuss "big" and "small", also "large" and "little."

Ask which circle is the smallest? Which is the biggest? Ask which circle is the largest? Which is the littlest?

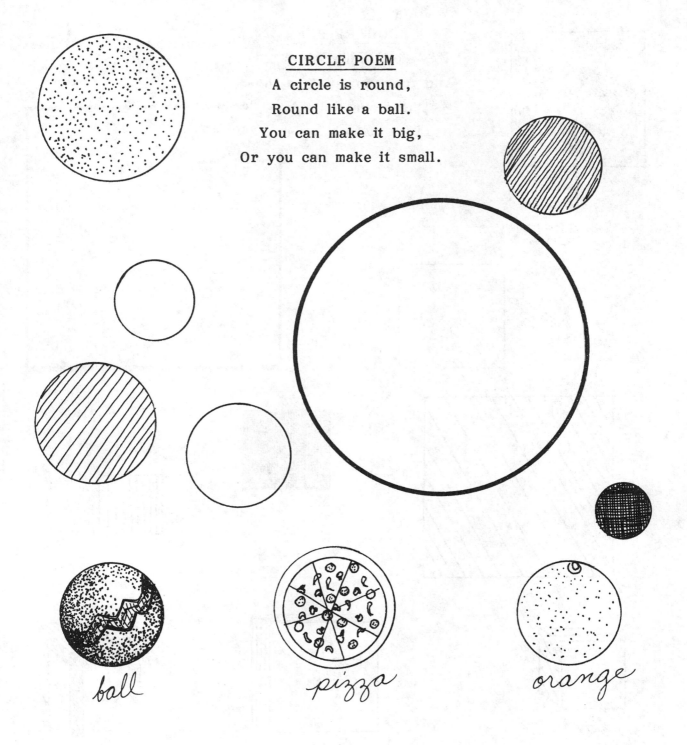

CIRCLE POEM
A circle is round,
Round like a ball.
You can make it big,
Or you can make it small.

ball   pizza   orange

5. <u>SQUARE</u>

A square has four equal sides and four corners. Make different size squares out of colored tagboard.

What are some things that are shaped like a square? Discuss square shaped things: a box, napkin, book, blocks, table, etc.

SQUARE POEM
Four equal sides,
And four corners are there.
These are the things,
That make a square.

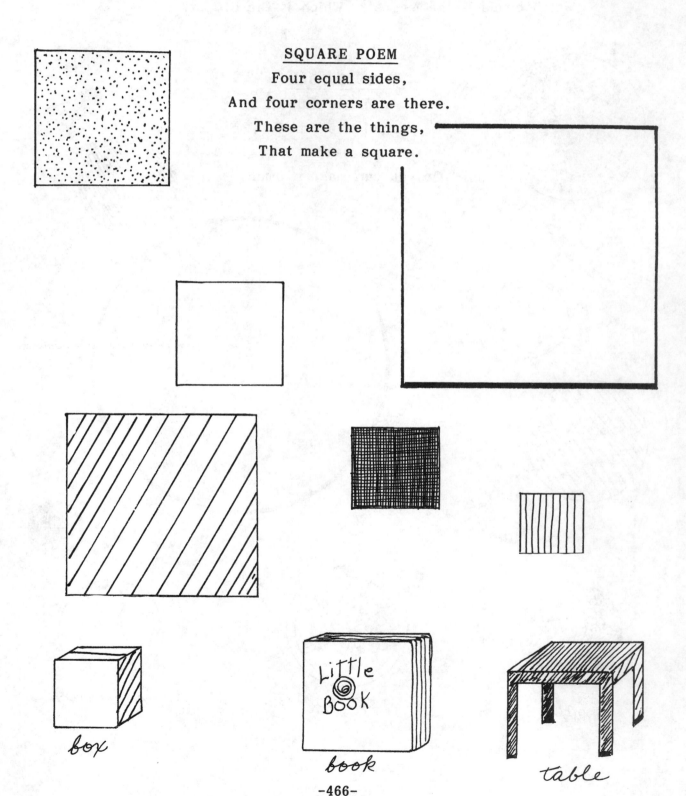

box

book

table

6. <u>TRIANGLE</u>

A triangle has three sides and three corners. Make some triangles of colored tagboard. Make these triangles different sizes.

Some things that are shaped like a triangle: a sailboat, piece of pie, witches' hat, etc.

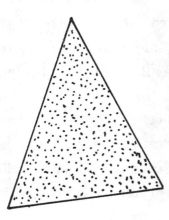

TRIANGLE POEM
A triangle's sides,
Number three.
Also, three corners,
As you can see.

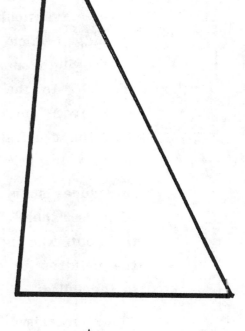

pie

witch's hat

sailboat

7. ORDERING

Collect eight Pringle cans (or similar type of can) and cut the cans into various sizes. Cover these cans with contact paper.

Object: Arrange the cans in a progressive order from the smallest to the largest.

Allow the children to each have a turn at the task. At first the child will probably start in the middle and work toward both ends. Eventually, with practice, the child will use his/her eyes to judge which cylinder he/she needs to start with, and then which will be next in line, and which ones will follow in the proper order. As the child works with the cans, he/she will learn to work from one and progress to the other. He/she will start with the smallest or the largest and continue to arrange the cans in their proper order.

Introduce "short" and "tall." Use cans to demonstrate to children what is "short" and what is "tall." Using the children in class, find out who is the tallest and who is the shortest. Arrange the children in order, starting with the shortest and progressing to the tallest.

Think of animals that fit each category. For example: giraffe, elephant, horse, brown bear, etc. Small animals: mouse, squirrel, cat, chipmunk, etc.

8. **A GAME ABOUT SIZE**

Ask questions that make a comparison of the sizes of things. Give each child a chance to answer a question or to make a statement about size.

1. Find something smaller than your hand.
2. Think of something larger than an apple.
3. I'm thinking of something tall. It is a flagpole. Can you think of something taller? (Have children answer until no one can name anything taller.)
4. I'm thinking of something short. It is a can of pop. Can you think of something that is shorter?

9. **WIDE AND NARROW**

Introduce the concepts of "wide" and narrow" by asking questions that make a comparison of these words.

1. I'm thinking of a loaf of bread. Can you name something wider?
2. I'm still thinking of a loaf of bread. Can you name something that is narrower than the loaf of bread?

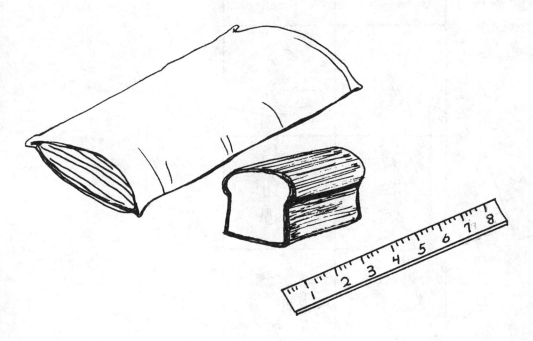

10. **LET'S PLAY MATH BINGO**

Materials needed: tagboard, scissors, ruler and magic marker.

Make enough tagboard cards so that each child has a card. Make extras so that they can exchange a card after a game.

Make small tagboard squares for covering the numbers.

Divide each tagboard card into eight squares. Put numbers from 1-10 on each card in a scrambled order. (Each card only has eight numbers on it.)

Make a Master Card with numbers 1-10 to use for checking.

Decide how you want the children to cover the card.

a.   Cover top half only.

b.   Cover bottom half only.

c.   Cover only the four corners.

4.   Cover only the middle four numbers.

5.   Cover all the numbers.

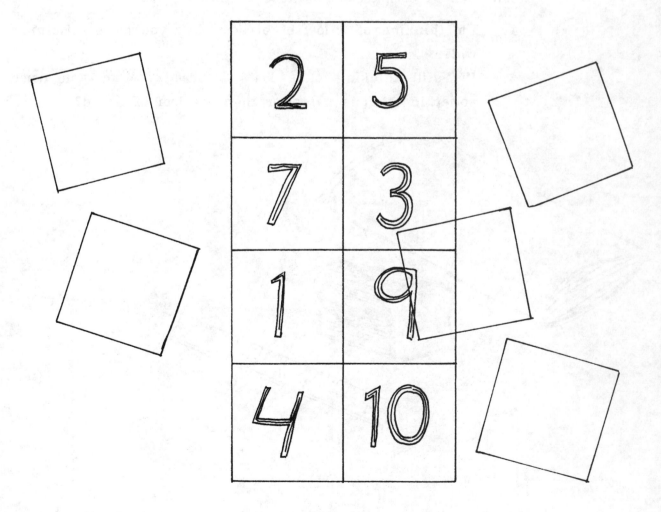

11. SEQUENCING WITH COLORS AND SHAPES

You will need a transparent plastic bag and colored tagboard. Also, you will need patterns of small and large circle, small and large square, and small and large triangle

Using patterns, trace and cut from the tagboard large circles of blue, red and yellow. Cut small circles of green, brown and purple.

Cut large squares of blue, red and yellow. Cut small squares of green, brown and purple.

Cut large triangles of blue, red and yellow. Cut small triangles of green, brown and purple.

When all of the shapes have been traced and cut, fill each plastic bag with the same materials so each child has the same objects to work with.

READY TO WORK

Child is to find a specific item. For instance: Find and put in front of you a large red circle. Next find a large blue square.

Gradually children will be able to follow a pattern of several items and colors in correct order.

Children will develop the ability to enjoy and gain knowledge from books.

1. **Favorite Fairy Tales Told In Greece**
   Haviland, Virginia
   Illustrated by Nonny Hogrogian
   Little Brown and Company, Boston, 1970
   90 pages, illustrations

   > Line drawings illustrate these Greek fairy tales which include: "Constantes and the Dragon," "The Princess Who Loved Her Father Like Salt," "Fairy Gardens" and five other tales. The author's note at the end of the book gives background information on the development of Greek fairy tales. This book is one of a series of fourteen books of fairy tales by Virginia Haviland, each from a different country.

2. **How Do You Hide A Monster**
   Kahl, Virginia
   Charles Scribner's Sons, New York, 1971
   Unpaged, illustrations

   > Rhymed story about a friendly sea monster named Phinney. When strangers mistake Phinney for a terrible monster, Phinney pretends he is a bridge. He flips the strangers in the air and they land in the water. After the townspeople save the strangers, they are warned to improve their bridges.

3. **The Secret In The Dungeon**
   Krahn, Fernando
   Clarion Books, New York, 1982, 1983
   Unpaged, illustrations

   > A true adventure story told only in pictures, no words. A little girl is on a tour through an ancient castle with her parents. She goes through a huge door and finds herself in the dungeon. Wheels and pulleys hurl her into a lower level where the fierce fire-breathing dragon seems to be taking a nap. The fire snorting out of his nose propells her out of the dungeon through a fireplace and into the tour once more. This is a fun book! The pictures are black and white drawings with red highlights.

4. Joji And The Dragon
    Lifton, Betty Jean
    Illustrated by Eiichi Mitsui
    Morrow, New York, 1957
    Unpaged, illustrations

    > The whimsical story of Joji the scarecrow, who didn't scare crows.
    > In fact, they liked him! Even though the crows promised Joji
    > they would not eat the rice he was guarding, the farmer didn't
    > trust the crows and advertised for a "spooky person" to scare
    > them away. A ferocious dragon was hired and Joji was thrown
    > in the corner of the barn. The crows got together and, through
    > heroic cooperation, scared away the dragon and restored Joji to
    > his rightful place guarding the rice.

5. Prince Bertram the Bad
    Lobel, Arnold (1933)
    Harper, New York, 1963
    Unpaged, illustrations

    > Prince Bertram is a very bad boy. He hits a witch with a stone
    > from his sling shot and she changes him into a small dragon.
    > He lives a hard life until he gets a chance to use his fire to
    > thaw the frozen witch. As a reward, she turns him back into
    > a boy. It appears that Bertram has learned his lesson, so the
    > witch returns him to his parents, gives them all a ride on her
    > broom, stays for lunch and wishes him good things as she leaves.

6. Have You Ever Seen A Monster?
    McInnes, John (1927)
    Illustrated by Tom Eaton
    Champaign, IL, 1974
    32 pages, color illustrations

    > The question in the title refers to all of the activities in which
    > monsters engage. "Have you ever seen a monster" ride a bike,
    > play, sleep, eat, etc? There is an element of one-upmanship,
    > because the answer is often that the responder has seen "something
    > better." The monster in this book is more fun and silly than
    > scary.

7. **Monster And The Baby**
    Mueller, Virginia
    Illustrated by Lynn Munsinger
    A. Whitman, Niles, IL, 1985
    22 pages, color illustrations

    Anyone who has tried to entertain and quiet a crying baby will appreciate monster's dilemma. The story is told mainly by the very amusing pictures, supported by a total of less than sixty very, very simple sentences. Since monster uses a combination of three blue blocks, two yellow blocks and one red block, the book could be a good introduction to number and color patterns.

8. **Custard The Dragon**
    Nash, Ogden (1902-1971)
    Illustrated by Linell Little
    Little Brown Inc., Boston, 1959
    30 pages, color illustrations

    Custard the timid dragon becomes brave when a pirate threatens his friends. But, it doesn't last and after eating up the pirate, Custard reverts to his timid ways. This is a story in verse by the famous humorist, Ogden Nash.

9. **No More Monsters For Me!**
    Parish, Peggy
    Illustrated by Mark Simont
    Harper and Row, New York, 1981
    64 pages, illustrated
    (An I-Can-Read book)

    A young girl is not allowed to have a pet. She finds a baby monster and hides it in her basement. Feeding the monster becomes a daily problem; as it eats, it gets bigger and bigger. The little girl gets it out of the basement and to the hills, which are it's rightful home, just before it becomes too big to get through the door. Her mother relents and buys two kittens.

10. <u>How Droofus The Dragon Lost His Head</u>

Peet, Bill

Illustrated by the author

Houghton Mifflin, Boston, 1971

46 pages, illustrations

This is a rather long story for very young readers, but could readily be split into several sections. Droofus is a dragon who becomes very domesticated while raising himself in the woods, where he landed because he couldn't fly and keep up with his family. He is kind and helps people and animals and must defend himself from those who think that he is like other dragons. All ends well!

11. <u>Why Won't The Dragon Roar?</u>

Rosenbluth, Rosalyn

Illustrated by Rosalie Davidson

Gerrary Publishing Company, Champaign, IL, 1977

Walter the Dragon's mother takes him to the doctor to discover why he does not roar. The doctor finds nothing wrong with Walter. Walter finally roars when he is forced to protect his defenseless friends from hunters.

12. <u>I'm The King Of The Castle!</u>

Shigro, Watanabe

Illustrated by Yasuo Ohtomo

Philomel Books, New York, 1981

28 pages, color illustrations

(An I-Can-Do-It-All-By-Myself Book; #4 - Playing Alone)

The little bear takes his shovel and pail to play in the sand. He builds a castle and digs a hole and makes a nice lake. He enjoys playing alone. Very few large print words and pastel drawings tell this happy, gentle story.